THE SNAKE AND THE SPIDER

The Snake and the Spider

ABDUCTION AND MURDER IN DAYTONA BEACH

Karen Kingsbury

RosettaBooks®

Copyright © 1995, 2014 by Karen Kingsbury

ISBN: 978-0-7953-0014-1

A NOTE FROM KAREN KINGSBURY

The story you are about to read was adapted from my days as a news reporter for the Los Angeles Times.

Sadly, the characters in this story are real. In most cases, the dialogue and events are real. Some scenes have been re-created to better tell the story. Always, the chapters were difficult to write, a very real look at the darker side of life.

Missy's Murder was the first of four true-crime books I wrote at the beginning of my career as an author. It allowed me to be home with my daughter, Kelsey, who was just an infant when I covered the trial.

I wrote three more, *Final Vows, Deadly Pretender,* and *Snake and the Spider.* After that, I decided I couldn't write another. I'd explored enough of the dark side.

All of my novels since then contain characters with serious trials and troubles, but they are written in context of the faith, light, and hope that I believe exists for us all—including the characters in this book. God Bless!

Karen Kingsbury

P.S. You can learn more about my other titles at KarenKingsbury.com or by following me on Facebook and Twitter.

Dedicated
To

Little Norm,
my sweetest song.
I love you, honey.

T.D.,
my baby boy
whom I love so dearly.

Donald,
my husband,
with whom life just
keeps getting better.

My parents,
for their loving support.

My Christian family at
WVCC and VVCC.

God Almighty,
who defines love.

And to the memory of
Jim Boucher and Daryl Barber.

ACKNOWLEDGMENTS

Much thanks goes to the people who helped make this book possible. First, and foremost, Marian Barber and Faye Boucher, who shared their lives and those of their sons so that their story could be told. May the telling of what happened to Jim and Daryl serve to keep Snake and Spider in prison forever.

A very special thanks also goes to Private Investigator Bob Brown, who opened up dozens of files and hundreds of documents for my inspection. Thank you for recreating your amazing work and providing me with details that I wouldn't have had otherwise.

I would like to thank Maria Amato for uprooting herself during the writing of this book and taking special care of my children for six long, hot weeks. I couldn't have done it without you, Moe!

Thank you, too, to Donald, my husband, who continues to make whatever adjustments are necessary so that I can break away from life long enough to complete a manuscript. You are wonderful and I love you!

My appreciation goes out to my parents, who believed in my writing abilities from the beginning and who will always be strong pillars in my support system. I love you!

And a sincere thank you to my dear friends Pat, Amber, Jo Ann, Sue, and Gina (who is anything but a slub). Your laughter, love, and encouragement are what help me keep focused through the difficult times. I love you all and thanks a million.

Finally, I would like to thank my editor, Tony Gangi, for his brilliant knack of turning the ordinary into the extraordinary, and also my agent, Arthur Pine, and Dell's Leslie Schnur. Thank you for believing in me.

(1995)

AUTHOR'S EXPLANATORY NOTE

The events described in this book are taken directly from court transcripts and other public records and documents, as well as from numerous interviews with the many people involved. In many instances, however, to better communicate the story and the atmosphere surrounding the events, incidents and dialogue have been dramatically recreated based on court testimony and other public records, and interviews with various participants or other knowledgeable individuals.

Snake's wife, Sandra; Mike Black and Rob; Jeff Kindel, Dick Kane, and the names of other minor characters are all pseudonyms. The author has chosen to change these names and disguise the identities of certain people involved in this story. This has been done to preserve privacy. Any similarity between the fictitious names and those of living persons is, of course, entirely coincidental.

THE PEOPLE YOU'RE ABOUT TO MEET

JIM AND DARYL DIDN'T KNOW WHAT WAITED FOR THEM... .

THE SPIDER-
A loser, a biker, a kid with
no conscience—what secret did
he know that could break a parent's
heart in two? What deal was
he willing to make to tell it?

THE SNAKE-
A thief, a drug dealer, a Pagan
leader—where did he get
Daryl's red Chevy Nova and traveler's
checks signed by Jim?

BOB BROWN-
A dedicated private eye who prayed
before taking this case—what did
he find out in a run-down trailer park
that made his blood run cold?

LARRY-
A fearless red-haired giant and a biker
on his own—could he find
the person called "Fat Man"
and the clue that would break the case?

SANDRA-
A pretty twenty-three-year-old who
was married to a man called
Snake—what was her birthday present
that was paid for in blood?

MURRAY ZIEGLER-
A hard-nosed homicide detective—why
was he finally brought into the case
of the missing boys?
What sickening facts did he
suspect … or know?

**SOME POISONOUS CREATURES
ARE HUMAN.**

THE SNAKE AND THE SPIDER

CHAPTER 1

Faye Boucher hummed quietly to herself as she made French toast in the kitchen of her rambling country home that August 12, 1978. This was going to be a special breakfast, the last one she would cook for her oldest son, Jim, before he and his best friend Daryl set out for Florida. Their dream vacation had finally arrived.

Faye considered the trip and decided she was not concerned about the boys' safety. After all, Jim was seventeen, about to start his senior year in high school, and Daryl was nineteen. Certainly the boys were old enough to take a one-week vacation.

She set her mind to the task at hand, dipping the slices of soft bread into the mixture of egg and milk and placing them on the hot buttered griddle. The sun shone bright in the early morning sky and the temperature had already soared into the eighties. She and her husband, Roy, loved summertime in Metamora, Michigan, and this day like so many others was going to be a beauty: the rolling deep green hills, maple trees in full bloom, and long, warm days of fishing or horseback riding or swimming at the nearby lake. There would be family picnics, barbecues, and endless get-togethers with the dozens of relatives who lived less than an hour away. Metamora summers made the snowy winter months tolerable.

But for two teenage boys who had spent a lifetime of summers in Metamora, the town offered very little in the way of entertainment. And so the dream vacation had been born. One week in which the boys would drive to Florida, spend a few days at Daytona Beach and then visit Disney World in Orlando. They had planned the trip for months and Faye knew her son had never been more excited.

"Hey, Mom, did you wash my blue jeans?" Jim walked past the kitchen wearing only a pair of shorts and headed toward the utility room where he began searching frantically through a load of clothes in the dryer. "I don't see 'em," he yelled. His body was now partially inside the dryer. "Hey, Mom! Can you help me here? I need my jeans."

At the same time, the youngest member of the Boucher family, seven-month-old Kristi, began to cry.

"Okay, okay, I'm coming," Faye said, flipping a batch of French toast and smiling to herself as she moved briskly toward the baby's playpen. "Be there in a minute, Jim."

Faye easily lifted her infant daughter onto her hip as she headed toward the utility room. She was a slim, pretty woman whose body showed few signs of having had five children. Tousling her son's brown hair as she walked past him, she picked up two neatly folded pairs of blue jeans off a folding table.

"This what you're looking for?"

Jim grinned. He was a slender, muscular boy, five-foot-ten, one hundred and forty pounds, with shoulder-length brown hair and sparkling brown eyes much like his mother's.

"Why don't you get Daryl and come to breakfast," Faye said. "It's almost ready."

"Good idea," Jim said, setting the jeans down. "Can you help me pack after we eat?"

"Sure. Now go get Daryl."

"Thanks, Mom." Jim flashed her a smile from beneath the sparse mustache he had grown a few months earlier and then dashed back down the hallway toward his bedroom. Faye wasn't entirely pleased with the mustache but she figured it was harmless.

"I'm nearly a man, now," he had told his parents when they both raised an eyebrow at the growth on his upper lip. "It makes me look older, don't you think?"

"What's the hurry, Jim?" she had said then. "You're only seventeen."

Jim had always been mature for his age and now he seemed to want nothing more than to be treated like an adult. But Faye feared that growing up in Metamora had not prepared him for the world he wanted so desperately to explore—another reason why this trip was such a good idea, she told herself as she set the table. It would give Jim a chance to feel independent.

In a matter of minutes both teenage boys were sitting at the butcher-block kitchen table consuming mountains of French toast, syrup, and melted butter. Daryl and Jim had been friends for seven years and although Daryl was two years older, neither boy had been away from home by himself.

Daryl was polite, a good-looking teenager who was the youngest of five kids and lived just a few houses down on Baldwin Road. He had been working as a machinist for the past year and was about to begin his first paid vacation. He had brought his 35-millimeter camera and planned to capture a lot of memories in the coming week.

The excitement in the sprawling kitchen was palpable.

"I think we're going to need at least a few bags of this French toast for the road," Daryl said as he stood up and took his plate to the kitchen sink. He turned to Jim. "Maybe she can come with us, you know, just so we can get a good breakfast each day."

Faye smiled. "Somehow I don't think you want me and four kids tagging along to Daytona Beach."

Jim stood up and set his empty plate in the sink. "Oh, we wouldn't mind at all," he grinned, leaning over and kissing his mother on the cheek. "Hey, Mom, you ready to help me pack?"

Faye wiped her hands on a dish towel. "Let's get to it while Kristi's taking a nap," she said.

For the next twenty minutes she gathered clean clothes from the utility room and helped Jim pack his spacious blue suitcase. In addition to the necessities, he was taking several T-shirts and pairs of shorts, a few tank tops, a bathing suit, and the blue jeans.

"Plenty of room for souvenirs," he said as he and Faye stood side by side surveying the contents.

"Well, don't buy too much," Faye reminded gently. "You have a car on order, remember?"

Jim had won a statewide bowling tournament in January and three months ago had received a check for ten thousand dollars as prize money. He had decided to take just four hundred dollars on the trip and set aside the remainder to pay for the brand new 1979 Camaro he had ordered.

"Who said anything about buying souvenirs," Jim said. "I'm bringing home live crabs!" He looked down at his little brother, John, who had joined them a few minutes earlier. John was about to enter first grade and he loved his oldest brother dearly.

"You want a crab, John?" There was mischief in Jim's voice.

The small boy's eyes lit up at the idea. "Yeah! Bring me a crab, okay, Jim?"

Jim laughed as he caught his mother's disapproving expression. "Okay. But I think Mom will make us keep it outside."

"Yeah, I'll make a cage for him," John said as he raced out of the room, intent on finding a place where he could store a crab. Seconds later they could hear him singing happily, "I'm getting a crab, I'm getting a crab. Jim's going to get me a crab."

The packing finished, Jim and Daryl hauled their suitcases outside and placed them in the trunk of Daryl's 1972 Chevrolet Nova. Although not flashy, the red sports car was easy to recognize with its shiny, black vinyl top.

Jim's father, Roy Boucher, had said good-bye to his son that morning before he left for work and Daryl's family had said their good-byes earlier, also. Now, the rest of the Boucher family lined up in the family driveway to watch Daryl and Jim leave. Timothy, fifteen years old, laughed and playfully wrestled with Steven, just two years younger than him. John, meanwhile, hovered beside Jim, struggling to help him pack a stack of towels and a blanket into the backseat of the car. The child worshiped his oldest brother and had not stopped talking about the idea of getting a crab when he returned.

"Are you sure, Jim?" the little boy asked, huge brown eyes searching Jim's for an answer. "A crab? A real live crab?"

Jim crouched down on one knee and put his hands on John's shoulders. "I'll try my best to find one for you, and you be a good boy for Mom, is that a deal?"

John nodded but then his lower lip began to quiver and a single tear escaped as his eyes overflowed. "How long is a week?"

Jim pulled the child into a hug as the others watched from nearby and Faye felt a lump rising in her throat. "Not very long," Jim said softly. "I'll be back before you know it."

John nodded and his sudden sadness seemed to pass as quickly as it had come on. Jim stood up and waved good-bye to his other brothers as Daryl climbed into the driver's seat and shut the car door. Faye walked up to Jim and took him in her arms. Kristi was up from her nap and she sat balanced once again on Faye's hip. The three of them stayed close for a long moment until finally, Jim pulled away.

"I love you, Mom," he said, leaning toward her and kissing her.

The lump in Faye's throat had grown larger and she was unable to speak. Her eyes grew damp and Jim could see how emotional she had become.

Faye smiled in spite of her feelings. "I love you, honey," she whispered, her voice raspy.

"Don't worry, Mom," he said, looking intently into her eyes. "We'll be fine."

Faye nodded quickly, swallowing hard. She did not want to cry. It was ridiculous to be so concerned over Jim's departure. But he had never been away from home, never been on his own without the help of his parents.

"Please call when you get there, okay?" she said finally, forcing herself to sound casual. The boys planned to travel more than five hundred miles that afternoon and arrive in Daytona Beach sometime late that night. Faye figured she should be getting their phone call at that time.

"We will," he said. "Soon as we get there."

Jim kissed her one more time and smiled.

"Have fun," Faye whispered, brushing her son's hair back from his eyes and smiling in return. "We'll miss you."

"Me, too." Jim slid into the passenger seat and waved at his family. "Bye!" he shouted. "See you in a week!"

Faye looked hard at Jim as the car pulled out of the driveway. He looked young and carefree, about to begin the adventure of a lifetime. A week wasn't long at all and then they would be back, sharing tall tales of their time in Florida. She raised her arm up once more, waving one final time.

"Bye, Jim," she said softly. "Love you."

And then she and her four remaining children stayed in the driveway waving to the boys until the red Chevy Nova with the shiny black top turned off Baldwin Road and disappeared from sight.

CHAPTER 2

The Eagles sounded loud and clear over Daryl's new car stereo and the boys sang along as they drove south down the interstate.

"I've got a peaceful, easy feeling, And I know she won't let me down. 'Cause I'm already standing on the ground."

When the song ended, Jim reached into the backseat and grabbed a paper bag. "Sandwich time," he said, tossing one to Daryl. "How long we been driving?"

Daryl glanced at his watch. "Three hours. Still got a long way to go."

Jim and Daryl were halfway across Ohio when they finished the sandwiches. They had made them the night before in an effort to save time and money and so their only stops would be to buy gasoline for the Nova.

Jim looked out the window and wondered what Jaime was doing. He wished that there had been some way she could have come on this trip, but he knew the idea had been impossible. Her parents would never have allowed her to spend a week's vacation with him. They had been dating very seriously for the past four months, but in many ways their relationship was still more like a friendship than anything else. They kissed a lot and occasionally made out after a date. But she drew the line beyond that. Jim sighed out loud as he thought of her. She was a beautiful girl with a heart that seemed perfect for his own.

Daryl glanced at his friend. "Oh, no. Thinking of Jaime already, aren't you?"

Jim laughed. "Okay, you caught me."

"Don't worry, Jim. You'll survive without seeing her for one week. I promise."

In fact, the trip to Daytona Beach had been Jaime's idea. She and a girlfriend had driven to Daytona during spring break several months earlier. They had spent the week lying on the hot, white sand and splashing about in the clear, warm Atlantic Ocean. She had come home tan and bursting with enthusiasm.

"It's great," she had said, her hands gesturing in excitement. "Beaches as far as you can see and everyone's our age. Everyone. It's like teenagers run the place. We must have met a hundred people. And there's the boardwalk and the shops. You've got to go!"

Jim had talked the idea over with Daryl, who had been to Florida once before with his parents, and in a matter of days the idea of a dream vacation had been conceived.

Jim stared out the car window as they passed one farm after another. Yes, he could imagine marrying Jaime one day. She was that kind of girl. A sweet, family-oriented girl who didn't mess around with her boyfriends the way some girls did. Jim smiled as he thought of her. It was probably just as well that she hadn't pursued the idea of joining them on the Florida vacation. A week of staring at Jaime in a skimpy bikini would probably have given him heart failure. Besides, this week was going to be a special time for him and Daryl. Just like old times.

"How's it feel to be on vacation," Jim asked, breaking the comfortable silence.

Daryl shrugged and grinned. "Considering I'm pulling in a paycheck for spending a week in Florida, it feels pretty good."

Jim laughed and looked out the window again. He and Daryl didn't have to spend a lot of time talking in order to enjoy each other's company. They shared a love for the same kinds of music, they participated in similar activities, and they had grown up playing together on the same street. They were almost like brothers.

The only problem was that for the past year, since Daryl had started working full-time as a machinist, they had spent much less time together. Once Jim had resigned himself to Daryl's new schedule, he had gotten a job also, working as a part-time clerk at Kmart so that he could save up extra money for the trip to Florida. Even after he received his bowling prize money Jim did not consider quitting his job. The trip was going to be expensive and he wanted to make as much money as possible before the school year started.

"Jim, why don't you relax a little and enjoy this summer," his mother had said. "You work all the time."

"I like to work," Jim had insisted. "It makes me feel good to know I can make money and buy my own things. I've had enough summers where all I do is sit around. Besides, I want to save for the trip."

With their heavy work schedules, the summer had gone by quickly and then, suddenly, the trip was upon them. By that time Jim had saved an additional five hundred dollars, of which he kept four hundred in cash for the trip and put the rest in the bank with his prize money.

The car was traveling at a steady speed and Jim casually felt his wallet to make sure he'd brought it. Then he remembered his traveler's checks. Suddenly he couldn't remember if he had taken them or not.

"Oh, no," he said. He rummaged through his duffel bag.

Daryl watched his friend with a puzzled look on his face. "What's up?"

Jim felt the smooth plastic check holder tucked in the bottom of the bag and he released a deep sigh as he held up the traveler's checks so Daryl could see them. "For a second there I thought I forgot these."

"Glad you didn't," Daryl said. He had resumed singing and was clearly enjoying the trip. He had several hundred dollars in cash with him but Jim's parents had insisted that one of them take some money in traveler's checks.

"You never know, son," his father had said. "You could lose your money or your wallet might get taken. Having traveler's checks, you won't have to worry about that. It's a good idea."

Jim had agreed and now, two hundred miles from home, he was glad to know he hadn't forgotten them.

"Tell me again what you remember about Daytona Beach," Jim said, turning sideways in his seat and reaching over and turning down the radio.

Daryl laughed softly. Jim had never been away from home except for family vacations to visit grandparents or other relatives. Now he seemed excited just traveling through Ohio. Daryl could only imagine what he would think about Daytona Beach once they got there.

"Well, I'll tell you this much," Daryl said. "There are definitely a lot of girls. And none of them are wearing much, if you know what I mean!"

Jim laughed and felt his face flush with embarrassment. Jaime had warned him about the girls.

"I know you're on vacation," she had said lightly, "But keep your hands to yourself, hear?"

Jim had agreed completely. He wouldn't mind sitting on a warm beach watching bikini-clad girls stroll by. But he wasn't looking to get involved with any of them. Not with Jaime waiting back home.

"What else?" he asked, anxious to change the subject.

"Well, they have parties on the beach," Daryl said. "You know, at the motels up and down the strip."

The idea of attending a beach party sounded wonderful to Jim. He had been to high school parties and get-togethers at friends' houses in Metamora and nearby Lapeer. But he had never been to a party like he figured they would have at Daytona Beach.

"And the water's warm, right?" Jim continued.

"You bet it is," Daryl said, grinning at the memory of the warm Atlantic water. "Nothing like our lakes back home."

The boys slipped into an easygoing quiet and Daryl turned the radio up. Minutes later they were both singing as loud as they could, their windows open so that the warm breeze whirled throughout the car. They were on vacation and life felt so very, very good.

Hours later they passed a sign that read, "Daytona Beach, seven miles."

Faye and Roy Boucher had finished dinner, done the dishes, and gotten the younger children in bed. Now, finally, they were alone at the kitchen table. They talked about Roy's workday and Kristi's latest accomplishments. Then, after a while, they slipped into making occasional small talk. But every few minutes Faye glanced up at the clock on the wall.

Why haven't they called, she asked herself. *They should be there by now and they definitely should have called.*

Finally, Roy took her hand in his and smiled.

"I know what you're thinking, honey," he said. "But it's only ten fifteen. The boys are probably almost there and they'll be calling us any minute."

Faye nodded slowly. "I know," she said. She was quiet a moment as she sorted her thoughts. "I'm not really worried. It's just that I wish I would have asked them to call sooner. Or maybe just to call at a specific time. That way we would be sure they would call at ten o'clock and we wouldn't have to sit here worrying."

Roy raised an eyebrow. "Who's worried? I thought you weren't worried about a thing."

Faye laughed at her own contradiction and moved closer to her husband, setting her head on his shoulder.

"Do you think they're okay?" she asked softly.

Roy stroked his wife's hair. "Yes, sweetheart. I do. They're big boys. They're smart and they're very responsible. They'll do just fine."

Faye nodded absently. "It's just that it's so far away. Maybe they should have flown or something."

Roy laughed. "Honey, really. They're going to be fine."

Glancing up at the clock again, Faye sighed. "I just wish they'd call, that's all."

"Maybe you should pray about this, just so you won't worry so much," Roy said, seeing that his wife was still nervous.

"You're right. God doesn't want us fretting like this."

The Bouchers were devout Christians whose children had learned more from watching their faith in action than from any of the hundreds of Sunday School lessons they'd received. The Bouchers lived their faith, believing that to be anything less than devoted to God and His son Jesus was to make a mockery of Christianity. As a result they did not merely participate in a religion. They shared a relationship with God and each of their children had grown to do the same thing.

Fifteen minutes passed and Faye spent much of that time in prayer, begging God for the boys' phone call. Still, when the telephone rang she released a sigh of relief as she jumped up to answer it.

"Hello?"

"Hey, Mom," Jim said, his voice sounding as clear as if he were standing in the next room. Faye felt instant relief as she strained to hear Jim above the sound of traffic in the background. "We're here. Made it safely."

"That's wonderful," Faye said. "How was the trip?"

"Well, I have to tell you," Jim said. "That's one long drive." Jim laughed. "But now that we're here it's great. The water is so warm, Mom, you wouldn't believe it."

Roy had moved into the other room and was listening in on the extension. "You mean you've already been down to the beach?" he asked.

"Oh, hi, Dad," Jim said. "Yeah, just for a minute. We wanted to feel the water before we called you. And guess what?"

At that instant, an operator interrupted the call.

"I'm sorry, but you are out of time. Please hang up or deposit more money."

"Operator, can you reverse the charges?" Roy asked.

"Yes, that'll be fine. I'll reverse them starting now."

"Thank you," he said. "Jim, are you there?"

"Yeah. Hey, thanks, Dad. I'm out of change. Anyway, guess what I found?"

"We give up," Faye said lightly, laughing as she enjoyed her son's obvious excitement.

"A crab! Can you believe it. Just walking along the beach. I saw it in the moonlight and caught it. So, you can tell John that I'll be bringing him the crab I promised, okay?"

Faye wrinkled her nose at the thought of having a sea crab in her house. But she didn't want to dampen Jim's enthusiasm. "I'll tell him," she said. "I'm sure he'll be thrilled."

Roy laughed. He could just imagine little John asking Jim to bring him a live crab from Florida. "Son, tell us where you are."

"Okay, we just got into Daytona Beach," Jim said, raising his voice above the sound of the heavy traffic. "We're going to drive down the strip a ways and find a motel. And that's about it for tonight."

"All right," Roy said. "Well, be careful, son. And have a good time."

"And please call us," Faye added.

"I will. I'll keep in touch and let you know how the trip's going."

"We'd appreciate that," Roy said. "Especially your mother. You know how she worries."

"Yeah, yeah," Jim tried to make light of his parents' concerns. "Don't worry about us, Mom. We'll be fine. We're having a great time already."

"Okay, honey. Well, good night then. I love you," Faye said.

"Love you, too. Good night, Dad."

"Good night, son. Talk to you soon."

Roy hung up the telephone and walked back into the kitchen and pulled Faye into a hug. She looked more relaxed than she had before.

"You okay," he asked.

"I'm fine," she answered, sounding almost surprised at herself. "I guess I was worried something would happen to them on the way there. You know, a car accident or car trouble. Something like that."

"Silly girl," Roy said, tickling his wife playfully. "The boys are fine. You have nothing to worry about. Now, come on, let's go to bed."

That night, in the moments before Faye fell asleep, she said a silent prayer of thanks. Roy was right. The boys were safely in Daytona Beach. There was absolutely nothing to worry about.

CHAPTER 3

After hanging up the phone and joining Daryl in the Chevy Nova, Jim suggested they find a motel before doing anything else. Daryl agreed and the boys looked south on Atlantic Boulevard at the dozens of places to choose from.

"Let's find something cheap," Daryl said. He had brought less money than Jim and didn't want to waste it on frivolous motel luxuries. "Just a place to sleep; sound good?"

"Yeah, but let's stay on the beach side," Jim said.

"Definitely." Daryl laughed as he pulled the Nova back onto Atlantic. "Can't stay at the beach unless you're sleeping over sand. Besides, the parties are usually on the beach side of the strip from what I hear."

The teens drove several miles, realizing that what they had thought was the heart of Daytona Beach was really only the outskirts.

"This place is huge," Jim said, his eyes wide as he soaked in the beach atmosphere. I love it!"

Daryl pointed toward a motel just a few hundred feet down the road. "There, that looks pretty good," he said.

"Thunderbird Motel. Sure, sounds good to me."

They pulled in, walked up to the front desk, and paid cash for a one-night stay in Room 109. The room had easy access from the motel parking lot. But more importantly it had a balcony which overlooked the beach and the famous boardwalk.

"I can't believe I'm really here," Jim said as they hauled their suitcases into the room. When they had finished setting up their things, Jim turned to Daryl. "Now what?"

Daryl smiled. "Let's hit the beach."

Jim looked at his watch. "Isn't it too late. I mean, the parties will already be going. Who's going to be on the beach now?"

Daryl shrugged. "Never know unless we go," he said, casually dropping his car keys into his pocket and grinning. "The night is young. Come on!"

Jim laughed and shrugged. Daryl was so carefree and fun to be with. Besides, it was only eleven o'clock and they were on vacation. Why not go down to the beach?

The boys took towels and walked down a flight of motel stairs to the beach below. The lights from the boardwalk flooded the sandy stretches on either side, and Jim and Daryl could see the silhouettes of several couples making out on beach blankets.

"I think I'm missing Jaime," Jim mumbled under his breath and Daryl laughed.

Jim had never imagined such a place existed. The sand beneath his feet was still warm from a day of intense sunshine. He gazed upward at the star-filled sky overhead and listened to the sound of the gentle surf. This beach had to be one of the all-time great places to bring a girlfriend.

Jim and Daryl spread their towels on the sand in a place where they could watch hundreds of teenagers riding the Ferris wheel and trying their luck at carnival games along the boardwalk.

"Imagine, a full-fledged carnival built right over the ocean," Jim said. "It's amazing!"

"Want to go up and join the fun?" Daryl asked, raising his eyebrows in anticipation. "That's probably where we'll meet people who can tell us where the parties are."

"Nah. We can go later. I just want to sit here and soak it all in. You know, get used to the place for a while."

"We won't hear about any parties sitting down here," Daryl warned again. "And it's still pretty early."

"Well, let's just sit here a little bit, all right? We just got here."

"Sure." Daryl didn't mind. There would be plenty of time for parties. Besides, he didn't have to go to a party to have fun at Daytona Beach. It was fun just being there. He leaned back on his towel, watching the boardwalk and enjoying the warm breeze that washed over him. The Atlantic Ocean was wonderful, so much warmer than the Michigan lakes. Daryl decided he could stay right there on the beach with his best friend beside him forever if he had to.

Suddenly a strange voice interrupted the moment.

"Hey, man, what's going on?"

Jim and Daryl turned toward the voice and saw a young man in his late teens or early twenties approaching them.

"Hey," Daryl responded.

The young man was wiry with thin, scraggly brown hair and he was dressed in a rumpled pair of shorts and a T-shirt. He looked dirty, as if he hadn't taken a shower in days.

"Mind if I sit down?" The young man did not wait for an answer but slid onto the sand near the boys' towel. Looking both ways, he quickly took out a marijuana cigarette and lit it, inhaling deeply.

He looked at Jim and Daryl and saw that they seemed nervous.

"Hey, relax, man," he said. "Listen, you wanna' go to this great party up the beach?"

Instantly he had Jim's and Daryl's undivided attention.

"Sure!" Daryl replied. "Where's it at?"

CHAPTER 4

Although they had no instructions to call home on a daily basis, both the Bouchers and the Barbers expected to hear from their sons several times during their vacation. So, when Sunday came and went and then Monday and Tuesday without word from either boy, their parents became somewhat concerned.

"Do you think they're in some kind of trouble," Faye asked Daryl's mother on Tuesday afternoon?

"Come on," came the reply. "They're boys, Faye. They're probably out having too much fun to call home."

Faye agreed with this logic, but still she was troubled. Besides, Daryl was the youngest of five children and Marian no longer got worried as easily as she once had. Jim, though, was her oldest and it was the first time he'd ever been away from home by himself.

Somehow Faye survived the rest of Tuesday. But when Wednesday passed and then Thursday and Friday, the Bouchers were no longer merely concerned. They were terrified.

Saturday finally came. The boys were supposed to be home by 8 o'clock that evening and now it was 10 o'clock, and the boys were two hours late. Faye stood up from the kitchen table where she'd been doing very little besides staring at her hands for the past hour and walked outside. She moved to the end of the driveway and gazed down Baldwin Road toward the spot where she had last seen Jim and Daryl. The boys had been so happy, so excited about their vacation.

She stood there now, the night air still and dark, a dense humidity shrouding the neighborhood in a suffocating way. She crossed her arms tightly around her body and strained to hear the sound of Daryl's car. Surely it was coming; it would be rounding the corner any minute.

But several minutes passed and there was only the sound of the frogs from the local ponds. Faye closed her eyes and prayed. Still, there was nothing she could do to shut out her fears. What if something had happened to the boys? It must have. Daytona Beach was a terrible place. Hadn't the city newspaper done a story on the crime in that area. And how come she hadn't remembered about any of that before the boys left? Who knew what kind of people were traipsing about the beach. And then there was Orlando. Wasn't that a tourist trap and weren't tourists oftentimes the victims of crimes?

Faye stood perfectly still in the same spot where she had kissed Jim good-bye just one week earlier and softly, soundlessly, she began to cry. A few moments later Roy walked outside and came up behind her. He took her shoulders in his hands and leaned close to her.

"They'll be home any time," he whispered. But his words sounded hollow even to him.

"They would have called."

Roy was silent a moment, helpless to say anything that might make his wife less afraid. Worse, he was trying desperately to deny his own feelings of fear.

"Maybe we could call someone," he suggested softly. "One of his friends, someone who might know something about where they are, why they're late."

Although the tears continued to stream down Faye's face, there was a strange, unnatural numbness to her voice. She did not sob or scream or cry out. Roy thought she acted almost as if she was paralyzed with fright.

"Jim is with his best friend in the whole world," she said, her words measured. "Who would we call?"

Roy considered her response and agreed. No one knew Jim better than Daryl. They had always looked out for each other, always come home safely whenever they'd gone out together. Besides, had the boys called anyone, they would have called home. If there was one thing he and Faye had taught their children it was to be responsible. At least have the respect to call home. Don't make mom and dad worry. He sighed out loud and bent closer to his wife, kissing her hair. Then, silently and a little more slowly, Roy went back into the house.

At that same time, a few houses down Baldwin Road, the Barbers were dealing with their own fears. Daryl was not the kind of boy to ignore his parents' feelings. And neither of them could think of a single reason why the boys hadn't called during the week and why now they were late coming home.

"Maybe we should call the police," Daryl's mother was saying to her husband.

"We've been through this, Marian. We call the police and they'll tell us they can't possibly know what happened to our son. They don't have jurisdiction over Ohio or Kentucky or Tennessee or any of the other states between here and Florida. They'll tell us to wait twenty-four hours, until they're at least one day late, and then they'll tell us to file a missing persons report. There's nothing they can do."

"Okay," Marian said quickly, brushing off her husband's response. "Then let's call the auto club." Marian was moving about her kitchen and dining room rearranging piles of cookbooks and magazines, scrubbing spots on walls, and straightening items that had already been straightened ten times. It was as if she had to keep busy so that she wouldn't have time to think about any of the terrible things that might have happened to her son.

"The auto club won't know anything at this hour, Marian. It's Saturday night after ten o'clock. They'll only have emergency dispatchers. And even if they had taken a call from Daryl, they would only know about the immediate area. He could have broken down two hundred miles or twelve hundred miles away from here and they wouldn't know a thing about it."

"Well, then?" Marian stopped suddenly in her tracks. For a moment she was unable to speak, searching frantically for options. "What do we do now? Who can we call?"

Ron stared at his wife, trying not to get sucked into the anxiety that was beginning to consume her. "We call no one. They're okay, Marian. Really. Just relax."

"You don't understand," she said, still staring at him.

"What?"

"We need to do something now!"

"Like what?"

"Oh, forget it." Marian shook her head and left the kitchen, moving into living room and taking a seat beside the telephone. She picked it up and dialed.

"Hello?" The voice on the other end sounded tired.

"Roy, it's Marian," she said quickly. "Are they home yet?"

"Uh, no." Roy's voice was steady but his tension was audible and it only made Marian feel more frightened.

"Well, where in the world could they be?" she asked.

There was no logical reason to ask such a question. But in those hours, when belief that the boys would come home was so real they could almost hear the Chevy Nova turning onto Baldwin Road, logic was not necessary. The Barbers and Bouchers were clinging to past experience, hoping that this time, like every other time in the boys' lives, they would come home safely. Or, if they didn't come home, there would be a reasonable explanation and one they would hear via telephone any moment.

Roy paused a moment. "I don't know, Marian. I'm sorry. I'll have Daryl call as soon as they get here."

"Where's Faye?"

"Outside."

There was another pause. "Is she worried, Roy?"

"Worried sick."

Marian sighed. "Well, tell her to pray. We've got to pray that they'll get home safely or that we'll hear something from them. Something. Okay, Roy?"

"Marian," Roy said kindly. "She's been praying for those boys since the moment they left."

Just then Roy heard Faye open the door and walk back inside the house toward the kitchen. Her eyes were red-rimmed and bloodshot and she was about to move past Roy when she saw him talking on the telephone. She paused and for an instant, a surge of hope shone in her eyes as she looked questioningly at her husband. Was it the boys? Had someone called to say where they were, why they were late? He could read her eyes and he shook his head sadly, pointing down the street toward where Daryl lived.

Normally, Faye would have gotten on the phone and said a few words to her neighbor. Instead, she turned down the hallway and walked away without saying a word. Her oldest child was missing and Faye could feel an emptiness growing inside her. It was as if only Jim could fill that place and without him she was nothing more than a barely functioning shell of her former self. Roy watched her disappear.

"I've got to go, Marian."

He hung up the phone and walked down the hallway looking for his wife. He glanced into each of the bedrooms until he found her in the last room on the right. It was the nursery where seven-month-old Kristi slept. Faye had taken the sleeping infant, bundled her in soft flannel blankets, and was now sitting in the rocking chair, holding her close and humming. She stared straight ahead, the fear painfully evident on her tearstained face as she turned and looked up at her husband. Then deliberately, Faye closed her eyes and bent her head toward her tiny daughter's, nuzzling her face into the child's fine hair.

As Roy watched, he thought he understood. Faye wanted nothing more than to hold Jim, to take him in her arms where she would know for sure that he was all right and had not come to harm. But Jim was gone; she hadn't heard from him all week and there was no way to know where he was or what had happened to him. But Kristi was right here. She was alive and real and warm. By holding her, Faye could remember a time when Jim had been that infant—a time when he had been completely safe. She could believe, with that tiny life living and breathing up against her chest, that everything really was going to be okay.

The sight of Faye clinging so desperately to little Kristi brought tears to Roy's eyes and he turned away so she wouldn't see them. He was not yet ready to admit that her fears were well founded. Jim would come home and when he did, he would find his father waiting.

Roy walked into the living room and sat in a chair that faced the driveway. The questions came in a torrent. What could possibly be keeping the boys from calling? Where were they? Had their car broken down or had they been having so much fun that they'd gotten a late start driving home?

Suddenly, at that moment Roy heard the sound of a car turning onto Baldwin Road.

"Thank God," Roy muttered, walking outside and into the driveway. He was filled with relief as he watched the headlights draw closer until finally the car was nearly at their house. But it wasn't slowing down and then, in a blur, it passed by. The car hadn't even resembled a Chevy Nova. Roy watched the car's red taillights and waited a moment until its engine could no longer be heard.

He looked back down the street toward the corner where he expected the boys to appear. Certainly they would be home any minute. He waited for what must have been half an hour and then turned and walked back inside the house.

Roy stationed himself in the same chair, his eyes riveted on the driveway, his thoughts began to drift back in time. Suddenly he could see Jim as an infant and then as an energetic toddler. Hundreds of snapshots flashed through Roy's mind. Afternoons of playing catch and hours of Little League practice. Countless man-to-man talks about serious matters—everything from riding bikes to dating girls. Jim was his firstborn son, the child in whom he had seen himself as a young boy.

He remembered how proud he had been when Jim won the bowling tournament last January. Then Jim had grown that scraggly mustache. Roy chuckled out loud at the memory. His son was growing up and trying so hard to be a man. Even now, with all the questions that plagued him, Roy was nearly bursting with pride at the kind of man his oldest son was becoming.

Finally, after mulling over these thoughts for nearly an hour, Roy sat straighter in his chair and convinced himself that everything was okay. Perhaps the boys hadn't planned to return until Sunday. Yes, that had to be it. He considered going to bed but decided against it. If they were coming tonight, someone should be up to greet them.

Roy sat perfectly still, his eyes fixed on the driveway, willing Daryl's Nova to appear.

"Come home, son," he whispered into the night. "Please come home."

Then he waited.

And that was how the Barbers and Bouchers passed the night, calling each other every few hours, taking turns sitting outside and then moving back inside. Watching, hoping, crying. But most of all waiting, almost as if it was a physical exertion to do so. Praying that the boys would return home, and doing everything in their power to shut out the images of what might have happened and the haunting questions for which they had no answers.

Days passed, then weeks. The Bouchers and Barbers contacted local police, state patrolmen, and even the governor's office. They devoted every waking moment to locating their sons and in turn were provided only with a terrifying lack of information. No one had seen the boys, no one knew where the boys had gone after telephoning their parents their first day in Daytona Beach, and no one knew where they might be now.

The same day Faye Boucher filled out missing persons reports on Jim and Daryl the families thought of another way to trace the boys' whereabouts. The traveler's checks. Roy went to the local bank in Metamora where he and Jim had purchased them and was given a telephone number for the central Michigan clearing house.

"If your son has used the checks, they should be at the clearing house," the bank manager told him as Faye sat anxiously beside him holding little Kristi. "Usually they're sent there within four or five days."

Roy thanked her for the information and squeezed his wife's hand. This was the first real lead they'd had and perhaps now they would find out where the boys were. The past forty-eight hours had been torture on both families and they had reached a point where they were driven to find out something about the boys' disappearance.

Roy dialed the number and waited several minutes before a researcher came on the line with the information.

"It looks like we have some of those checks, Mr. Boucher," the researcher said. "They cleared late last week."

"Can you tell us where they were cashed?" Roy was hopeful.

"Yes, I'll go over them one at a time. Are you ready?"

"Go ahead." Roy reached for a pencil and pad of paper.

"The first one was cashed at Majik Market in Daytona Beach, Florida, on Sunday, August thirteenth," she said as Roy scribbled the information for Faye to see. "Then, let's see, looks like the next one was cashed Thursday, the seventeenth, at Road Runner Pit Stop and Grill in De Funiak Springs, Florida."

As Roy wrote down this latest detail Faye looked doubtful. "De Funiak Springs?" she whispered. "Where's that?"

Roy shrugged and continued to listen.

"Next there was a check cashed that same day at the North Beach Street Trailer Park."

Again Faye looked concerned. The boys had said they were going to stay in motels the entire time. Why would Jim have used one of his traveler's checks at a trailer park? The researcher was continuing the list.

"Then it looks like one on Friday, the eighteenth, cashed at Dobbs House, a diner in Pascagoula, Mississippi," she said pleasantly, "and another at the Ocean Springs Kustom Cycle Shop in Ocean Springs, Mississippi."

Roy's hand was beginning to shake as the woman relayed the information. Mississippi? Cycle shops? What did this mean? Had the boys decided to take a side trip and head over to Mississippi?

Faye meanwhile had grown quite pale. The boys had never intended to visit Mississippi. It would have been hundreds of miles out of their way. Suddenly she thought of something. Perhaps the checks had been stolen and signed by someone else.

"Ask her who signed the checks," she whispered, "Tell her to check the signatures."

"Uh," Roy interrupted. "Before you go any further could you tell me who signed the checks please."

"Certainly. They were originally signed by a James Boucher. And, let's see. Yes, they were all countersigned by James Boucher as well."

Roy glanced at his wife and nodded.

"So they were signed by James Boucher," he repeated for Faye's benefit. "Can you tell if it's the same signature. Maybe it was forged."

The researcher was silent. "I'm trained to identify forgeries," she said. "These look like the real thing to me, but I'll have them checked out by my supervisor."

"Fine. Thank you," Roy said. "Are you sure those few checks were cashed in Mississippi?"

"Yes, sir. The establishment uses a stamp with its address and bank information. Several checks were cashed in Mississippi."

Roy nodded, releasing a heavy sigh as he did. "Okay. Were there any others?"

"No. Looks like some are still outstanding."

"All right. Thanks for your time." Roy hung up the phone and turned to his wife. "Well, time to start digging."

First, they contacted the Michigan State Police and passed along the information about the traveler's checks.

"Look, we'd like you to follow up on this information right away," Roy said urgently. "We know the boys weren't planning to go to Mississippi. Something's definitely wrong."

Jim remembered another detail that might help the officers in their investigation. He whispered to Faye to get their recent phone bill which had come in the mail on Saturday. Faye quickly brought the bill to Roy. There near the end of the bill was the phone call Jim had made from a place called Ormond Beach. Since he had reversed the charges midway through the phone call, the telephone number of the phone booth was on the printed statement.

"Here's one more thing," he said. "The number of the phone booth Jim used when they first got to Daytona Beach." Roy gave the number. "The strange thing is that it says here, on the bill, that Jim called from Ormond Beach. I don't know where that is. The boys said they were in Daytona Beach."

At the other end of the line, Officer Ray Burnham wrote down the information. "We'll check it out this afternoon and call you back."

"Okay. Thank you. We'll be waiting."

Next he called the Barbers and told them what was happening.

"What can we do while they're checking out the information you gave them?" Marian asked, her voice shrill and nervous.

"All we can do is wait," Roy said. "We'll call you when we hear back from the police."

"I want to do something more than that." She was frustrated and Roy could understand. But at this point there was nothing they could do but trust the police. With all those places that had taken Jim's traveler's checks something was bound to turn up. Perhaps the boys had been in a car accident in Mississippi or were stranded on some deserted stretch of highway.

"The police have done this kind of thing before, Marian. They'll probably have good news for us by this evening."

"Well, I hope so. We're going crazy over here."

"I know, believe me. We feel the same," he said.

"I know," she said. "Hang in there."

When the conversation ended, Marian buried her head in her hands and began to cry. Her husband moved quietly beside her and stroked her head.

"They're going to be fine, sweetheart," he said. But he had lost his conviction in the matter and Marian could hear it. She looked up, tears spilling onto her face. For the first time since the boys had gone, Ron Barber wasn't completely calm about the fact that his son had not returned home from vacation.

"You say they're fine, but you don't believe that, do you?" she asked fearfully. "You don't really believe they're all right."

He waited a fraction of a second too long and then, unable to speak, his eyes grew watery.

"I want to believe it, Marian." His voice cracked and he clenched his fists. "You don't know how badly I want to believe it."

He had taken the day off so they could make phone calls or drive somewhere or do whatever had to be done to find the boys. But only now had he finally admitted to himself that something was wrong. It was one thing to go an entire week without calling and even to be a few hours late coming home. But Daryl and Jim would never have been two days late without calling. Besides, it was Monday. Daryl was supposed to be back at work.

Ron had called his son's boss earlier in the day and asked if they had heard anything from him.

"He's late for work, I know that," the supervisor had said a bit gruffly. "What happened? I thought they were on vacation."

"Well, we don't really know what's happened," Ron had said. "He said they'd be back Saturday, back in time to get to work and all."

"He's not here yet and normally he would have been here an hour ago."

"Would you mind calling us if you hear anything from him?"

"Sure," the supervisor said. "And if he goes home first, tell him to call me. I need to know if he'll be here tomorrow."

"Okay. Just so you know, we do have the police looking for them, too."

At the mention of police, the supervisor had seemed to soften. "Gee, sure hope everything's okay."

"It is, I'm sure," Ron had said. "Just probably one of those stupid things kids do."

But now, several hours later, Ron had lost all his optimism. He reached out for his wife and as they embraced, they both began to cry in earnest.

Meanwhile, Officer Ray Burnham at the Michigan State Police office had spent two hours making phone calls and was frustrated at the lack of information he'd been able to get. He had been assigned the missing persons reports on both teenage boys and so far had learned just one thing—the location of the phone booth in Ormond Beach where Jim had called his father. Ormond Beach, Burnham had learned, was the first town one comes to when driving from the north toward Daytona Beach. It would have been easy, he reasoned, for the boys to reach the city and call home thinking they were in Daytona Beach when they were actually still several miles away.

Apparently that was the last time anyone heard from the boys and this concerned Burnham a great deal. He did not know Jim and Daryl, but he knew several of their brothers and sisters, many of whom had been friends with his children over the years. The Barbers and Bouchers were good people with a strong allegiance to family. Boys like that would have called home. Especially when in the days that followed they were seemingly busy cashing traveler's checks.

Burnham had also contacted each of the establishments which took the traveler's checks from Jim. He made a point of talking to whoever was working the day the checks were cashed, in hopes of finding someone who might recognize the boys.

"We're looking for two teenagers who cashed a traveler's check at your business on the thirteenth of August," he informed the manager of Majik Market. He went on to describe the boys' appearance and then he paused. "Sound familiar?"

"Look," the man said. He had a thick New York accent. "I was working that day so maybe I should have remembered those kids. But I don't remember nothing. We get traveler's checks around here all the time. Don't take time to remember every face that comes through the place. Understand?"

Burnham thanked the man for his assistance and called the other establishments. Each time, after describing the boys, he was met with the same response. No one could remember two teenage boys having been in their business and having used traveler's checks. Finally, Burnham was out of leads. He sat back in his chair and gazed out the window at the lush green that surrounded the station.

The way he saw it, there were two problems with this missing persons case.

First, the boys were usually responsible kids who under normal circumstances would have called home every few days. Actually, the way these kids were, they probably would have called *every* day and maybe even every night. Since they hadn't, Burnham could hear bells going off.

The other problem was that although the traveler's checks were signed by James Boucher, no one at any of the establishments where they were cashed remembered the boys. That led Burnham to one rather obvious conclusion: The boys hadn't cashed the checks. If someone else had cashed the checks, it was possible they had been stolen and that the signature of James Boucher was actually forged.

Those two details made it almost impossible to consider this merely a missing persons case. But still, there was no concrete evidence to suggest that the boys had been victims of crime. And considering the fact that they were teenage boys—as were so many runaways—Burnham knew what most officers would do when given the case. Shelf it. Keep an eye out on the streets for the kids, but never put any real time into investigating the case until there was proof that a crime had been committed.

Unfortunately for the Barbers and Bouchers, Officer Burnham knew the case would not likely receive much attention. The parents were worried sick and he wished there was something he could do to ease their fears.

Finally he did think of one way he might be able to help. He picked up the phone and dialed the Daytona Police Department. Dispatch connected him to the department that handled missing persons.

"Detective Mikelson," a voice said.

"Yeah, this is Officer Ray Burnham, Michigan State Police. Got a missing persons case for you."

He rattled off the information, promising to mail pictures of the boys and copies of the missing persons reports that afternoon.

"Listen, Mikelson," Burnham said before he hung up. "Put some time into it, will you? These were good kids, boys got along with their parents, good jobs, money in the bank. The thing smells real fishy from where I'm sitting."

"Yeah, yeah. I know." Mikelson sighed. "Every time a kid disappears in our precinct it smells fishy. This is the beach, remember, Burnham? Daytona Beach."

It was the not knowing that was so very difficult, causing a frantic feeling that only worsened with each passing hour. There is something internal built into a parent that connects them to their child. And when that child is missing, the parent searches every horizon, every hiding place, everywhere possible in an effort to find the child. Constantly searching. Because as long as that child is missing, there is no rest, no peace. It matters not whether the parent has lost a toddler or a teenager. The child must be found if life is ever to regain any semblance of normalcy.

When two months had passed, with the police in Michigan and Florida working to no avail to find the missing teens, their parents finally reached a breaking point. They were losing precious time with each passing day, and the pressure of not knowing where their sons were, if they were alive or dead, was destroying them. Day and night they racked their brains for possible explanations for their sons' disappearance. And in return they were continually assaulted by waves of panic as they realized that, indeed, there were no explanations, nowhere even to begin to look for them.

And so on Monday, October thirtieth, disillusioned by the efforts of law enforcement, they hired Private Investigator James Byrd of Detroit. They were not for a moment concerned about the price of such an investigation, but only about finding their sons. Their entire lives had been reduced to a single goal, a single purpose. The boys must be found, whether they were alive or not. They agreed that nothing could be worse than not knowing the answers, regardless of what those answers were and what it might cost to get them.

"Don't worry," Byrd said when he spoke with the parents that morning. "I'll do whatever I have to do to find your boys."

Ten minutes later Byrd did just that.

He called Private Investigator Bob Brown of Orlando, Florida, and hired him to solve the case.

CHAPTER 5

Bob Brown was not surprised when he took the phone call about the missing teenagers. He was, by that time, a nationally recognized private investigator and many times other investigators hired him to work on local cases.

Of course, as far as the clients were concerned, hiring an investigator who then hired another investigator was not very ethical. It would have been better, most clients believed, for their investigator to recommend the other one. Otherwise a lot of unnecessary money was spent in overhead costs. For instance, in Byrd's case he planned to keep three dollars for every one he paid Bob Brown. But Bob knew nothing of this because he made a point of never getting involved in the financial arrangements between other investigators and their clients. His job, he believed, was simply to solve cases.

And it was something he did with remarkable success.

Other investigators had not always been so willing to take piecework or entire cases to Bob Brown. But over the thirteen years since Bob began doing private investigations, a nationwide network of investigators had come to trust his judgment like none other.

Their original hesitation about the man had not been because of his ability. He was a brilliant investigator from the beginning. Their doubts had been because he wasn't like other private investigators. He didn't act like them, didn't work like them, and certainly didn't look like them.

At forty-eight, Bob was a soft-spoken man who looked more like Bob Newhart than Magnum PI. He was known to bow his head and say grace in restaurants and he was active at his local church. Rather than sporty jackets or denim jeans, Bob wore a nondescript suit to work most days of the week. And in place of the usual sports car, Bob drove a white sedan which was almost as clean as he was. The only way to tell that Bob was a private investigator was the small-handled revolver tucked underneath his suit coat.

Even if one used a tremendous amount of imagination, one would almost never be able to picture Bob running through alleys or up fire escapes or being shot at in dramatic chase scenes. For that matter it would have been difficult to imagine him climbing over fences and surveilling subjects in the middle of the night.

Yet over the years, Bob had done all those things and then some. He laughed—softly and with a great deal of politeness—when someone had the nerve to ask him how he had mastered a profession that seemed so foreign to his nature.

"It's easy," he would say. "I've been on both sides of the fence."

It was true. When Bob was a teenager he had no intention of investigating criminal activity. He was too busy partaking in it.

Bob was born in 1932 and grew up in a suburb of Chicago that housed mostly low-income families. His father, a truck driver, was gone most of the time and his mother, Helen, was busy caring for her four children. So it was that Bob found it easy to slip away and spend a great deal of his afternoons with a shady group of neighborhood boys.

By the time he was a teenager, Bob had joined a group of "bad" boys who wore black caps and jackets bearing a skull and crossbones. They talked of having a motto: "Death Before Dishonor." Although theirs was not a gang of organized criminals, anyone in their neighborhood would have agreed on their potential to be so.

From time to time, the police would catch the "Bad Boys" in a dark alley talking about secret things and perhaps planning violent crimes. Wanting to keep a handle on the situation, the officers would grab the boys, toss them into the patrol car, and beat them with rubber hoses. Then they would take them to the station and telephone their mothers.

Apparently none of this bothered Bob much because when he was fourteen years old he and three older boys broke into a gun shop. Police responded to the scene and the boys took off on foot. Two of the boys were caught but Bob got away. For two weeks Bob looked over his shoulder, afraid he was going to be arrested at any minute. During that time his Uncle Jim, a police officer, had been watching Bob with a wary eye.

"You did it, didn't you?" he said one afternoon when they were alone.

"What?"

"Don't play dumb! You were in on that break-in at the gun shop."

Bob paused too long and then, caught in the truth, hung his head in shame. "You going to take me in?"

Jim resisted an urge to laugh. They would not arrest a fourteen-year-old boy whose role in such a crime had only been to look out for the others. But Bob didn't know that and his uncle wanted him to be worried about the consequences of his actions. "I won't," he said. "I want you to go down to the station yourself and tell them what happened."

Bob looked horrified. "Uncle Jim, I couldn't do that!"

"Either that or I take you in myself."

And so reluctantly, Bob went to the station and met with a man who worked with his uncle. Jim had arranged the meeting and asked the other officer to scare the boy. For the next thirty minutes the officer seemed to ponder the notion of throwing Bob in jail. Finally, he let him go and warned him to leave the gang for good.

For once, Bob listened.

Even when he was dying to run with his old friends, he stayed out of trouble. Finally, he was old enough to join the army, where he was almost immediately recognized as a talented photographer. Within a few years he was sent to

South Korea so he could participate in a covert operation involving his skills as a photographer. The U.S. Army would take over a section of land previously occupied by the Koreans and before the military would move in, Bob and his crew would go through the area taking pictures. The subjects were not pleasant. Most of the photos were of American soldiers who had been bound with barbed wire, gagged, and shot to death by Koreans.

It was a highly secret mission and none of the pictures were released to the public until decades later. Bob's superiors were thrilled with his work. Not just his brilliant eye for photography and detail. But the fact that he understood the importance of keeping the mission secret.

When Bob left the army he married his first wife and throughout his twenties he worked his own photo studio, bringing in more than enough money to feed his wife and daughter, Vicky. When the pressures of running a studio became overwhelming, Bob and his family moved to Florida where, using the byline "Charlie Brown," he became the photo editor for the *Sarasota News*.

One of his assignments was to ride with the local highway patrol squad and shoot a photo essay. Bob's excitement for the job had nothing to do with the pictures he took. Rather he was thrilled with the idea of police work. He had come full circle from his days in the suburbs of Chicago, all because his Uncle Jim had been willing to steer him on the right path.

He received his training while still working for the newspaper and less than a year later he was hired by the Manatee County Sheriff's Department. He spent most of his time investigating accidents, but from the beginning he wanted to be a detective. He worked his way up to a position in the crime lab and then, after a few enjoyable years, he quit because of a disagreement over pay.

Bob spent the next few years working for the *Orlando Sentinel* as a photographer, but his heart was no longer in it. He had come to a crossroads and he considered his options.

He had known life on the dark side, and he had developed an ability to work secretly, to photograph crime scenes, and to investigate. So, in 1966, now married to his second wife, Bob moved to Orlando and began working as a private investigator.

As a means of supporting his private investigation business, Bob—always the entrepreneur—started a business called Central Security Police. He developed that business from a two-guard operation to one that employed three hundred guards in three cities. His guards were logging seventeen thousand hours a month but still he wanted to be a private investigator. That year, he sold the security business and with the proceeds put all his time and energy into private investigations.

At first business was slow, but eventually the calls began coming in quite regularly. Most of his jobs involved domestic cases in which one spouse believed the other to be unfaithful. When this happened, Bob was uncannily successful at following the spouse in question and developing proof of the infidelity. His reputation grew and in time more clients found their way to his humble office.

In those early years he was shot at twice, both while doing surveillance on private properties. He played a role in numerous real-life chase scenes in which he had to track down a subject who preferred to remain anonymous. And when the people weren't exciting, his equipment was. He used cameras that could photograph the face of a person in a motel room with the blinds closed at more than a hundred yards away. There were tracking devices, transmitting devices, and nearly invisible tape recorders.

But by the early 1970s, although he thoroughly enjoyed his work, Bob had reached a point of concern regarding his career. Because he handled mostly domestic cases, he had begun to fear that his reputation was at stake. Bob had not considered the sleazy aspects of investigating domestic affairs and at times the pictures he was forced to take turned his stomach.

About the same time, Bob became a Christian. He wanted to do everything in a way that would please God, and almost overnight he began to question the ethical aspects of his work as an investigator.

"God," he prayed one day, "please show me if you want me out of this field. I will only stay in it if I can do your work here."

The answer came in dramatic fashion. The morning after putting the issue before God, a woman came into his office in tears. She needed to know, she said, if her husband really had been unfaithful as she suspected.

Bob saw her tears and the pain she was in and suddenly he could relate. He had been through divorce and knew the hurt of a torn marriage. He pulled up a chair and took the woman's hand much the way a father would do with his hurting child. He told the woman he would do what he could but that even if her husband was cheating on her, there could be nothing better than a reconciliation.

Indeed, after confirming the woman's fears, he arranged for the couple to meet in his office. That meeting led to another and eventually the couple agreed to get professional counseling and some time later they were reunited. Bob had his answer.

After that, with what Bob knew to be God's divine assistance, his reputation and income began to grow at a dramatic rate. Nationally, he became recognized as an authority on private investigations. Bob intended to keep doing investigations as long as there was someone he could help.

This was still true the morning he received the call from James Byrd. After listening to the sketchy details of the case, Bob knew it would fit that criterion. Somewhere, four parents were suffering a great deal of pain over not knowing the fate of their sons. There was only one way to ease their pain and that was by finding them—alive or dead.

With a confidence that was purely founded, Bob knew it was only a matter of time before he found the boys. And then, as with his other cases, he could put an end to their awful pain.

CHAPTER 6

In addition to being a phenomenal detective, Bob Brown prided himself on being a good father. He had two beautiful daughters, Vicky and Cindy, and years later, he and his second wife, Lois, had been blessed with a son. Over the years Bob had learned how different boys were from girls, how anxiously they sought their freedom and how they craved adventure.

Most of the time, Bob and Lois obliged their children by allowing the necessary experiences to help them gain their independence. There were vacations with friends, overnight trips, and other typical teenage activities. But there was one place Bob never allowed his kids to go and that was Daytona Beach.

Bob had never needed a newspaper article to understand the statistics about Daytona Beach and how it was considered one of the most dangerous cities in the United States.

Many of his investigations took him to that area and he had seen firsthand the types of people and kinds of behavior that made the city what it was. He had seen teenage girls selling their bodies for drug money, had known of teenage boys who had gotten caught up in the motorcycle gangs and then wound up in jail for committing crimes. He knew that for the most part Daytona Beach consisted of motels and bars and drug-infested video arcades. As far as he was concerned, his children had no business being in any of those places.

On Wednesday, November 1, he received a package of information from Byrd regarding the disappearance of Jim Boucher and Daryl Barber and everything their parents had been able to tell him about their sons.

Bob Brown had one rule he followed religiously: know the missing people before making a move. There was no point investigating the disappearance of two teenagers without first knowing everything there was to know about the boys. And by the time Bob was finished, he planned to know them better than even their parents did.

Although still working as a subcontracted investigator for James Byrd, Bob spent hours on the telephone talking to the boys' parents, their friends, girlfriends, teachers, and relatives. Finally, after a week of intensive efforts, he felt that he knew Jim and Daryl thoroughly. He knew where they would go for a good time, what restaurants they would eat at, who they would befriend, and, especially, what dangers they would be unaware of.

The boys' Florida dream vacation was the culmination of a seven-year friendship, the details of which Bob committed to memory. The boys were utterly loyal to that friendship and the close relationship they had built as children. They knew each other's strengths and weaknesses and one never failed to stand up for the other in times of trouble.

Naturally, their parents had figured there could be no better traveling companions. Certainly no one would bother two grown boys when one was always looking out for the other? Jim was younger than Daryl by two years and that alone brought comfort to Roy and Faye Boucher. In Daryl's company, Jim would always have someone watching over him, helping him should anything go wrong while they were away from home.

What their parents hadn't seen, and what Bob now found painfully obvious, was how their friendship might have worked against them. Both teens were equally naive, equally trusting of people they met. And neither had the ability to recognize the potential dangers that lay hidden like so many explosives across the sparkling sands and motel-lined streets that made up Daytona Beach.

This was largely because the boys had grown up in Metamora and spent little time outside the township limits. Bob researched the town and found that it offered no training in the ability to recognize criminal types. Very simply, there were no criminal types and no crime in Metamora or its neighboring communities.

Metamora, Michigan, was founded in 1832 after a pioneer named Jesse Lee moved to what was nothing more than an area of wilderness and built his wife a log cabin. Fifty years later an additional seventeen people had moved to Metamora, and in the years that followed, the township grew at only a slightly faster pace. So that by the 1970s, when Jim and Daryl were growing up, there were still less than five hundred people in the township of Metamora and another two thousand five hundred in the surrounding areas. So small was Metamora that when townspeople wanted to get out of town and head for the big city, they went to nearby Lapeer, which with 6,500 people was a regular metropolis in comparison.

Actually, the nearest big city was Detroit, some sixty miles south. People in Metamora heard rumors of the things that went on in Detroit: riots, armed robbery, killings. But for the most part there was never anything they could actually prove, because there were many people in Metamora who had never in all their lives traveled as far south as Detroit. After all, they had a civic center in Lapeer and there were clothing shops, auto repair garages, and certainly grocery stores. What possible reason could there be, most people reasoned, to leave a beautiful place like Metamora, or even Lapeer for that matter, and travel to a forsaken place like Detroit?

For all its big-city problems, Bob figured had even one of the boys been from Detroit he might have seen Daytona Beach for what it was. The drug dealers and thieves would stick out as clearly as if they carried billboard signs.

Instead, upon their arrival at Daytona Beach, Jim and Daryl probably saw the same thing Jim's girlfriend had seen: a teenage playground the likes of which had never been seen in Metamora or anywhere else in Michigan.

The playgrounds where Jim and Daryl sought a good time in the early days of their friendship had been much safer.

Daryl, the youngest of five children, had grown up in his family's sprawling home on Baldwin Road. The Barbers owned quarter horses and kept them on their ten-acre lot. They also had what was probably one of the only private swimming pools in all of Metamora or the surrounding townships. For that reason, Bob learned, the Barber children always had a stream of friends flowing in and out of their home, and there were times it seemed more like a clubhouse than the family's private backyard.

Daryl's parents loved the busyness of their home and did all they could to encourage it. They believed that if their children were spending time at home, they weren't spending it in places where they might get in trouble. The theory had proved effective and as Daryl's siblings grew to be productive adults, the Barbers never regretted having opened their home to the neighborhood children.

With his four older brothers and sisters entertaining their friends at the house, Daryl often hung around kids who were older than he. In addition to his place in the family birth order, Daryl's friends were older because the children who had grown up on Baldwin Road tended to be older, also. Most of the families had purchased land and built homes at about the same time and at first none of them had children Daryl's age.

Outgoing and personable even at the impish and mischievous age of seven, Daryl never minded or even noticed that he lacked friends his own age. He enjoyed playing with the friends of his brothers and sisters and thrived on the attention they gave him.

"Your little brother is so cute," his brother's girlfriends had said on more than one occasion.

Bob could imagine how Daryl's brown eyes must have danced, his dimples punctuating his precocious grin. Who needed friends one's own age when one was getting that kind of attention from older girls? When he wasn't spending time with the older kids, Daryl rode horses or fished from the family's private pond. He was an athletic boy with tanned skin and an easy, friendly smile. Especially as he grew older, more than one girl in the neighborhood began paying attention to the handsome youngest son in the Barber household.

Bob smiled at the picture of Daryl. Indeed, the boy had lived a charmed childhood, one which only got better the summer of 1971—the summer Jim Boucher moved into the house down the street.

Ron and Faye Boucher had lived in Troy, Michigan, since shortly after getting married. Although Troy was not the city Detroit was, it seemed to be heading that way and the Bouchers were not pleased. Sometime after Jim and Timothy were born they began dreaming about moving to the country: vast open space, trees to climb, horses to ride, friendly neighbors. In Troy, they feared that soon enough there would come the crime and violence and crowded conditions that accompany life in the city.

By 1971 the Bouchers had four children, all of them boys, and they were ready to make their dreams of owning a country home a reality. That year the Bouchers spent many weekends piling the boys into the station wagon and driving through the countryside. Eventually they located several areas, each of which would be a wonderful place to raise their sons. Their favorite place was Metamora, with its rolling green hills and houses set back on several-acre lots along country lanes. Ron began searching for work in the area.

In a few months things fell into place. Ron was hired by G. P. Plastics in Lapeer, just six miles from Metamora, and the family purchased an old farmhouse on ten acres along Baldwin Road. Jim discovered Daryl the same day they moved in.

At that time, Jim was ten and Daryl, twelve. While his parents were unloading boxes from the moving truck and rearranging their new home, Jim wandered down the street and found a sandy-haired boy about his age walking along the road carrying a fishing pole. Bob had heard the story from a few people.

"Where are you going?" Jim had asked, hurrying his pace to catch up.

"Fishing," came Daryl's answer and he turned toward Jim with a curious glance. "Who are you?"

"Jim."

"Oh." There was a pause as the boys continued to walk together. "Well, where you from?"

"Just moved in. Down the street."

Daryl nodded appreciatively. "Good. We can do a lot of fishing. My brothers and sisters don't fish much anymore. You like to fish?"

"Sure," Jim shrugged. He had wondered if there would be guys his age on Baldwin Road. He had left behind his entire Little League team, not to mention his fifth-grade class in Troy.

"Go get your swimming trunks," Daryl said, still walking toward the pond and pointing toward a break in land several hundred yards ahead of him. "I'll be up that dirt road a ways."

So was born a friendship that came as easily as the fish from the clear, cold pond behind Daryl's house, as naturally as the maple trees turned colors each season. The friendship between Jim and Daryl was effortless from the beginning, almost as if they had lived down the street from each other all their lives.

They spent summers fishing and playing baseball, and in the middle of winter when the pond froze over, the boys would ice-skate, using a tennis ball for a puck and pretending to be professional hockey players. In the spring there was Little League baseball and flag football. The boys were always together, always in motion, their friendship grew until their parents rarely saw one boy without the other.

In his research Bob came across several people who said the boys were more like brothers than friends. But there was a difference: brothers fought with one another; Jim and Daryl did not. Even when they reached their teenage years and were sometimes interested in the same girl, nothing came between them.

It was during those early days of friendship that they grew fiercely protective of each other, completely loyal to the bond they shared. If someone threatened Jim they would have to face Daryl. And if Daryl missed a fly ball in center field during a Little League game, then Jim was the first one defending him in the dugout.

Of course, much of the time Daryl was the one looking out for Jim, since Jim was two years younger. Bob thought it must have been an interesting switch for Daryl, who as the youngest in his family had always been watched over by his older siblings. Likewise, Jim was not used to having someone to look up to, a role model older than himself. As the oldest in his family, he had always had to set the example and take care of his younger brothers. But with Daryl it was different and Jim thought the world of his older friend.

There was nothing, it seemed, that Daryl couldn't do. He could hit home runs easier, run faster, and swim farther than any of his peers. He caught the biggest fish and was an experienced horseman before he hit his teenage years. He could talk his way out of a punishment and if necessary fight his way out of an argument. In Jim's eyes, Daryl was larger than life, the older brother he never had. As time passed, Jim knew from years of experience that whenever they were together he had nothing to worry about.

Bob decided that was probably how Jim felt about traveling with Daryl to Daytona Beach in the summer of 1978. After all, Daryl had been to Florida before, even if he had been quite a bit younger then, and even if his parents had been with him. Jim figured Daryl was worldly and wise, and beyond that Daryl knew how to have a good time. There was probably no one Jim would rather have gone with on his first trip away from home without his parents.

Jim was quiet and reflective. If Bob knew the younger boy like he thought he did, Jim had probably considered the trip and the things that might go wrong. They could run out of gas or have car trouble. They might get lost or sick or lose their money. And once they were on the beach they might encounter deadly riptides or a man-eating shark in the Atlantic Ocean.

But as far as Bob could tell neither Jim nor Daryl ever voiced such concerns. After all, Daryl had been to Daytona Beach before and successfully returned without any problems. And because of that Jim probably believed that with Daryl in control they could also steer clear of any trouble this time.

In Bob's opinion the flaw in that thinking was obvious. Neither Jim nor Daryl would recognize Daytona Beach trouble if it walked up and introduced itself.

CHAPTER 7

As Bob learned about Jim and Daryl, he quickly realized that the boys shared more than common interests and pastimes. They were both responsible teenagers with a deep respect for their parents. This was no accident in Bob's opinion. The teens came from large families in which having respect for one's siblings and parents was equally important as doing one's chores. Children did not have an option when it came to being respectful or responsible. It was simply expected.

As a result, Jim and Daryl were the types of boys to do their chores as asked and clean up after themselves, all while practically thanking their parents for the opportunity to help. And if they weren't perfect, they were certainly not rabble-rousers and they certainly did not possess the kind of defiant attitude that some of their peers often expressed toward their parents.

But above all, Bob learned, they never made their parents worry about them. Both sets of parents developed a system as soon as their children were old enough to leave home by themselves. It was a system that guaranteed the parents would always know the children's whereabouts. To break the rule would be to have privileges taken away for upwards of a month or more. Besides, letting parents know of one's whereabouts was a matter of courtesy, and for the children in both households it was something they took for granted and never complained about.

The system worked this way. Note pads were left on the kitchen tables at both homes so that children coming and going could always leave messages. Even if previous permission had been given, the children were to write down where they had gone, when they had left, and when they would be home. If they were running a little late, they were to call home immediately. Never, under any circumstances, was one of the ten children belonging to the Barbers and Bouchers ever to go somewhere without notifying their parents. None of the Barber or Boucher children ever thought this a strange way of life. It was a matter of respecting their parents' wishes and being responsible enough to obey them.

When Jim and Daryl made plans for their trip to Florida, Faye Boucher could remember several times asking Jim to please telephone home every now and then. Because they were trying to give Jim his freedom, they did not insist their son call every day. But it went without saying that the boys would most likely call several times during the vacation. Probably every day, because that was the kind of teens they were. Respect and responsibility.

All of which led Bob to another aspect of the boys' lives he had figured out. Neither teen was a drug user.

Even in Metamora, a town of less than a thousand people, some of Jim and

Daryl's friends smoked marijuana now and then. Bob had not been surprised to learn this. It was, after all, the summer of 1978 and youth nationwide were still feeling the effects of the drug-induced rebellion that began a decade earlier. That year and for years afterward there were still a good deal of people who viewed drugs the way people had viewed them in the late 1960s: merely a form of entertainment.

Jim and Daryl had been around people who smoked pot but they never participated. They played sports together in high school and had decided to avoid taking drugs or doing any excessive drinking.

Nevertheless, they didn't mind associating with people who drank excessively or even used drugs. So the idea of partying in a place where people might be doing drugs did not strike either teenager as being a problem. And this concerned Bob deeply. He was only too aware of the hard-core drug parties that took place in Daytona Beach and the numbers of naive kids that attended. Often the parties allowed those kids to try drugs for the first time only to be sucked into an underground world of highs and lows and living for the moment. He did not think Jim and Daryl were the type of teenagers to be cajoled into drug use, but he wasn't sure. After all, the boys were on their very first vacation away from home. Anything was possible.

Still, even if they had dabbled in drugs or drinking while at the beach, Bob thought they would have come home at week's end. Especially because the teens had every reason in the world to return to Metamora.

Daryl, for instance, had a close relationship with his parents and siblings and a full-time job as a machinist. He had worked carefully for the past year and had received an excellent evaluation after almost no absences or late arrivals. He had been thrilled to have a paid vacation and before leaving he had voiced intentions to stay with the company for some time.

But if Daryl had reasons to return home, Jim had ten times as many. First, there was his family. He was very close to his brothers and enthralled with his little sister, Kristi. Six-year-old John looked up to Jim in such a way that Jim knew his absence for any length of time would be hard on the child. He was also very close to his parents.

Then there was Jaime, the girl he'd been dating. The two had been on very good terms and Bob knew the girl hadn't heard from Jim since he'd left.

And if the people he loved were not enough reason to believe Jim wanted to return home, there was his money. Jim had won ten thousand in a bowling tournament, nine thousand six hundred of which was sitting in a bank account in Metamora. He had ordered a brand new 1979 Camaro, which was going to be ready in a few months.

Bob was convinced that there was not a boy anywhere with that kind of money and expecting that kind of car who would simply turn his back and disappear.

It made no sense. Perhaps if Jim had taken his money with him. But not with $9,600 in the bank and a brand new car en route to his parents' house.

Back in his Orlando office at the end of the week, Bob thought about the boys and all he had learned, and picked up a picture of Jim Boucher. The interviews had been helpful, but a person could learn what they wanted about Jim from his eyes, Bob decided. They were filled with laughter and typically danced with energy. But they were, at the same time, utterly innocent and naive. The eyes of a child trying to adjust to his nearly adult body.

In light of all that he had learned, Bob knew the boys were not runaways. And so that left just one other option. For some reason, Jim and Daryl must be unable to call home. Whatever the reason, Bob was certain the teens were in some kind of trouble and needed assistance.

He thought about the townsfolk of Metamora and how taken they were with the boys' disappearance. Bob had spoken with several of them and knew that they were worried about Jim and Daryl. Although the residents of Metamora remained largely sheltered from the happenings of city life, they discussed in great length the happenings in their immediate community.

Bob knew that when people in Metamora said that everyone knew everybody else, they were serious. So that if someone walked into the market and mentioned that Joe was having trouble with Diane, everyone in earshot knew exactly who they were talking about and probably what the trouble was. Despite this, nothing of much interest ever occurred in Metamora in all the years that the Barbers and Bouchers lived there. But that was before Jim and Daryl disappeared.

Once word got around about how the boys had gone to Florida on vacation and then were never heard from again, people in Metamora were horrified. Suddenly, it was as if the boys had two hundred sets of parents, dozens of siblings, and probably a thousand or so close friends. Everyone had their opinion about what might have happened to the boys, which by itself was not so interesting given the nature of the town. What was interesting was that, despite their lack of exposure to such things, their consensus—and it was one Bob had to agree with—was rather dark.

If the boys had left loving families, loving friends, jobs, and girlfriends, and in Jim's case nearly ten thousand dollars, back in Metamora and still had not called home, then there was only one likely explanation.

Something terrible had happened.

CHAPTER 8

The first thing Bob Brown did after learning all he could about the boys and their backgrounds was go over the groundwork that had already been laid by the boys' parents. He read copies of the missing persons reports they had filed with the Michigan state police and learned that that agency had in turn filed a report with an Officer Mikelson in Daytona Beach. Then he began sorting through a myriad of other aspects involving the case.

Eventually, he would contact Mikelson, although he didn't expect to learn much from the detective. People disappear daily along Daytona Beach and missing persons cases were as common as sunbathers. The way Bob figured it, Mikelson would be doing well if he'd even read the case by now.

In fact, by then Daytona Beach Detective Wes Mikelson had not only read the case but also given it more thought than most.

He was not unaware of the fact that while life in the Barber and Boucher homes was slowly falling apart, the entire burden of finding the missing teenagers had fallen squarely on his shoulders.

Mikelson had always enjoyed the beach and had even been mistaken for a regular along the beach when he was off duty. He was tall and handsome with dark good looks and bronze skin. But when he was in uniform, the thirty-five-year-old Mikelson's deep brown eyes looked hard and ruthless. If one was going to work Daytona Beach, one needed to be ruthless, even on the good days.

Daytona Beach, being what it was, offered a plethora of opportunities for Mikelson to do what he enjoyed doing best—solving crimes. There was a limitless supply of crimes happening every day in Daytona Beach and over the years Mikelson had had a hand in solving more than a few major cases.

In fact, there was much that Mikelson enjoyed about his job as detective for the Daytona Police Department. He liked being near the beach, liked being near young people—especially when his watchful eye played a part in turning some of them away from a life of crime. He even liked the fact that he stayed so busy.

What Mikelson disliked most about his job was the missing persons cases. As with other police departments, each of the detectives was responsible for an equal number of missing persons cases in addition to his regular workload. The problem was, in Daytona Beach that number was incredibly high. For instance, currently, in addition to the murders and rapes and robberies that Mikelson was personally working on, he probably had nearly a hundred missing persons cases. Maybe more.

If that number had been something more manageable such as, say, five or even ten cases, Mikelson knew he would put in overtime trying to figure them out. He would read them carefully, make telephone calls, and contact friends and relatives. Anything to find the missing people and give peace of mind to those who had filed the report.

But *one hundred cases.*

Mikelson was overwhelmed by the number. Since his colleagues had an equal number of missing persons cases, they had developed a system by which all such cases were handled. An officer would be assigned to the case. He would take down the information regarding the physical appearance of the missing person, and he would pass it along to everyone in the department.

Then, instead of actually working the case, they tried to keep in mind the descriptions of several hundred missing persons each time they were on the streets. Mikelson thought this a sad way of dealing with cases that might, in fact, involve criminal activity. But they had so many cases to solve, so much work to do, that there really weren't any options.

And so on the morning of August 22, 1978, when Mikelson received in the mail the information involving the missing persons reports of Jim Boucher and Daryl Barber, he shook his head sadly. He remembered what the Michigan officer had said about the case smelling fishy, and he wished once again that he had time to actually work this case and any of a dozen of the more interesting missing persons cases to which he'd been assigned.

The problem was, most of his hundred cases involved teenage boys. And much of the time, these missing persons were only kids who had come to Daytona Beach and gotten caught up in the drug culture or who had perhaps moved into one of the local flophouses where they suddenly were without any responsibility whatsoever. Many kids used Daytona Beach as an escape from their real lives. It was a place where kids from all over the country went when they ran away.

Because of that, Mikelson knew he could not justify spending time on a missing persons case involving two teenage boys. Glancing through the file he looked at their pictures: Daryl's handsome face and bright grin; Jim's gentle brown eyes and shy smile.

Mikelson sighed out loud, frustrated by the ineffectiveness of what he was about to do. Then he unceremoniously tossed the folder in a box with dozens and dozens like it. As he did, he remembered the boys' faces. They looked like nice kids. Probably came from nice families. What in the world, then, were they doing in Daytona Beach?

CHAPTER 9

Like Detective Mikelson, Bob Brown could hardly understand why the Michigan boys would have gone to Daytona Beach for their vacation. After one week on the case he had researched the teenagers thoroughly and gone over what little information had already been obtained about their disappearance. In all he had one conclusion. The teens were totally unprepared for the fast and dangerous life that was Daytona Beach.

By the time Jim and Daryl took their August vacation, crime in Daytona Beach had actually decreased from the previous two years when it had reached a truly atrocious level. The problem was that even with the decrease, Daytona Beach was still a significantly dangerous place, whether a person was planning to live there or just stop by for a hamburger and a quick swim in the Atlantic.

So bad was the condition that four months later, on December 16, the *Sentinel Star* (now the *Orlando Sentinel*) ran a story on the front page of its metro section titled, "Seven of 25 Nationwide Top Crime Areas Are in Florida."

The lead paragraph of the story read, "The FBI says you are more likely to be the victim of a crime in Daytona Beach than in almost any other metropolitan area of the country. In fact," the article continued, "you even have a greater chance of being a crime victim here than in New York City."

The report went on to say that although there were fewer people in Daytona Beach—or more specifically, Volusia County—than many of the big cities around the country, crime was happening at a much more rapid pace. But even at that, Daytona Beach apparently had reason to be proud of the fact that they had less crime than in the recent past.

Daytona Beach police were certainly proud of the fact that in 1978, crimes had slowed down so that the area was now only the second most dangerous place in America. The statistic seemed like a victory because in 1976, Volusia County had been far and above the rightful owner of the No. 1 spot on the list of most dangerous places.

This information came as no surprise to Floridians, many of whom would never consider taking a vacation in Daytona Beach, let alone allowing their children to vacation there by themselves. Although located on a beautiful stretch of white sand and warm, clear water, in the 1970s Daytona Beach was a transient town. It was the unofficial headquarters for several biker gangs and ninety percent of the country's runaways. With those people making up much of the population, Daytona Beach became a place which lent itself to competitive drug dealing, easy robberies, and, with a fair amount of frequency, even murder. Many times, when a Daytona Beach resident needed money, bank withdrawals were not the only option.

In fact there were people who considered the entire place a barbaric setup which had long since spiraled out of control and would probably be best off closed down completely. But, since Daytona Beach was still a tourist trap and still brought in a great deal of capital for the state, no one ever acted on such suggestions. Instead they tried to curb the crime.

Which was why Volusia County Sheriff Ed Duff was so upbeat about the crime statistics reported in the December article. Despite the fact that his community had received nationwide attention because of its crime rate, Duff was quoted as saying that the statistics for the area really weren't "too bad." Especially when one considered the transient types attracted to the beach area and the fact that four thousand people had been added to his county since the previous year.

But Sheriff Duff's perspective and that of the Bouchers and Barbers were as different as Daytona Beach and Metamora. How Jim's girlfriend, Jaime, had come and gone without incident was almost remarkable in light of the statistics. In fact, if either of the boys' parents had known anything about Daytona Beach's crime rating or about the transients that frequented the area, Jim and Daryl never would have gone on the trip—not because their parents would have forbidden them to go, but because once the teenagers knew the truth about Daytona Beach, being responsible, respectful young men, they would have made the decision on their own.

Instead, their parents never learned the dark secrets about Daytona Beach until after their sons had disappeared. And by then, whether they were ready to admit this to themselves or not, it was far too late.

CHAPTER 10

It was not enough for the Barbers and Bouchers to hire a private investigator. The nightmare continued and so, they agreed, must their personal efforts to locate their sons. Even if that meant merely keeping alive the hope that one day they would come home.

Around the Barber home the older, married children, who had long since moved away, took turns coming by and comforting their parents. At times, the family would sit around the kitchen table brainstorming about ways to locate the boys. Other times, they attempted to carry on other conversations involving other matters. But nothing, not a single word, was ever said that wasn't weighed against the prevailing burden that Daryl was missing.

Marian and Ron took turns being supportive for each other. But inevitably, each day was longer than the one that preceded it and more depressing in light of the fact that there was no news about the boys. Nights were the worst. The couple would lie in bed, awake but lost in their own private worlds of agony. Instead of sleeping, they would rack their brains thinking of some way they could find their son. And when they weren't doing that, they were busy remembering the past, reliving memories of Daryl as if by doing so they might preserve his presence in their lives another day.

The most vivid memories were those of Daryl and his motorcycle. He had purchased the bike prior to the trip and had enjoyed riding along the country lanes that wound their way through Metamora. Each evening, on the days when he went riding, Daryl would take a damp cloth and dust off the bike's body, taking special care to keep it in perfect condition. Now the motorcycle sat unused in the Barbers' garage and the cleaning was done by his parents. Marian and Ron took turns caring for the bike, almost as if by doing so they could keep it ready and waiting for the moment Daryl would return home.

And there was the pond out back, where Daryl and Jim would fish, and the horses that Daryl had always liked to ride. Everywhere the Barbers looked there were memories of their son.

Sometimes, when she thought no one would miss her, Marian would go outside, sit on the front porch, gaze down Baldwin Road, and cry. Daryl was her youngest son, her baby. It seemed like just yesterday that he was toddling around the house trying to keep up with his older brothers and sisters. She missed him so badly there were days when she didn't believe she could go on. She was certain, as much as she tried to deny the fact, that something very, very bad must have happened to her son to keep him away from home so long.

When she wasn't sitting outside looking for Daryl to return or polishing the chrome on his motorcycle, Marian would look through photo albums: toothless baby Daryl celebrating his first birthday; six-year-old Daryl riding proudly on his new bicycle; thirteen-year-old Daryl in his Little League outfit swinging a bat for all it was worth; nineteen-year-old Daryl standing beside his motorcycle grinning from ear to ear.

But the pictures stopped there, followed by empty unfilled pages. Marian prayed with everything inside her that one day there would be more pictures. Daryl would come home and they could go on living like a normal family again.

Things were no better at the Boucher home. In fact, if possible, they were worse.

Jim's younger brothers had begun to fall apart in light of their older brother's disappearance. Timothy and Steven had started doing poorly in school and had begun moping about the house in a way that was completely uncharacteristic for them. Neither boy wanted to believe that something bad had happened to Jim. But by the end of September, they had trouble imagining any other possibilities.

Then there was John, the first grader who idolized his older brother. John had been almost completely unable to attend school since Jim and Daryl disappeared. He was very aware of what was happening and knew how worried his parents were. As a result, he had convinced himself that Jim had been "hurt by bad guys" and that the bad guys, whoever they were, would try to get him, too. Each morning Faye would get John ready for school while he protested the entire time.

"No, Mommy," he would say, his innocent brown eyes filling with tears. "The bad guys will get me! I want to stay home and wait for Jimmy. Please! Mommy, the bad guys will be there!"

And Faye would have to explain to him, despite her own fears and heartache, that there were no bad guys waiting for him outside his first-grade classroom.

"You need to go to school, son," she would say. "Let us worry about Jim. We're going to find him as soon as we can."

But John would only cry louder until finally, with her little boy still sobbing, Faye would strap him in the station wagon and take him to school.

The separation was another thing.

"Don't leave me, Mommy, please!" he would cry. And there wasn't a day that went by when Faye didn't leave John's classroom in tears herself.

Each day, about an hour later, Faye could expect a phone call.

"John's terribly upset," the principal would say. "I think you'd better come and get him."

Finally, under advice from a counselor, Faye and Roy decided to take John out of school and keep him home. But even then the child's torment was relentless. At night he would wake up screaming that the bad guys were coming or that they were in his room ready to get him.

"Help me, Mommy! Help me!" he would scream and Faye would go running into his room.

"It's all right, honey," she would say, holding him closely, trying to give him the security that had been ripped from his very existence the day Jim disappeared.

Then when John had calmed down enough and was ready to get back to sleep, he would drag his pillow and blanket into his parents' room and, still emitting tiny childlike sobs, he would fall asleep next to them on the floor.

If Jim's absence was seriously harming the mental health of his brothers, it was taking a tremendous toll on the physical health of his father. Roy Boucher was a diabetic and had always been able to control his disease through insulin shots. Roy knew that excessive sugar and a sedentary lifestyle contributed to the harmful effects of his disease so he exercised regularly and was always careful about what he ate. Those were the ways a person could control diabetes.

But the most damaging risk factor for a diabetic was something Roy had no control over at all. Stress. When a person suffering from diabetes is forced into stressful situations, especially long-term stressful situations, that person's blood sugar rises dramatically. That in turn plays havoc with the body's pancreas, which in a normal person produces the proper amount of insulin to keep blood sugar levels normal.

With elevated blood sugar, a diabetic must take more insulin to compensate; otherwise he could slip into a diabetic coma. But even when high blood sugar does not result in a coma, it weakens the body's immune system, leaving the diabetic susceptible to an assortments of ailments. Worse yet, it is difficult for a person with diabetes to overcome these ailments because a diabetic does not heal as quickly as most people.

When the weeks began to pass and Jim still had not returned home, Roy's blood sugar levels began to rise. His son was missing and the idea of not knowing where he was, was actually killing him. Eventually his blood sugar levels began to skyrocket. At that time, Roy began to get sick and had to take a medical leave of absence from his job as foreman with G. P. Plastics.

There was absolutely nothing the doctors could do to stop the ravaging toll diabetes was taking on his body. Stress was to blame. And there was just one thing that could eliminate Roy's stress: his son's return.

Sick much of the time and battling his raging blood sugar levels, Roy said very little of how he felt about Jim's disappearance. Obviously he was devastated, worried sick in a literal sense. But he never talked about his feelings, never screamed about the unfairness involved or the irony or the heartbreak. He remained stoic and quiet, while his body slowly destroyed itself.

Faye, meanwhile, found herself in the position of counselor. She was the one who talked with her remaining sons when they had questions. Most often, she was the one who comforted John when he began to cry about the bad guys. But there were many times when she could no longer be the comforter, times when she could not go another minute unless there was someone to comfort her.

Those were the times when Faye would sneak into the nursery, take Kristi from her crib, and hold her tight. What had started as a way to ease the pain that first night when Jim and Daryl hadn't come home had become a way of dealing with life. Kristi, so new and innocent and unaware of all that was happening around her, would smile and coo at her mother, happy and peaceful in her mother's arms.

There, with the tiny baby close to her body, Faye would allow the tears to come. She would cry and cry, tears spilling onto her baby daughter as she tried to ease the pain and ache that Jim's absence was causing her. Sometimes Roy would find Faye like that, rocking Kristi and crying soundlessly, and he would pause a moment and then shut the door, leaving her to deal with her grief in private. But he never spoke to her about it, never asked why she did that or if it helped any.

And so, with each of them struggling individually to deal with the pain and frustration of missing their children and with none of them having any idea where to find the boys, they agreed on a plan. They had been in contact with the Michigan State Police Department daily and had learned nothing. For that reason, Faye made a decision to write to the governor, asking him to intervene. She had read once of a family who had done that and then received so much attention that their child was eventually found.

One afternoon on a crisp day in early November, Faye took out a stack of stationery and wrote a letter to Governor William G. Milliken. The letter wound up in the hands of one Larry C. Burkhalter, a member of the Michigan House of Representatives. He read the words and thought for a moment that he could feel the woman's pain. So he took an hour that same afternoon and wrote a letter to the governor detailing the circumstances surrounding Jim and Daryl's disappearance.

> We have been requested by these families to do all in our power to see that this case be given all possible attention. Thus, I am requesting that your office contact the Governor of Florida to inquire as to what the law enforcement agencies in those states are doing to pursue this case. It is my hope that the state police and all local law enforcement agencies of that state will be made aware of this case and begin to participate fully its investigation.
>
> Thank you, in advance, for your assistance. I await your response.
>
> Sincerely, Larry Burkhalter.

Then Burkhalter contacted the Bouchers and told them to remain posted. He was certain, being a friend of Milliken's, that the governor would respond. When that happened, Burkhalter would let them know what happened next.

Faye Boucher felt a sliver of hope after speaking with Burkhalter. By then she had sent duplicate letters to the Michigan State Police, the Daytona Beach Police Department, the Michigan House of Representatives, the state assembly, and the governor's office. After that she took another leap and sent letters to the vice president and even to the Oval Office to be read by the President himself.

Burkhalter's phone call assured Faye that someone was listening to her. And that maybe, if the chains of command began to work properly, someone would find Jim and Daryl and take care of the bad guys—whoever they were—once and for all.

CHAPTER 11

The time had come for Bob to pay a visit to the Daytona Beach Police Department. He knew a report had been filed with the department, but now he had to see what work if any had been done on the case. Bob thought he knew the answer to that question. There were hundreds of missing teenagers reported each year in Daytona Beach and more likely than not this one hadn't received any more attention than any of the others. But it was worth checking.

Besides, in a case where Bob suspected criminal activity, he liked to keep the police apprised of what he was doing. He didn't need their help to solve his cases, but he would need an officer who knew the details of the case on the chance that someone might need to be arrested. And Bob figured that before this case was finished there would be at least one arrest.

With the file tucked neatly inside his briefcase, Bob climbed into his sedan and set out for Daytona Beach, an hour northeast of Orlando.

At one o'clock that afternoon, Detective Wes Mikelson was sitting at his desk doing paperwork. He had been busier than usual, trying to catch up on an extreme workload that summer. While some people talked about Daytona Beach's alarming crime and other people wrote about the statistics, Mikelson and his peers were busy handling it.

At the top corner of his desk was a three-tiered document holder. The top section was overflowing with new missing persons reports. The documents that didn't fit in that section were stacked beside him, spilling out of a cardboard box. The missing persons case involving Jim and Daryl hadn't crossed his mind for weeks.

So many other such cases had come his way that he wouldn't have had time to think about the Michigan teenagers at all. Finding a missing person in Daytona Beach was, in those days, virtually impossible. Especially because there were so many other crimes for detectives like Mikelson to investigate.

He was sorting through one such criminal case when Bob Brown entered the office, walked up to his desk, and pulled up a chair. The police in Daytona Beach knew Brown, even though most of them had never worked with him. Brown handled domestic cases and, not surprisingly, there were a lot of domestic problems in Daytona Beach. For that reason the police had crossed paths with Brown on several occasions.

Bob pulled out a badge from his pocket and identified himself.

"Right," Mikelson said politely. "You work a lot of domestics out here. How can I help you?"

Bob set his file on Mikelson's desk and opened it. "I understand you're working the Boucher-Barber case."

Mikelson's expression was blank. "Who?"

"Boucher-Barber."

"Uh," Mikelson searched his memory. "Doesn't sound familiar. What's the case about?"

"Missing persons. The boys came here from Michigan and never returned home."

Suddenly Mikelson remembered the case. "Oh, right, right," he said. "The family's been calling, checking everything out. Real worried."

"Is it your case?"

"Yeah," Mikelson sounded somewhat defensive. "Look, Bob. The kids are nowhere."

Bob raised an eyebrow. "Exactly how much investigation time have you put into it, if you don't mind me asking?"

Mikelson shook his head in a way that suggested he was disgusted about something.

"None. No time at all. It just hasn't been possible," he said. "You know how many missing persons we get out here along the beach?"

"Well, this case is a little different."

"That's what everyone says. Every case involves someone who would never disappear. Relatives call and they want us to put the entire department on hold while we find their family member. Same story each time. Listen, Bob. It's just not possible."

"Okay, but let's talk about it for a minute. You do have a minute, don't you?"

Mikelson threw up his hands. "Sure. Why not?"

Bob opened the file and showed the detective the money sitting in Jim's bank account and the brand-new motorcycle sitting in Daryl's garage.

"They had good relationships with their parents, lots of friends, jobs, and girlfriends," he said. "And not one person has heard a word from them since August twelfth. Doesn't that sound a little bit like something criminal may have happened here?"

Mikelson sighed, closing the file he'd been working on and taking a closer look at the one Bob had brought in. After a minute he looked up. Bob could read the detective's eyes and he saw that the man was greatly frustrated. "What do you want me to do?"

"Well, first I thought you'd be interested to know that the governor of Michigan has contacted our governor. The big boys are getting interested in this one. Sort of using it as an example, a reason to tackle the criminal activity on the beach once and for all," Bob said, leaning back in his chair.

"Second, I want you to know that I'm not going anywhere until I find those boys. I'll be in your office, walking your beaches, checking your flophouses.

You're going to get so sick of seeing me you'll do anything to help solve this case. And finally, I want you to know that when I find out who's responsible for the disappearance of those kids, you're the first person I'm going to call. You'll get the arrest, Mikelson, and that will look just swell on your track record, don't you think?"

Mikelson was looking weary as he listened to Bob. "Sure. Swell."

"So when I need a little assistance, you're going to give it," Bob was not looking for approval, but rather stating a fact. "Sound good?"

"Sure," Mikelson said. He was massaging his eyebrows and staring at a blank spot on his desk. As Bob got up to leave, Mikelson looked up. "Hey, Bob, just remember one thing. I can't make any promises. My schedule is packed as it is and I can't be taking time to find those boys."

Bob smiled confidently as he turned and left the office. "Don't worry, Mikelson. You won't have to."

CHAPTER 12

If not knowing where their sons were was sucking the life out of everyone in the Boucher and Barber families, by the second week in November there was something that seemed even worse. There seemed to be nothing they could do to change their situation.

Yes, they had a private investigator working on the case. But there had to be something else they could do to find their sons. Finally, that week, they hit upon an idea. They would contact the media, make a plea for publicity. And maybe then someone would know something and they could finally find their missing boys.

For the most part they were met with indifference by various editors and television news producers. Two teenage boys take a trip to Daytona Beach and don't come home as expected. It wasn't exactly the type of story that drummed up sympathy and an urge to react on the part of readers and viewers. When the missing children were young and helpless, that was one thing. But when they were nearing their twenties, people figured they probably disappeared on purpose.

So, despite the families' efforts, the local newspapers and television stations ignored the story. With one exception.

The K-Liner, a national newspaper for and about Kmart employees agreed to run a small story and picture on the front page of its October issue. The editor reasoned that since Jim had worked for a tremendous company like Kmart that past summer and had not yet reported back for work, something must truly be amiss.

Jim's picture ran alongside a three-inch article titled, "Jim's Missing." The article stated only the basics—the day Jim and his "traveling companion" had disappeared, the fact that Jim had worked for Kmart number 9088 in Lapeer, Michigan, and that he was about to start his senior year in high school. Then, in case anyone recognized him, the article listed a telephone number of the Michigan State Police in Lapeer.

One week later, in East Birmingham, Alabama, the manager of the local Kmart received the K-Liner newspaper and, as was procedure, tacked it up on the store's bulletin board. The next day, shopper Margie Barrett saw the article and immediately recognized Jim's picture.

Jim was the same boy she had hired to help her around her farm sometime in the middle of August. She was positive. Immediately, Margie copied down the information in the article and returned back home. She checked her records to see what day she had hired the boy and whether his name was Jim Boucher or not.

Her records showed the boy's hire date as August 15. He had used the name Walter Alexander and had only worked for her a few days. She remembered that when he had left, he had said he was going on to work at a cement plant in Tarrant City, Alabama.

Margie was certain the boy was Jim Boucher. She quickly dialed the number that had appeared in the article and was eventually transferred to Officer Ray Burnham. Burnham had dealt with the case since the missing persons reports were originally filed. Now, after listening to the woman and taking down her information, he needed to ask a few more questions regarding the boy's attitudes and any other factors that might identify him as Jim Boucher of Metamora.

"Now, you say the boy you hired looked like the boy in the newspaper," Burnham asked.

"Yes! I'm positive. It's him!" The woman was excited and Burnham couldn't help but feel the same way. He would love nothing more than to call the parents of those boys with word that their sons had been found.

"Okay, fine." Burnham was scribbling notes as he spoke. "The missing boy was traveling with a friend. Did you see another boy at any time?"

"Well," Margie said, puzzled at this detail. "I read that he had been traveling with someone and I do remember another boy coming by the farm a couple times. The two of them would go off and do things together after work. But I never got a good picture of the other boy, never got his name or anything. Now, Jim, he was another story. He came to me looking for a few days' work and I gave it to him. Said he wanted to pick up a little cash before heading over to Tarrant City and the cement plant."

"Did Jim talk about running away from home?"

"No. But something was wrong with the boy. I knew it the minute I hired him. Now that I think back, he must have been running from something. Else why would he be plumb out of money?"

"Right." Burnham was anxious to get through his questions so he could decide what to do next. "Just a few more questions. This other boy, the one who would come and visit Jim and go out with him after work. Can you tell me how tall he was?"

"Sure, he was about the same size as Jim. Looked like two peas in a pod, they did! At least from what I could tell."

"Okay, fine," Burnham said. "That's all the questions I have. We may be in touch again and certainly if you remember any other details give us a call."

"I hope I helped you some," the woman said, her voice smothered in southern charm.

"Well, we'll certainly check it out. I want to thank you for taking the time to call. The boys' parents will probably want to thank you, too."

Burnham hung up the phone and considered his next move. He wanted to call the families, but he didn't want to get the parents' hopes up if this was a false alarm. Whatever he did, he would have to move quickly. If the boys had decided to run away, there was no telling how often they might pick up and leave. Burnham decided to contact the cement plant first. He picked up the telephone and began dialing. A few phone calls later he had the number for the cement plant. A secretary answered on the first ring.

"This is Officer Burnham, Michigan State Police," he said. "We need to know if you have a Jim Boucher working at your plant?"

The secretary did not hesitate but answered the officer immediately. "Why, yes!" she said, anxious to be of help. What would a Michigan police officer want of Jim? she wondered. Suddenly the day did not seem quite so dull. "Jim's a great guy. Works for us, sure does."

Burnham could hardly believe his good fortune. The boys' parents were going to be thrilled.

"Could you tell me what Jim looks like?"

"Oh, sure!" Her voice was bubbly and Burnham hoped she would be able to identify the teenager. "He has brown hair, a mustache," she paused. "You know, kind of thin and stuff."

Burnham felt another surge of excitement. Based on his description of the boys, that was definitely Jim.

"Now, what about Jim's friends. Any friends of his working there? Guy named Daryl, for instance?"

The girl gasped. "How did you know?" she asked. Burnham was struck by how thick the girl's southern accent was. He could hardly understand her. "Daryl and Jim are best friends. They work together all the time, same shifts and everything."

"Okay, tell me what Daryl looks like."

"Well, pretty much the same size and all. Just a little bit bigger, and no mustache or anything." Then the girl paused and her tone of voice changed and she gasped once again. "They're not in trouble with the police or anything are they?"

"No, nothing like that. Hey, could you tell me when they work next."

"Just a minute." The girl paused a moment, checking the work schedule. "Yes, here it is! They work tomorrow afternoon. Two o'clock."

"Okay, thanks for your help. We'll be in touch."

"Is there a message, anything you want me to tell them?"

"No." Burnham was afraid the girl would notify Jim and Daryl and that they would disappear again before their parents could reach them. "Don't bother the guys. I'm just doing some research, that's all."

When he hung up the phone he felt better than he had in years. It was one thing to solve a case in which the subject was a criminal. But this was something new, finding two boys whose parents were worried sick about their disappearance. Burnham thought this next phone call might possible be the most rewarding in his life.

CHAPTER 13

About a week before Margie Barrett saw *The K-Liner* newspaper, Faye's relatives decided to get involved in the search for Jim and Daryl.

Faye's sister, Jessie, and her husband, Craig, were especially close to Jim. Craig, in addition to being Jim's uncle, was also his bowling partner and friend. Several years earlier Craig had taught Jim the proper technique for rolling a bowling ball, working with him several hours each week.

As Jim grew older and stronger, he mastered those techniques until finally he surpassed Craig at consistently bowling a high-scoring game. Craig enjoyed spending time with Jim, treating him as an equal despite their age difference. And in his presence, Jim felt special. There was nothing quite like an afternoon at the bowling alley with Uncle Craig.

It was Craig who convinced Jim to enter the Detroit Motor Bowl contest in which the grand prize was ten thousand. Craig had competed, too. When Jim won the contest Craig was so proud he told everyone he knew.

"Hey," he'd say. "Remember my nephew, the one who bowls with me? Well, get this. He won the Detroit Motor Bowl. The whole thing. Ten thousand! What a kid, eh?"

Craig had immediately begun making plans to help Jim improve his skills for next year's competition. Wanting badly to be a repeat winner, Jim had spent much of his spare time prior to the vacation with his Uncle Craig.

So, when the boys disappeared, Craig had wanted to do whatever he could to find them. When weeks passed, he had grown fearful and frustrated. He agreed that the boys had no reason to want to run away. And, like the police and the boys' parents, he could not understand why they hadn't come home yet. By the end of October, he could no longer sit by while other people investigated his nephew's whereabouts.

"I'm going to Florida, Faye," he told her one day. "Jessie's coming, too."

Faye sighed. "Craig, I appreciate your concern, really," she said. "But for now I think we'd better let the police deal with this."

"I'm not doing this for you, Faye," he said softly. "I love the kid. He was like my little brother." There was a pause and Faye could tell Craig was crying. "I miss him so much, Faye. Please, understand. I've got to do this. For me."

Faye was in tears, too, and she struggled to speak. "I know how you feel. But please be careful."

"You know we will."

"When will you leave?"

"We're packing now. I'm taking next week off so we'll leave tomorrow. Drive the same way they did, check out the beach, talk to people. Anything is better than sitting here isolated from everything and waiting for the police to find them. For all we know they're not even working on the case."

"They're trying, Craig. I have to believe that," Faye said. She still clung to the hope that Burkhalter or one of the other politicians she had contacted was putting in overtime trying to find the boys.

"Well, we'll see."

"Will you call?"

"Every day."

Craig and Jessie did almost everything they intended to do.

They drove to Daytona Beach, stopping at rest areas and diners and talking to people about the boys. They walked along the beach looking for them and asking questions of the locals. Then they went to the police station, where they discovered that absolutely nothing had been done on the case. In fact, the boys were not even registered with the national computer listing which contained all missing persons. They talked with Detective Mikelson and begged him to look for the boys. And they called Faye each night with an update.

The only thing they didn't do was find Jim and Daryl. No one they talked to had ever heard of the boys. Not the vendors or the motel operators or any one on the boardwalk. It was as if the boys had never been there at all. Frustrated and discouraged, Craig and Jessie came home with none of the answers they so desperately wanted.

The couple was sitting in Faye and Roy's living room the morning after their return, talking about all they had seen and done, when the phone rang.

"Hello?" Faye answered the phone.

"Mrs. Boucher, this is Officer Burnham." The two had spoken daily for the past two months and knew each other's voices well. But in the past, Faye had always done the calling. Now, hearing the officer's voice, she felt her heart skip a beat.

"Yes, what is it?"

"I think we've found the boys?"

"Oh, dear God," Faye said, clasping her hand over her mouth and moving slowly toward the nearest chair. Her husband and Jessie and Craig stood up at the same time and moved closer. Obviously there was some news about the boys. And everyone braced themselves for the worst.

"Are they alive?" Faye asked, tears springing instantly to her eyes. Her hands were shaking and she felt as if she might faint.

"Yes. It seems they ran away. We've located them at the cement plant in Tarrant City, Alabama."

A hundred questions flooded Faye's mind and she struggled to think clearly. "Are you sure? Jim and Daryl didn't have any reason to run away."

"We haven't seen them yet, but I talked to a woman who works with them and she confirmed it," he said. "But I have to agree with you. They didn't seem like the type to run away. Of course, we see this once in a while in police work where kids do something completely out of character. I don't know what they were thinking. Kids are hard to figure out sometimes."

Faye began to sob. Never had she felt such a feeling of relief. She moved the phone away from her face and looked at the others. "They're alive, they're okay," she whispered. Immediately Roy sank weakly to his knees in silent relief. Craig put an arm on his shoulder and pulled Jessie close to him. They were all sobbing, grateful that the ordeal was finally over.

"How in the world did you find them?" Faye asked.

"A woman saw the article in the Kmart paper. Called us and told us she'd hired Jim for a few days. He had a friend who came by once in a while and the woman thought both boys acted strange. Like they were runaways. She told us about the cement plant and we called up to verify. Both of them took jobs there."

Faye was crying so hard she could barely talk. "How can we ever thank you?" she sobbed. "How can we thank that woman?"

Burnham swallowed a lump that had been growing in his throat since Faye answered the phone. "Let's take first things first. Why don't you call the Barbers and then book a flight to Birmingham, Alabama. I'll arrange for the police to pick you up and take you to the cement plant. The boys work tomorrow at two o'clock."

"I can't believe this is happening," Faye said, wiping her eyes, her tears now mixed with elated laughter. "Officer, I have to tell you, we thought we'd never see them again." She paused. "We thought they were dead."

"You weren't the only ones who thought that," he said. "I'm just glad things turned out all right."

Faye thanked the officer again and then hung up the phone. The others moved toward her and the four of them remained locked in a group embrace for several minutes. After that, Faye called Marian and Ron Barber.

The scene at the Barber home was much like the one at the Boucher house. Marian screamed for Ron, who happened to be spending the day at home. Ron had his own business and had been spending much of his time at home since the boys disappeared.

"They're alive!" she shouted.

"What?"

"Ron, they're alive! The police found them in Alabama, working at a cement plant."

Ron wanted desperately to believe what he was hearing, but he shook his head. "Wait, you mean they just left the beach and decided to get a job in Alabama without calling? That's not our boys."

Marian nodded furiously. "Yes! The police said it happens once in a while where teenage boys just need to test their wings, spend some time on their own."

"Are they sure it's our boys?"

"Positive."

Clinging to Marian's confidence, Ron covered his face with his hands and began to cry. His son was all right. Daryl would be home in a matter of days and they could all go on living. He knew what he would do the moment he first saw Daryl again. He would run up to him, take him in his arms and hold him, just like he'd done when Daryl was a little boy.

Marian, meanwhile, was still talking to Faye and working out the details of how they'd get the boys home. Finally, the phone call was over and the plans were made. All four parents would fly to Birmingham, Alabama, on the first flight in the morning. They would meet up with police and go directly to the cement plant, where they would wait for the boys to arrive for their scheduled work shift. Then, for the first time in nearly two months, they would all be together again.

The rest of the evening was a flurry of excitement in both households as the parents packed their suitcases and made arrangements for baby-sitters for the Boucher children. That night before climbing into bed, Faye took a picture of Jim from her bedside table and looked at it lovingly.

"You know, I'm not even mad at him," she said to her husband, who was lying awake in bed beside her.

"I know. Me either," Roy said.

"I can't understand why they would have done such a crazy thing. But none of that matters. I thought I'd lost him," Faye said. "And right now the farthest thing from my mind is anger."

Roy smiled and Faye looked at her husband closely, her eyes filled with concern. "You were worried sick, Roy," she said, caressing his shoulder.

He nodded and took her hand. "I love the boy, Faye," he said quietly. "I want him home."

The next morning, the Batbers put their things together and headed for the Bouchers' house where they had planned to meet. They were loading the car with their belongings when the phone rang.

"I'll get it," Roy said, setting his small suitcase on the ground and darting back into the house. He picked up the phone sounding happier than he had in weeks. "Hello?"

There was a pause and for a minute Roy thought the caller might be a prankster. Then someone spoke.

"Uh, Mr. Boucher?"

"Yes?"

"This is Officer Burnham. None of you have left for the airport yet?"

"No, we're on our way." Roy leaned against the kitchen wall and closed his eyes. He could tell from the officer's voice that something was wrong. "We'll be there on time, though. Everything okay?"

"Well …" Burnham closed his eyes and rubbed his temples with his thumb and forefinger. If the last phone call to the Bouchers had been his best, this was by far his worst. "I think there's been a mistake."

Early that morning, just as a precaution, Burnham had decided to call the boys' supervisor at home to be sure they had the right kids. Yes, there were two men working at the plant named Jim Boucher and Daryl. But they were in their forties and had been working there for nearly a decade. Burnham wondered at the odds of such a coincidence.

Then he had asked the supervisor if a Walter Alexander worked for him. That was the name the boy had given Margie Barrett when he worked for her in East Birmingham. Yes, he was told. Walter was nineteen and about six-foot-two. He was a new employee and, no, he wasn't a runaway. He had family in the area and his parents had been by the plant several times.

Burnham could have kicked himself. The only question he'd forgotten to ask the secretary was about their ages. One simple question and he could have avoided getting the families' hopes up.

As soon as he knew the truth, Burnham had hung up the phone and immediately dialed the Bouchers. Now he felt sick to his stomach having to explain the error to Jim's father.

"We did some further research on the boys in Alabama," he said. "The Jim and Daryl I was told about are in their forties. They've worked at the plant for ten years."

Roy was silent, feeling as if some part of him had suddenly died.

"They're not your boys, Mr. Boucher. I'm really sorry about all this."

"But someone identified them." Roy's voice was weak, his blood sugar rising by the minute. He wanted so badly to cling to the hope he'd felt moments earlier.

"The identification was almost the same. But their ages were different. I'm so sorry. Really."

By then, the other parents had joined Roy in the kitchen. By the look on Roy's face and the tears forming in his eyes, they knew something had gone terribly wrong. And before Roy finished talking to Officer Burnham they each knew the truth.

Jim and Daryl were still missing.

After the shock of the disappointment wore off, life for the Barbers and Bouchers seemed almost more unbearable. There were days when none of them knew how they could go on. They were in daily contact with Investigator Byrd but they knew little of the overtime hours Bob Brown was putting in. And by the end of that week, they realized that whatever the police and politicians and hired help were doing to find their boys, it clearly wasn't enough.

CHAPTER 14

Bob had promised Detective Mikelson he would do whatever it took to get a lead on the case and he lived up to his word. Operating from his car, which was equipped with a telephone, a police radio, and a tracking device among other gadgets, Bob and two assistants began combing the beach first thing Thursday morning. Byrd had told him to spend whatever money necessary to locate the teenagers, and by that morning he had printed up posters offering a five hundred dollar reward to anyone with information leading to the whereabouts of Jim and Daryl.

Bob was aware of the fact that he did not look anything like a Daytona Beach resident. He also did not look like a tourist. In fact, if anything, he looked like a narcotics officer. So starting Thursday, Bob left his suits in the car and instead put on tourist attire. Wearing a Disney T-shirt and Bermuda shorts, and with a camera, and a map in his pocket, Bob set out for the sandy strip determined to find someone who knew something about Jim and Daryl's disappearance.

He instructed his assistants, Mike and Rob, to dress the same way as he had and to pass out flyers while talking to everyone they saw. He would do the same from the other end of the beach and they would meet back around noon. By eight o'clock in the morning he had found his starting point and he began his beach walk.

"Excuse me." Bob nudged a teenage boy lounging against the wall that divided the sandy beach from the row of arcades. The boy had tattoos across his caved-in chest and he was smoking a cigarette. A lovely example of American youth, Bob thought. He cleared his voice, appearing hesitant in order to maintain his tourist image. He hoped the teens would think he was a parent.

"These boys were here a few weeks ago," he said. "They're missing now and we're offering a reward if anyone knows anything."

"Reward?" The boy had seemed uninterested but at the mention of money he sat up straighter and took one of the flyers from Bob. He scanned the sheet and looked at Bob with narrow eyes.

"Anonymous?"

"Completely anonymous."

"Five hundred dollars?"

"For the right information."

"That's it? Then five hundred dollars?"

"Right."

"Thanks, man!" The teenager took four more flyers and passed them to his friends. "We'll see what we can do. We'll call you, okay?"

"Please do."

Bob spotted a group of teenage girls ahead and he trudged through the sand to where they were sitting. They wore skimpy bikinis and had covered themselves with oil. He had seen these girls talking with some of the locals earlier so he knew they weren't tourists. He wanted to talk only to locals since a new group of tourists filled the beach each week and those there now would not have been on the beach when Jim and Daryl were in town.

"I'm looking for a couple of boys," Bob said, handing flyers to each of the girls. "You live around here?"

"Yeah," one girl said and the others nodded. A few of them were smoking cigarettes and Bob thought he could smell marijuana. "You a narc or something?"

"No," Bob laughed lightly. "Just looking for my boys, here. Got a reward for anyone who can help me find them."

Like the first teens to whom he'd spoken, the girls' interest was piqued by the mention of cash.

"Five hundred dollars?" one girl squealed.

"Gee, they're pretty cute, too," added another as she stared at the pictures of the boys.

Then the first girl spoke for the group. "We'll work on it, okay? If we hear anything we'll give you a call."

"Anything at all. I gotta find them."

"Sure. Sorry they're missing." As she spoke, the girl nearest her began to giggle.

Bob thought he knew why. They were probably runaways and somewhere someone was looking for them, too. Kids who had run away from home stuck together along Daytona Beach. If someone's parents came looking, no one would give them information. It was sort of an unspoken rule. But rules disappeared very quickly when cash was involved, and Bob believed that the kids he'd talked to so far would call him instantly if they thought they had a chance at earning the reward money.

As the morning sun grew hotter, Bob talked to several more groups of teens both up and down the beach and along the boardwalk. At noon he met with his assistants and agreed to let them continue the beach coverage. He was going to check the hospitals. If he found nothing there, he would visit the morgue.

Bob changed into a shirt and dress pants and headed for the first of Daytona Beach's two hospitals. Getting information from a hospital could be tricky. Many hospitals have policies against releasing information regarding a patient to anyone other than family members. Although being a private investigator did not entitle a person to any legal advantages, Bob had seen dozens of doors opened because of his title. He went immediately to the business office and showed his identification. The man in the office examined the badge, smiled, and welcomed him in.

"How can I help you?"

"I need to know if two boys, Jim Boucher and Daryl Barber, have been patients here at any point since August twelfth."

The man hesitated a moment. He was tall and very thin and looked a little like a cartoon character. "Actually, that's not something we usually share with the public." He thought a moment and lowered his voice, looking from one side of the room to the other to make sure no one could hear him breaking the rules. "But you *are* a private investigator, and this is important to your case, right?"

"Right."

"Okay." He was nearly whispering. "If you'll keep quiet about it, I'll check that out myself, right away."

Bob smiled and waited patiently while the man checked. He did not expect that the boys had been in the local hospitals. For one thing, unless they had been completely unconscious and without any identification, someone would have known who they were and contacted their parents. Still, the hospitals had to be checked even if it was only to rule out the possibility that the boys had been in an accident and had been hospitalized.

"No, no one by that name," the man replied. He was relieved that he had not been forced to divulge any patient information.

"You sure?"

The man nodded quickly. "Positive."

"Okay." Bob shook the man's hand. "Thanks."

Bob drove quickly to the other hospital and received the same information from its business office personnel. That meant it was time to visit the morgue. Although three months had passed since the boys disappeared, it was possible they had been killed more recently. Besides, when morgue officials suspect homicide as the cause of death of an unidentified body, efforts are made to preserve the body as long as possible.

The first thing one noticed upon entering a morgue was the drastic drop in temperature. It did not take a rocket scientist to understand why those who operate morgues need to keep the building cool. But there was something else, a certain septic smell and a stillness in the air, that Bob never quite got used to. He shuddered involuntarily as he walked up to the front window and identified himself.

The clerk needed only a few minutes to determine that Jim and Daryl had never been at the morgue. That much did not surprise Bob, because if they had been able to identify the boys' bodies, they certainly would have contacted their parents. It was the unidentified bodies that contained the greatest potential. If the boys had been robbed of their wallets and then killed, they could very easily be sitting in a morgue awaiting identification.

"How many John Does do you have?" he asked.

The young man checked the records again. "Fifteen," he said. "You want to see them?"

No, Bob thought. "Yes."

"Follow me, then."

The bodies were stacked in refrigerated compartments built into a number of walls throughout the morgue. The two passed several autopsy rooms before the clerk stopped at a section marked, "John Doe."

"There they are," he said, handing Bob a key and smiling. "This key fits each of the John Doe compartments. Take your time."

Bob looked at the young man and saw that he was serious, almost as if he were a sales clerk urging a customer to take his time in the shoe department. Bob watched him walk away and briefly wondered how long one must work at a morgue before one's sense of humor began to fade. He read the tag on the outside of the first compartment.

"John Doe. White male. 5-foot-ll. 175 pounds. Brown Hair. Undt. eye color. 20 years."

Great, Bob thought, taking a deep breath. Undetermined eye color meant that probably the body had been partially decomposed when it was found. But he had determined to check every John Doe body that even somewhat resembled the description of either boy. He slid the compartment open and pulled back the cotton covering. Even though the body had rotted away in sections, it was easy to determine that this was neither Jim nor Daryl. The body was fleshy and overweight and neither boy had carried any excess weight. He moved to the next compartment.

After nearly an hour of examining bodies, Bob was convinced that the boys were not in the morgue. This puzzled him. He had hoped he might find the boys at the morgue. But now hope surged through him. If Jim and Daryl weren't in the morgue, there was a chance they were, still alive. Bob knew where he would look next.

He climbed into his car and headed for the beach-side flophouses.

Scattered throughout every residential block along the streets that paralleled Daytona Beach were homes recognized by police and locals as flophouses. They were not places one could find by checking the Yellow Pages. But they had a distinct look about them that left little question as to their purpose.

Most of the flophouses were owned by people who lived no where near Daytona Beach. Through a variety of methods these owners rented each room in their houses to different people. Often, those tenants invited a handful of tenants of their own so that as many as six or seven people might be combining funds for the cost of one bedroom in such a house. After that, it was easy to lose track of who was actually living in these homes, and they became places where people could flop or crash with merely an invitation.

Bob—and anyone who worked at the Daytona Beach Police Department—knew that the flophouses were often sites for raging parties twenty-four hours a day and in many cases all-out orgies involving young teenagers partaking in illegal drugs and illicit sex. They were sickening places, to be sure. But if anything had seduced Jim and Daryl away from the security of their homes, it quite possibly could have been the flophouses.

Bob met up with his assistants at the beach and the trio drove to the north side of the strip. There they started with the first flophouse, intent on working their way down the block. They strode up the front walkway, ignoring the assault of marijuana smoke, and knocked on the door. When no one answered, Bob lifted his knee and kicked the door open.

"Way to show 'em, Bob," Mike said, grinning. Mike was considerably younger than Bob, with an athlete's build. He was always surprised at how agile his boss was when they were out in the field.

As the light invaded the dark, dank interior of the house, several startled couples moved to cover themselves. Others, too drugged to realize they had visitors, continued their sex acts out in the open. Bob waited for his eyes to adjust and then looked around the room in disgust.

"Productive citizens of the future, I'm sure," Bob mumbled to Rob and Mike as he moved to the first unconscious body.

He grabbed a fistful of the teen's hair and looked at his face. Not Jim. Not Daryl. He dropped the boy's head and moved to the next body, which was lying atop an unclothed female. He grabbed the boy's hair and checked his face. Not Jim. Not Daryl.

"Hey, man!" the teenage boy protested, yelling a handful of profanities and swiping aimlessly at Bob's hand.

"Good night," Bob said as he dropped the boy's head and moved across the room. The three men continued this until they had checked every teenager in the dwelling, twenty-three in all. Not one was Jim or Daryl.

It was three o'clock in the afternoon and Bob knew they would be checking flophouses into the night. He told his assistants to take a meal break and he went to his car and dialed his office.

"Get a map of Interstate 10," he said. "The guys are taking a trip tomorrow."

He had decided to finish the flophouses that night. No matter how long they had to work. Then tomorrow he would send Mike and Rob up to Mississippi. They were college students working for Bob for the summer and he knew they would appreciate taking the trip. He would have them stop at every exit, showing pictures of the boys to every gasoline pumper and convenience store cashier. After all, there had been traveler's checks cashed along that route. Someone had to know something.

* * *

At four o'clock they resumed their search through the flophouses and three hours later Bob thought they had probably examined the faces of hundreds of drugged teenagers. No wonder there were so many missing persons reports stacked on Mikelson's desk.

Just after dusk, Bob and his assistants kicked down the door of one of the more infamous flophouses along the strip. Immediately they began checking for Jim and Daryl but before they could finish a man approached them from another room.

"What the heck you doing?" he shouted. He looked like a professional linebacker with an attitude.

"Bob Brown, private investigator." Bob flashed his identification badge and resumed his activity.

"This is private property! Now get out before I throw you out."

Bob, who was probably eight inches shorter than the man and weighed easily one hundred pounds less, stood up and stared the man in the face. "I'm checking for a couple of missing teenagers." Again, he returned to his work.

The man was furious now and his face had begun to grow red. "I'm the owner of this place and I said out!" he bellowed. "Get out or I call the cops."

Bob stopped what he was doing and looked calmly at the man. "Now there's a good idea," he said, sounding as if the owner had just made his job that much easier.

"What?"

"Yes, go ahead. Call the police." Bob looked around the room at the drugs being smoked, the beer bottles, the couples lying naked on top of one another. "I think the police would very much like to visit your home."

The man seemed to think about this as he glanced uncomfortably about his home. Then, without saying another word, he turned around and returned to the room he had come from. The police were never called.

And so it went throughout the night. Bob knew he had probably found dozens of missing persons. Maybe hundreds. But none of them had been Jim and Daryl. This did not discourage Bob, because he knew he had covered an immense amount of territory in one day. He would find the Michigan teenagers. He was certain about it.

It was just a matter of when.

CHAPTER 15

For the first time since their sons' disappearance, the Bouchers and the Barbers felt as if something productive was being done to find them. They were checking in each day with James Byrd, their private investigator, and knew exactly what progress was being made. Although the boys had not been found, there were many places that the investigator had ruled out. The parents knew that Byrd was hiring people to help him with the investigation. But they had no idea that the entire case was actually being handled by Bob Brown. Technically, Byrd's role was only that of the middleman.

"Any news today?" Faye was the one who did most of the calling. Then that evening she and Roy would meet over at the Barbers' house and share the information. They no longer spent much time discussing the missing boys in front of the younger Boucher children. John was having a hard enough time without discussing the specifics of the private investigation in front of him.

"Well, looks like we sent a few operatives up Interstate 10 checking with the cashiers and such at every off-ramp," Byrd said, reading from a report he'd gotten from Bob.

"Any news, anything at all?" Faye was not ready to give up hope. She could never give up as long as the boys had not been found.

"Not yet. We'll find them, Mrs. Boucher. Don't you worry about it." He paused a moment. "Uh, by the way. We're going to need another ten thousand dollars by the end of next week." Byrd was paying Bob about one-fourth of the money he was taking in from the families so he needed plenty of cash in order to give Bob the flexibility to buy information as needed.

"Ten thousand dollars?" Faye could not believe the money this investigation was costing. They had already used all their savings and had listed a section of their land with a real estate company.

"Yes, ma'am. These investigations are very expensive. But they do give you peace of mind. And there's something to be said for that."

"Yes, yes, I know," Faye said, tears spilling from her eyes. "Please call us if you hear anything."

"Oh, I will. Don't you worry."

Faye broke the news to the Barbers that night about the added expense. Already the investigation had cost twenty thousand dollars and now another ten thousand. Neither couple could imagine what was costing so much money, but the investigator had said that he was using several operatives to find Jim and Daryl. They would simply have to find the money to keep the investigation alive.

Had the circumstances been different, the families might have switched investigators or researched exactly how the money was being used. But Byrd was always ready with what seemed to be a logical answer regarding his expenses and the parents were committed to seeing the investigation through. Even if it left them with nothing, at least they could go on being a family again. If they found the boys alive, they could be reunited and all of them would move on from this terrible nightmare. And if the boys were found dead, they could grieve and feel and begin the process of letting go of their sons.

But this life of not knowing was killing them all. Especially Roy, who had grown even sicker in the past weeks as his blood sugar soared out of control.

By then, both families had begun to accept the worst possible scenario. Jim and Daryl might be dead. Even though the boys had not been found at the local morgues in central Florida, it was possible they were in a different morgue, out of state somewhere.

Of course, none of them liked to talk about the possibility that their sons were dead. As long as they hadn't been found, there was still a hope that they were alive somewhere. But with each day, indeed with each passing hour, that hope grew dimmer.

Bob Brown, meanwhile, remained completely optimistic that eventually he would find the boys. As with all his cases he had prayed about this one and he believed with all his heart that he would solve the case. Over the years Bob had developed the nickname "Investigator of Faith" because he openly discussed at national investigative seminars his strategy of praying about a case before setting out to solve it.

If he was going to commit his work to the Lord and be successful at helping people who were hurting, he would have to ask for God's help first.

It was Thursday, November 9, and Mike and Rob had long since finished their trip up Interstate 10 with no luck. Bob had finished searching through the flophouses and checking with concession stand operators and souvenir shop cashiers and managers.

No one had seen the boys or heard of their whereabouts. All of this meant that whatever had happened to them must have occurred in the hours after they arrived. Otherwise, with an investigation as intense as he and his assistants were performing, something would have turned up by now.

That afternoon he was planning to continue his hunt through the motels along the strip. The boys had told their parents they were going to check into a motel after talking with them that August 12 night. So it would be up to Bob to locate the motel and from there retrace the teenagers' steps.

He was taking a late lunch break when he remembered something else that needed checking. The Michigan State Police had already investigated the locations where each of Jim's traveler's checks had been cashed and found nothing to go on. But the police hadn't gone to the establishments in person.

Suddenly he made a change in plans. He would finish searching the motels later. For now he was going to visit the places in Daytona Beach that had taken the traveler's checks.

Majik Market was the first on Bob's list. He went through his file, took out a copy of the check that had been cashed there, and talked to the cashier. Yes, the cashier said, he had been working that afternoon. He worked every afternoon. Yes, he had probably taken the traveler's check. He wished he could remember what the person had looked like, but he had no idea.

"I've been through this before, man," the young clerk said in an irritated voice. "Talked to the police a couple months ago. I just can't tell you who brought that check in. We get traveler's checks all the time."

At that instant, a customer walked up with long greasy hair and no shirt. He purchased a six-pack of Budweiser beer and paid for it with a rumpled traveler's check. The clerk gave the man his change as Bob watched from a distance.

"See? We get 'em every day."

Bob's next stop was the trailer park on North Beach Street. As Bob made his way to the area, he chided himself for not doing so earlier. This was perhaps the strangest place of all for two out-of-state teenagers to cash a traveler's check. He drove into the parking lot and saw that the trailers were, for the most part, very run-down. Shady characters milled about the grounds working on old broken cars and sitting in lawn chairs drinking beer.

Bob walked up to the manager's office.

"Can I help you?" A man stepped outside on the porch, shutting the door behind him. He was slightly disheveled and his clothes smelled of perspiration. Buttons had popped on part of his shirt from the pressure of his extended stomach.

"Yes." Bob pulled a copy of the traveler's check out of his suit pocket. Now that he was no longer trudging along the sand every day he had once again taken to wearing suits. "Someone spent this traveler's check at your establishment."

The man examined the copy of the check closely.

"James Boucher," the man repeated to himself. "Say, weren't the police asking about that check?"

"Yes, probably about two months ago."

"Right," the man said. "I remember. But I told them it must have been a mistake. We've never had a James Boucher living at the trailer park. Don't know how it got our stamp on the back. Must have been a bank error or something." He handed the document back to Bob. "Anything else I can help you with?"

"Yes," Bob said, placing the document once again in the manager's hands.

"Please check your records and see if anyone used a traveler's check to pay for rent on August seventeenth, the day the check was cashed."

"Listen, I never took a traveler's check like this one. I'd recognize it. We don't get these kinds of checks very much around the park."

"Are you the only one who collects rent checks?"

The man thought about this a moment. "Well, I guess not. Once in a while the wife takes a payment or two. Depends on who's in the office. Almost always it's me and like I said I know I didn't take that check."

"Your wife around?" Bob was moving past the man toward the office and the man held up his arm.

"Stay here," he said. "I'll get her."

When he returned a few minutes later he had his wife and the payment record book from the office. The woman was a smaller, disheveled version of her husband and she looked at the copied traveler's check, studying it for twenty seconds. Then, suddenly, her eyes lit up.

"Why, yes, I remember that," she said; then she turned to her husband. "You can take the record book back inside. I know who gave me that check."

"Who was it, ma'am?" Bob asked. He was so close to his first real lead in the case he could feel it, and now he could hardly wait for the woman to tell what she knew.

"Got that check from Snake," she said confidently.

"Snake?"

The woman looked up, squinting in the bright Florida sunshine. "Yeah, Snake."

The woman's husband looked slightly embarrassed by this revelation.

"Honey, the check's signed by someone else. James Boucher, I think." The man sounded uncomfortable. "Why in heaven's name would you take a check from Snake when it was signed by someone else?"

She put her hands on her hips and glared at her husband. "Look, you know as well as I do that rent's hard to come by. Snake was always late. Always. So when he wanted to pay a week in advance, I took the check, no questions. Good as cash as far as the bank's concerned. You'd have done the same thing."

The man looked helplessly at Bob, who had been taking notes throughout the conversation.

"I need Snake's real name," he said.

The couple stared at him blankly and then looked at each other and shrugged. "That's it, just Snake," the man finally said. "Everyone called him Snake. In fact, he and the wife and a few others moved out a couple months back."

Bob was amazed. "You mean you'd rent a furnished trailer to a man named Snake without taking any kind of first or last name?"

"No, 'course not. We got the trailer park owner for that part. She handles all the applications and then we handle the rent. Week to week. That's all anyone's good for around here."

"I'll need her name, please." Bob stared at the couple, waiting until one of them turned back into the office and returned with the woman's name and telephone number.

Bob copied the information into his notes and then pulled out the pictures of Jim and Daryl.

"Recognize either of these kids?" he asked as the couple leaned closer and examined the photos.

"Yeah," the man said, pointing to the picture of Daryl. "I know I seen him before." There was a pause while the man seemed to be lost in deep concentration. Then he looked at Bob excitedly.

"Yeah, he was here one night in August. Snake threw a party one night," the man said. "That's it! That's where I saw him. One of the cars was parked in the middle of the roadway near Snake's trailer so I go over and ask the driver to move the car. Nice car, too. Especially for these parts."

"What kind of car was it?" Bob could hardly believe the information he was getting. It was the biggest break of the case and he was still getting more information.

"Oh, nice car. Red, black top. If I remember right it had Michigan plates." The man pointed again to the picture of Daryl. "That young man came out and moved the car for me."

"What else did you see?"

"That's about it. Snake disappeared for a long time after that night. Thought he'd skipped out on us."

"What did he drive, do you know?"

"Well, Snake drove a blue bike, you know, Harley-Davidson. California plates."

"Did you see him leave on the bike after the party?"

"Nope, can't say that I did. But I heard from some of the guys that Snake had gone up to Mississippi with the boys."

"Did you ever see the boys again after that?"

The man concentrated again for a moment. "No. But I saw Snake. He came back with the boys' car."

Bob put his pen down and stared at the man. "Did you contact the police?"

"No."

"Didn't that seem strange to you? A couple of out-of-state teenagers visit Snake, Snake disappears, and then he shows up with the car and the boys are gone?"

The man was suddenly defensive. "Listen, I ain't no cop! I take the rent and after that I don't ask no questions unless someone breaks the rules. And there's no rule against driving someone else's car!"

Bob decided to try another approach. "Did you ask Snake about the car?"

"In fact, I did." He was indignant. "Snake said he got the car fair and square in a big drug deal."

"A drug deal?" This confused Bob more than anything else he had just learned. Jim and Daryl were not involved in drugs and Bob could think of no reason why they would have given away their transportation in exchange for drugs. The only viable explanation was that Snake had been lying.

"Yeah. Then he paid his rent—"

"With the traveler's checks?" Bob asked.

"With the traveler's checks," the woman inserted.

"And after that he and Spider and Fat Man and the girls moved out."

"Spider, Fat Man, and the girls?"

"His roommates. Snake had a lot of roomies while he was here. Those were just a few of them."

"Do you know their real names?"

The man and woman both shook their heads.

"Have you heard from Snake?" Bob asked. "Since then?"

"No, nothing."

"Okay," Bob checked over his notes. "Can you tell me anything else about Snake?"

The man and woman paused and moved about nervously. "Well," the man began, "he's not a real nice guy, know what I mean?"

Bob had guessed as much. "Tell me about him."

"He's a Pagan, rides with the gang. You heard of them?"

Bob felt his stomach sink to his feet. The Pagans were one of the most horrific gangs in Daytona Beach, and in many cases they were known for their ruthless behavior. "I know the gang."

"Let's see, he's a Pagan and he has brown hair, brown eyes. Lots of tattoos."

"How old is he?"

"Maybe twenty-eight, twenty-nine," the man said. "Hey, has he done something wrong?"

"That's what I'm trying to find out. The boys have been gone for ten weeks and no one has heard from them. Right now Snake's the last person who's seen them," he said.

The couple looked uneasy with the prospect.

Bob gave them his card. "Call me if he comes back around, or if you see Spider or Fat Man or the girls, okay?"

"Sure."

Bob thanked them for their help and returned to his car. It was after six o'clock and he used his car phone to call the trailer park owner.

Yes, she knew who Snake was. His real name was John Cox, according to his rental application.

"Do you have a forwarding address?" Bob asked.

"No. He left pretty quickly from what I understand," she said. "You have to know, Mr. Brown, our tenants are very transient. We're lucky to get a name and almost never does anyone leave a forwarding address. If I hear from him I'll notify you."

Bob thanked her and gave her his number. His next call was to James Byrd. For the first time since the boys had disappeared there was something to go on. Someone had seen the boys with John "Snake" Cox and days later Snake had been seen with the car but the teens were nowhere to be found.

After detailing the information to Byrd, Bob hung up the phone with mixed emotions. He knew he was far closer to solving this case now than he had been that morning. But his hope that the boys might still be alive had all but vanished. The boys had dared to tangle with one of the Pagans and in the process come across the path of a mean and ruthless Snake.

CHAPTER 16

In the late 1970s, anyone who knew anything about Daytona Beach knew enough to respect the Harley-Davidson motorcycle gangs. Not the way citizens might respect a civic group for its contributions to a community. Instead they respected the gangs in a way that many times proved beneficial to their health. *Never mess with a gang member,* was the city's unofficial slogan.

This was especially true for the two rival gangs who were possibly the most ruthless of all: the Pagans and the Outlaws.

Daytona Beach was an unofficial center for motorcycle gang activity and what the Outlaws were capable of, the Pagans were capable of. If the Outlaws had no problem accepting responsibility on the streets for a murder or for some other heinous crime, the Pagans were equally willing. For the most part they were a fearless, heartless band of bikers who loved their bikes above all else, their fellow gang members above their women, and who thought nothing of breaking the law. The only things that distinguished the two gangs were their names and the fact that each held an intense, often deadly, dislike for the other.

So fierce had the rivalry become that by the summer of 1978, the Pagans had actually begun migrating to sections of Maryland, where they apparently could terrorize communities in peace, without the incessant threat of running into an Outlaw along the way. That summer, about the same time Jim and Daryl left Metamora for their dream vacation, the Outlaws were in prime form.

In December, an article ran in the *Orlando Sentinel* titled, "Outlaws: Terror on Two Wheels." The article related two events that had occurred in or just outside of Daytona Beach that past summer.

First, a group of men and women were being questioned after having drunk through the night at a biker member's living room while in the next room three men beat a woman senseless. The woman was found dead hours later with fourteen stab wounds to her body, her throat slit from one end to the other. Two women in the house later testified that they had intentionally ignored the victim's cries for help because they feared if they intervened the same thing would happen to them.

Also that summer, ten white gang members had gotten into an argument with two black men one evening when the gang would not let the black men pass through a stop sign. These men were then taken from their cars, and in the middle of a deserted two-lane highway they were beaten with chains. Somehow, the men lived. When they reported the incident to the police, they met with little shock over the matter. Knowing who was probably responsible for the attack, the police showed the men pictures and dossiers on the likely suspects—all gang members. When the victims realized who they were up against they decided not to press charges.

In both cases, the Outlaws were involved so that when the police told people, as they did whenever asked, that the Outlaws were one of the largest and roughest motorcycle gangs in the country, they had examples to prove it.

The local chapter of Outlaws, the article went on to say, had only about twenty-five actual members with an unknown number of associate members. According to police, the gang—which again was almost identical in nature to the Pagans—had taken on the characteristics of an organized crime outfit. These traits included the fact that the motorcycle gang ruled by fear, intimidated witnesses, staked out territories of operation, and then dealt drugs and illegal weapons. Also the gang typically did its best to eliminate the competition—in particular, the Pagans.

A man named "Dirty Tom," identified by police as the Outlaws' chapter president, vehemently denied these reports.

"We don't look for trouble; we try to avoid it," he was quoted as saying. "People pick fights with us and all we do is try to defend ourselves."

Rumor had it the police clipped that quotation from the newspaper and tacked it up in the station so that whenever they needed a good laugh, they could simply walk by and read it.

"Dirty Tom" also confirmed that he and his fellow gang brothers were dropouts from the mainstream of society and many times at odds with local police. "What a club member wants is to be left alone and to ride the streets," he was quoted as saying. "It's not against the law to be an Outlaw."

But Sheriff Melvin G. Colman of nearby Orange County was quoted as disagreeing with the chapter president on many points.

"These aren't a bunch of fun-loving motorcycle riders," he said. "These are a bunch of brutal animals."

One need only examine the lifestyle led by the Outlaws—and very likely the Pagans—to understand the utter truth of this fact, Colman noted. In particular, one need only look at the way the Outlaws treated rival gangs and the way they treated women.

For instance, Steve Almond, who once rode on the fringes of both the Outlaws and the Pagans, said that nothing was done in either group without the permission of the local president. A group retaliation against a rival gang was not only something that required permission, it was something that was orchestrated in detail.

Almond was a Pagans pledge in the summer of 1974 when he and two Pagans were kidnapped by members of the Outlaws. They were taken to the Outlaw clubhouse, tied up, and then beaten and kicked. Almond escaped. The other two were dumped in a local forest where their skeletons were found a year later.

Almond chose to testify against the six Outlaws charged with the beatings and killings. As a result, he remains in hiding, taking part in the U.S. Federal Witness

Protection Program. During the trial he was able to identify his attackers and shed some light on the inner workings of the gang lifestyle.

Almond said that although rival gang members were hated, it was women who received perhaps the worst treatment of all by the gang members. The "brothers," he said, believed that women were "nothing." Because of that, they were often required to support the gang with earnings from prostitution and topless dancing. Women were treated as objects and could be bought or sold like pieces of property. If one member owned a particular woman, he could sell her to another member and even collect half of the money she might bring in from outside activities. In addition, many of the women were beaten on a regular basis by the men.

For the most part, police said, the women stayed with the gang out of fear. The beatings and constant string of threats made them victims of control. Many women had heard of or seen for themselves women who were killed for acting out of line. Therefore, the smart "honey" or "old lady" kept quiet and stayed in her place.

One police officer was quoted as saying that he didn't think there was any point in trying to develop a program that would assist the gang members in altering their behavior.

"These guys are happy doing what they're doing," the officer said. "My guess is that they are quite similar to psychopaths. Only they happen to share an interest in motorcycles."

By the summer of 1978, many of the Outlaws and Pagans were considered to have become very dangerous psychopaths. Indeed, police believed a number of gang members had started carrying illegal automatic weapons. And that summer they had launched heavily into drug trafficking, especially along Daytona Beach.

Sadly, Jim and Daryl knew nothing about the Pagans and the Outlaws. They were simply two kids from Metamora looking for the time of their lives. Obviously they knew nothing about the reasons why the locals feared and respected the motorcycle gangs. And they knew nothing about how dangerous Snake and Spider were.

Because Snake and Spider were Pagan bikers.

And if Jim and Daryl had even suspected what that meant around town, they probably would have fled the beach altogether.

CHAPTER 17

At about the same time that James Byrd was informing the Barbers and the Bouchers that he had made some real progress on his investigation, Bob Brown was arriving at his Orlando office earlier than usual. He had received an additional packet of information from Byrd's Michigan office regarding the missing boys, and he wanted to read through it before returning to Daytona Beach.

Private investigation work depended on fresh leads much the way the game of solitaire depends on fresh cards. One lead might lead to five which might lead to twenty-five. As long as there were viable leads, the investigation was still alive. If the leads dried up, so did the case. For that reason, he could not ignore this new information about the boys. Sometimes even the most mundane material had hidden within it the very lead that might crack a case. Bob hoped that was so with this material.

He opened the packet and sorted through dozens of documents. Much of the information was repetitive, detailing the boys' character traits and favorite hobbies. Bob was beyond leaning on that type of information at this point in the investigation. But that morning an obscure detail jumped off the pages of the report and suddenly Bob knew he had one more lead to follow up on.

In a section of the information that contained comments from the boys' parents regarding the kindhearted nature of their sons, one of their mothers said that Jim and Daryl had even been kind to members of the Hare Krishna group. The report from Byrd's office read:

> Subject Barber's parents, in stressing their point of Subject Barber's friendliness, related that Subject Barber purchased a Krishna book in the amount of $5.00 rather than insist to the seller that he did not want the book.

Bob thought about that detail for a minute. If Daryl had purchased the Hare Krishna book at some time, perhaps he had read it. And if he had read the book, it was possible that he and Jim had gotten mixed up with the Krishna group in Daytona Beach. Bob knew from previous investigations that the local cults were very aggressive in their pursuit of beach-going teenagers.

The modus operandi for most cults was to convince new recruits to cut off all communication with anyone outside the cult. Next, the newcomers would be instructed to sell their possessions and donate the money to the organization for the good of the group.

So it was possible, Bob reasoned, that the boys had joined the local Hare

Krishna movement, been forbidden to call home, and then sold Daryl's Nova to Snake for cash. Bob picked up the telephone.

"Jeff, this is Bob Brown," he said.

"Sure, I remember. Did you get me some work?"

Bob laughed softly. "Yes, I think so. I need you to check out a few of the local cults, Hare Krishna group, that kind of thing."

"Wow! That's great, man!" Jeff, a full-time college student, had always dreamed of doing private investigations. He had come into the office a month ago and asked Bob to call him if he ever needed a young operative for any of his jobs. "Is this like an undercover thing or what?"

"Right." Bob was impressed with the young man's enthusiasm. "Undercover."

"Great," he nearly shouted. "Sign me up! When do I start?"

He spent ten minutes giving Jeff the details of when and how to infiltrate the Hare Krishna group. When he was finished, he grabbed his briefcase, walked outside to his white sedan, and set out for Daytona Beach. It was time to pay another visit to Detective Mikelson.

Not much had changed for Mikelson since his last meeting with Bob. His workload was still as significant, his missing persons reports still spilling over from the places where they were kept, and he had still put no effort into solving the case involving the disappearance of the two Michigan teenagers. There were times when he thought about the boys and even wished he had enough time in the day to pursue the case.

He had spoken to Bob Brown twice since the investigator first appeared at his desk.

"Nothing new. No breaks in the case. Just wanted you to know I haven't given up," Bob would say. "And I hope you haven't either."

Each time Bob called, Mikelson felt the implied pressure for him to join in the investigation. But it just wasn't possible. And this bothered Mikelson.

He remembered the grief-filled faces of the boys' relatives when they had visited. He hadn't been an officer long enough to feel immune to that kind of pain. And although he didn't have time for the case, he sincerely hoped that Bob would find the boys. No one should have to live like their parents were probably living, wondering each day whether their sons were still alive and, if they were, whether they needed help or not. Because he had no time to work on it, Mikelson tried not to think about the case. But when he did, it was in hopes that Bob Brown would find the missing teens before so much time passed that it would be impossible to do so.

Despite Brown's sometimes annoying phone calls, Mikelson was comforted knowing that there was a private investigation regarding the teenagers—and, more importantly, that Bob Brown was handling it. And Bob knew that if there were ever any real breaks in the case, anything that needed Mikelson's assistance, the detective would do whatever he could to help.

That morning, November 10, Mikelson looked up to see Bob striding toward his desk. He was busy, he had other cases to work on, but he could tell by the look in Bob's eyes that something had happened. There had been a break in the case and, deep inside, Mikelson was elated.

"How's it going, Bob?" Mikelson leaned back in his chair and pushed himself a few feet away from his desk.

"Got a lead," Bob said, grabbing a nearby chair and pulling it up.

Mikelson raised an eyebrow. "Okay, tell me about it."

"Remember, I told you some of the boys' traveler's checks had been cashed, signed by Jim Boucher?"

"Right."

"Seems the people at the trailer park remember a man named John Cox, more commonly—and from the sounds of it more appropriately—referred to as Snake," Bob said. "Seems Snake used the signed checks to pay his rent."

As Bob spoke, Mikelson sat straighter in his chair, his eyes suddenly filled with a knowing look. "Snake Cox?"

Bob nodded quickly. "I figured you might know him."

Mikelson released a deep sigh and closed his eyes for a moment. "Yes."

Bob waited for Mikelson to elaborate.

"Snake's a dangerous guy, Bob. Fully capable of killing."

"That's what I thought. What do you know about him?"

"He's wanted by our department, the state police, drug enforcement. Oh, also the FBI for possession and illegal sale of drugs and weapons. Talk on the street is you don't mess around with Snake if you value your life. On top of that, he's a Pagan."

"So I heard."

"What in the world were those teenagers doing around Snake?"

Bob shook his head sadly. "You haven't heard the worst of it."

"There's more?"

"Lots more. Landlord says the boys and their red Nova were at Snake's house sometime around August twelfth—the last time their parents heard from them. After that, Snake disappeared for a few days and when he came back, he was driving the Nova and the boys were nowhere to be seen."

The two men sat in silence.

"Doesn't sound real good," Mikelson finally said.

"No."

Suddenly, Mikelson pounded his fist on his desk. "Why would those kids do a stupid thing like letting Snake Cox show them around town?"

"The answer's pretty obvious, Mikelson," Bob said.

"What's that?" The detective was frustrated.

"Those boys wouldn't know a poisonous Snake if it bit them."

Mikelson sighed and stood up. "We arrested that guy last year some time, before he had these warrants out." Mikelson moved toward the main filing area. He quickly found the section he was looking for and began searching for Cox's arrest record.

"Here it is!" he said, yanking a sheet up from a file drawer and staring at it. According to the report, John "Snake" Cox was wanted by several law enforcement agencies for a number of crimes. Mikelson read the arrest record and snorted in disgust.

"Take a look at this!" He thrust the report toward Bob.

The arrest record was a lengthy account detailing a ten-year crime history which by 1971 included several counts of breaking and entering and possession of stolen property. Then there were drug arrests and more charges of breaking and entering. But it was the last item on the report that caught Bob's attention and made him fear for the lives of the Michigan teenagers.

On February 29, 1976, Snake was arrested for possession of a deadly weapon—a gun.

Bob had seen enough. He turned toward Mikelson, who was still silently berating himself for not pursuing the missing persons report in the first place. "If there's an arrest record, there's a photo, right?"

Mikelson grinned. "You bet!"

"I don't have a forwarding address on the guy," Bob said anxiously. "But maybe, if we have a photograph, we can comb the beaches and find someone who knows him!"

"It's worth a try," Mikelson said, pointing across the room. "Let's get it."

The two men walked quickly through the department toward the photo area and looked up the file on John Cox.

"It's empty." Zachary opened the file but the only thing inside was a small, handwritten note that read:

"No picture available. Police department camera broken."

CHAPTER 18

Certain methods were used in private investigation that absolutely could not be employed by police. Most of the time, Bob did not have to resort to such methods because most cases could be solved with basic police techniques. Typically, he asked questions and got answers. But in this case, Bob was fairly certain he had exhausted all his routine options.

He wanted to find Snake. And if Mikelson and the trailer park couple were right, anyone who might know anything about Snake's whereabouts wasn't about to talk. Unless, of course, one might make some cash in the process. In that case, even the fear of Snake Cox might be eased enough to say something.

Yes, Bob decided as he left the police department that morning, it was time to pull out the stops. Time to start waving crisp one-hundred dollar bills around the haunts of Daytona Beach.

Although there were no laws to govern such a practice, there was an unwritten, time-tested rule in private investigations that said a person will not take a bribe unless they can fulfill their end of the bargain. Regardless of that person's character.

Therefore, if a person was offered one hundred dollars in exchange for the whereabouts of another person with the promise of an additional sum of money when that information was delivered, the person almost never took the money unless they were certain they could deliver.

James Byrd had given Bob permission to use the offer of a reward if necessary, telling him that his clients—the Barbers and Bouchers—were willing to spend whatever money necessary to find their boys. And so, before setting out on the beach, this time still in his three-piece suit, Bob stopped at the bank and withdrew two thousand dollars in hundreds from his business account.

He was looking for several things. First and foremost, the whereabouts of Snake Cox. Second, the real identity of Spider and Fat Man. And third, the whereabouts of those two and anyone else who might have been seen with the boys or who might be considered friends of Snake, Spider, or Fat Man.

He parked his car behind McDonald's and walked out onto the cement walkway that separates the arcades, gift shops, and fast food joints from the sandy beach and boardwalk area. He was no longer looking for any local group of teenagers. He wanted to find people who wore their hair long and unkempt, with little regard to their appearance. People who wore tattoos on their arms and legs and who seemed to be perpetually stoned on marijuana. People who rode Harley-Davidson bikes. That was it, really. He wanted to find bikers.

He scanned the strip and saw two young men who matched this description.

Without hesitation, Bob walked boldly up to them. The key was to hold back from flashing the money until they had heard the question.

"I'm looking for Snake," Bob said.

Immediately the young men seemed to grow nervous, shifting from one foot to the other and glancing about as if looking for some kind of escape route.

"Never heard of him, man," one of the two said, peering out at Bob from behind a curtain of blond, greasy hair.

Bob reached into his suit pocket and smoothly pulled out a handful of one-hundred dollar bills, fanning them discreetly but in clear view of the men. Their eyes grew wide and they looked up at Bob.

"This some kind of setup, man?" the other one asked. He wore a tattoo of the devil on his cheek.

"No. I'll give you two hundred dollars if you find out where Snake is. Hundred now and a hundred when you deliver the information."

The blond man shifted again, clearly uneasy with the proposition. "Hey, listen, man, we don't know where he is."

"You know him?"

The man shrugged toward his friend and pushed his hands deep into his pockets. "Sure," he said uncertainly. "Everyone knows Snake."

"Then someone knows where he is." Bob moved the money closer to the man.

"Wait a minute," he said, holding his hands up and rejecting Bob's offer. "You got the wrong guy. I mean, I know Snake. But I can't tell you where he is. Ain't a guy on this beach knows where Snake is. He just disappeared."

"Ever heard of someone named Spider or Fat Man?"

The two men grinned at each other and chuckled deeply for several seconds, slapping their knees and punching each other the way people do when the drugs they're on have compromised their ability to judge humorous moments.

"Sure, everyone knows Spider and Fat Man," the one man said when he'd caught his breath. Then, as if he suddenly realized that Bob was not laughing, the man straightened up and cleared his throat.

"Where are they?"

"Don't know that, either, man," the tattooed biker said. "Sorry."

"Find me their real names and the money's yours."

The men looked at each other again and shrugged. "Sorry, man."

Bob put the money back into his pocket and shrugged. "Your loss."

He turned around and walked away completely confused. Buying information had always worked in the past. Even in Daytona Beach. And it was obvious that these men knew Snake, Spider, and Fat Man. So why weren't they talking? It didn't make any sense. Unless of course the risk of talking was greater than their desire for cash.

Bob suddenly felt a chill race through his body and he silently began to pray, asking God to direct his investigation and protect him. Because from this point on, Bob was very certain he would need divine protection.

Later that afternoon, when no one on the beach had been willing or able to offer any information about Snake and the others, Bob headed for the motorcycle bars. Certainly that section of town would contain hundreds of people who knew Snake and his cronies and probably their whereabouts. What Bob wasn't sure of was how the bikers would react to his presence.

Like any bar, biker saloons in Daytona Beach were dark inside. But instead of beer and sports signs hanging on the walls, there were dozens of Harley-Davidson pictures posted about. Inside, there was a machismo that went beyond that in almost any other culture. Men, their egos larger than themselves, often sat atop bar stools while someone's skimpily dressed "old lady" waited on them.

By anyone else's standards, the inside of a biker bar was a slothful den of oftentimes cruel men who were really nothing more than overgrown bad boys. Of course occasionally there were solitary bikers who passed through Daytona Beach and frequented the bars. Those men and women usually bore none of the traits of the gang members. But in Daytona Beach a vast majority of the bikers belonged to a gang and hence were a despicable group.

Bob did not even consider changing his clothing style before venturing into the biker bars. He could tattoo his body, don a false beard and leather clothing, and cover his face with dirt, and still he would only look like a minister at a costume party. Better, he decided, to go as he was and make a straightforward approach.

It was just past five o'clock on Friday afternoon and Bob knew the timing couldn't be better. Bikers tended to gather early on Fridays and stay late. By now, the action had probably already started to pick up. He sat in his car outside the Boot Hill Saloon adjacent to the old cemetery and began to pray.

"Lord, protect me and give me wisdom as I search for this Snake," he whispered. "Only you know how best I can solve this case. Please lead me and direct me. In Jesus' name I pray."

He felt his pocket for the money, none of it spent yet, and walked toward the front door where a row of polished Harley-Davidson bikes were parked outside. Bob stood a bit straighter and walked inside.

The moment the door closed behind him, Bob felt as if he had entered another world. The eyes of a dozen large faces were instantly on him and all conversation and movement in the room had stopped completely. Bob looked around, allowing his eyes to adjust to the darkness, and then walked up to the bar. He decided not to waste any time in getting to the point.

"I'm looking for Snake." He leaned forward over the bar and allowed the bartender to catch a glimpse of the cash he was holding.

"Who are you?" The bartender moved closer to Bob and narrowed his eyes menacingly. "You got an invitation, mister?"

"It's a public place," Bob stated calmly. A thin layer of sweat had begun to break out across his forehead. He was definitely out of his usual realm. Even those people who had fired guns on him in the past had not represented the kind of pure danger he felt in this bar.

"You tellin' me my bar's a public place?" The bartender raised his voice and several muscle-bound bikers moved in around Bob, glaring at him from where they stood.

"Yes." Bob ignored the threats. "I need to know where Snake is. I'm willing to pay for the information."

"You hear that boys?" The bartender laughed heartily. "Mr. Mighty Mouse here in the suit is going to pay *us* so he can find out where Snake is!" He towered over Bob, staring straight down at him. "Now, tell me, Mighty. What you gonna do when you find Snake? Invite him to dinner? Take him to the movies?"

The entire room seemed to burst into spontaneous laughter and backslapping at the bartender's words. Sensing that he had overstayed his welcome and realizing that no one was about to give him any leads in this setting, Bob stood up to leave. As he did, he was immediately circled by a wall of bikers.

"Where you going, Mighty?" one asked, moving forward and pressing his chest into Bob's face. Bob reached his hand under his jacket and felt the handle of his loaded revolver. If they wanted trouble, he was ready.

"None of you wants to make some money, so I'll find someone who does," he said, squeezing his way past the man. He kept his hand on his hidden gun.

As he moved toward the door, two or three bikers kicked him and pushed him so that Bob lost his balance and fell onto the floor. He stood up and stared at them. Despite the danger they represented, Bob was not afraid of them. They disgusted him, everything about them. Besides, he had his gun if he needed it. He stared each of them in the face.

"I'll find Snake," he said as he opened the door. "And maybe bring a few of you reptiles down with him."

The guffawing quieted and several bikers appeared puzzled, as if they were trying to understand the significance of what Bob had said. Then they shrugged at each other and resumed their laughter. Whoever the little gray-suited man was, they weren't going to worry about him now. It was Friday night and the celebrating had only begun.

After receiving the same reception at two other biker bars, Bob stumbled upon a lone biker in one of the bar parking lots.

He cleared his throat as he approached the man and held out his hand. The man glanced down and saw a single hundred dollar bill. In a matter of seconds he related to Bob a conversation he'd overheard in a biker bar around the time the boys disappeared.

He had been at a nearby table when two bikers walked in and took seats at the bar.

"Hey," the bartender had said to the newcomers, leaning forward and lowering his voice. "Either of you seen Snake?"

The men, both dressed in jeans and leather jackets, both with tattoos covering their bodies, shook their heads.

"Well," the bartender continued, "word is they scored a heavy lick over the weekend."

Bob looked confused and the man smiled, holding his hundred dollars tightly, and explained.

In biker lingo of the late 1970s, the man told Bob, a heavy lick was something spoken of in hushed tones. Even in an area like Daytona Beach where bad things happened on a regular basis, a heavy lick meant that something very big, very bad, and very illegal had happened. It also meant that the person responsible had made out with a significant windfall in the process. And so it was with raised eyebrows and awe-filled voices that the men at the bar listened to this information from the bartender.

"Oh, yeah," one of the two men had said, downing the remainder of his beer. "What happened?"

"I don't know, man. But Snake disappeared Saturday night and no one's seen him since."

"Heavy lick, huh," the other man had said, shoving his glass toward the bartender for a refill. "Anyone hurt?"

"Don't know." The bartender turned to fill the glass with draft beer. He spun around again and raised his eyebrows. "But knowing Snake, I wouldn't be surprised."

That was it. The biker in the parking lot knew nothing more. He pocketed his hundred dollars, flashed a crooked smile at Bob, and walked into the bar. Bob considered the information and decided the money was well spent. He was definitely on the right trail.

He walked back toward his car and climbed inside. He needed more information, new leads. Maybe he'd have more luck talking with bikers who didn't hang out at the same places Snake and Spider frequented. Maybe rival gang members would be more willing to talk.

That was it! He should have realized it sooner. Bob chided himself for not first thinking like his potential informants. The only way to find out about Snake and his associates was to get the information from a rival gang. Of course, the people he would have to talk to would be just as dangerous. But their hatred for the rival gang might be enough to cause at least one of them to act as an informant. Especially if it meant bringing down a rival gang member.

He started his car and cruised slowly up the street toward the beach. Since Snake was a Pagan, he would need to talk with an Outlaw. He read the insignia on the bikes and jackets of people hanging around outside the different bars until finally he saw a trio of bikers, two men and one woman, lounging against motorcycles. Emblazoned across the back of each of their jackets was the single word, "Outlaw."

Bob circled around the block once and then parked his car just a few feet from the group. He ignored their blatant stares and the whispers they exchanged under their breath. Apparently this was protocol for biker gangs and by ten o'clock that evening Bob was getting used to it. He walked up to the group and began to speak.

"I'm looking for Snake." His eyes moved from one biker to the next, checking for a response.

"What's it to you?" one of them asked.

Bob took out a few bills and showed them to the group. "I've got two hundred dollars if one of you wants to tell me where he is. A hundred now. Hundred when I get the information."

For the first time that evening, this group of bikers did not seem offended by the idea.

"He in some kind of trouble, man?" the woman asked. Her top was very low cut and Bob noticed she had a tattooed rose on her chest.

"Might be." Bob didn't want to share too much information. There was a silence while the bikers exchanged glances with each other. Bob used the moment to add to the offer.

"I've got the same deal for anyone who knows the real names or the where-abouts of Spider or Fat Man."

One of the men leaned toward the other and said something Bob couldn't understand. Then he looked up at Bob and smiled.

"Deal," he said.

"What do you know?"

"Nothing about Snake. Too bad, too. I'd love to bring that Pagan to his knees."

"So what do you know?" Bob was not interested in small talk. There was only a sliver of moon in the sky and the number of bikers in the area was growing by the minute.

"Where's my money?" The man leaned back on his bike and crossed his arms defiantly.

"Here." Bob handed the man a one-hundred dollar bill. "You talking or you getting someone who will?"

"I'll do the talking. Spider. His real name is Earl Smith. Oh, yeah. About Snake. He's dangerous, man. Real bad. Carries two loaded guns—a .38 in his waistband and another pistol in his boot. Most of the time he has an ice pick with him. Bad, bad, bad."

Bob stared at the man and determined that he was telling the truth. He peeled off another bill and handed it to the man.

"Anything else?" Bob was hopeful. He wanted to get the most for his money.

"Nope. That's it." The man was looking down, examining the cash in awe. It was the fastest money he'd ever made and he seriously wished he knew the answers to this man's other questions.

At that moment another trio of Outlaw bikers joined them and stared at Bob angrily.

"Who's the narc?" one man asked.

Another moved closer to Bob. "I don't think you belong around here, mister."

The man who had revealed the information about Spider suddenly spoke up on Bob's behalf. "Tourist," he said to his fellow bikers. "He was just asking for directions."

The man turned and stared at Bob knowingly. "And now you're leaving, right?"

"Right," Bob said, nodding cordially. "Thanks for the directions."

Bob smiled to himself as he got into his car. He had his lead, even if he did have to buy it. And that, Bob thought as he drove back to Orlando that evening, was something a police detective never could have done.

CHAPTER 19

The meeting took place late Friday night at the Barbers' house. The investigator had notified the families that he needed more money. Twenty thousand dollars to continue the investigation another four weeks. And it was time to examine the facts for what they were.

Around the dining room table sat all four parents, empty-eyed, their faces drawn. It would have been impossible to pick out the couples from among the four adults because they each sat by themselves, their pain forcing them into isolation even from the people they loved the most. Ron Barber spoke first.

"We have to make some decisions," he stated flatly. He was staring at a pad of paper upon which were scribbled dozens of figures and calculations. He held a ballpoint pen and twirled it mindlessly as he waited for their response.

"Let's look at what we *do* know," Faye said. Her eyes were bloodshot from what had become three months of sleepless nights. She had not been eating well and her hair had lost its shine. She was thin and frail-looking and she barely resembled the upbeat, pretty young woman she'd been the morning Jim and Daryl left for Florida.

"That's easy," Ron said. He flipped through his notepad until he came to an outline.

"The boys left here August twelfth. They arrived in Ormond Beach outside of Daytona late that evening and telephoned us from a pay phone. After that, it seems they hooked up with a character named Snake." Ron took a deep breath and sighed. "People saw our boys at this Snake's trailer home, a place where Spider, Fat Man, and some girls also lived at some point. After that Snake disappeared for a while and when he came back he had Daryl's Nova. The boys were not seen again as far as we know."

There was silence as everyone considered these facts. Faye crossed her arms tightly around her body and began rocking. Roy, weakened from so much illness in the past weeks, leaned back in his chair and folded his hands behind his head.

"Do you think they're dead?" he asked softly.

Marian sat up straighter and leaned closer to the others. "I think they could be alive," she said. When no one acknowledged her statement she shook her head angrily. "I know it doesn't look good. But we owe it to our sons to believe the best. There has to be a chance, doesn't there?"

"Marian, I want to believe, too." Faye reached across the table and took her friend's hand. "We all do."

Ron stood up and began pacing near his chair. "Of course we want to believe they're alive, Marian. But we have to look at the facts. We've spent forty thousand dollars and they still haven't found the boys."

"They're closer than they were!" she said defiantly.

"Yes, they're closer than they were. But we need to decide how much more money we'll spend so that they can bring us street information about someone's nickname. We don't have a thing to really go on."

"Suppose they're somewhere being held as hostages or captives or something," Faye said. She had begun to cry and this only frustrated her husband. He could not take much more of this. Especially when Faye cried. He was her husband, the man who had promised to love her and cherish her and take care of her. But when it came to stopping Faye's grief, there was nothing he could do. He could stand by her, be strong for her sake. But otherwise he was completely helpless. He moved closer to her and put his arm around her shoulder.

"Faye's right," Marian said. "We have to see this through. If they're alive, then they need our help right away."

Ron nodded and returned to his seat. "Okay, have we all agreed to continue the investigation?"

The others nodded their heads.

"All right, then let's look at the cost. Mr. Byrd says it's going to cost another twenty thousand dollars to keep investigating another four weeks. We have to get the money together somehow."

"How long do we have?" Roy asked.

"Two weeks. He says since we've paid so much up front he'll give us some leeway."

None of them said anything. The cost was overwhelming, but so was their desire to find their sons. They had been in a perpetual fog, a haze of shock since the boys had failed to return. And so they were neither thankful nor resentful about the investigation. If they'd had their way there wouldn't be any investigation. The boys would have come home like they were supposed to and they'd be discussing Christmas presents right now.

"Roy, are you and Faye going to be able to come up with your half?" Ron asked the question as sensitively as he could. He and Marian could more easily afford the expense, even though it would mean something of a sacrifice. But the Bouchers were probably beyond sacrifice. They had already sold land to pay for the initial investigation.

"Well, Ron, it's like this," Roy said. "We've had a lot of help from the community, church friends, that kind of thing. The church raised a couple thousand dollars; some of it's been given to us by fund-raisers. Then there was the land." At this point Roy's voice cracked. He had hated the idea of selling the land. After all, they had purchased it for their children, especially the four older boys. Selling half their property had been like selling their dreams. But they hadn't had a choice. And their dreams were dead anyway if they couldn't find Jim.

Roy steadied himself and continued. "Now, it looks like we're left with just one choice." At this point, Roy's eyes filled with tears. Throughout the past three months, none of them except Faye had ever seen Roy cry. He held so much in, trying desperately to be strong for Faye and the others. But now, with what he was about to say, he could no longer hold back. The tears welled up in his eyes and spilled over the edge of his chiseled face.

"We're going to have to use Jim's money," he said, his voice choked with emotion. "I never wanted to do this. That's his money. My name's on the account, too. Still, I guess I feel like spending it now is almost like admitting he's not coming home. But I don't see any other way."

He hung his head and buried it in his hands. Around the table the others were silent, each sharing in Roy's grief. Faye began to sob and Marian had moved close to her husband, streams of tears pouring down her face.

"I'm so sorry, Roy," Ron said. "Are you sure? Is that what you're going to do?"

Roy nodded, wiping his tears and trying to compose himself. "I want my son to have his money," Roy said. "But more than that, I want my son."

CHAPTER 20

Jeff Kindel also wanted to find the missing teenagers.

It was Sunday morning, November 12, and he had placed himself on Daytona Beach near where two robed men with shaven heads were soliciting teenagers. Bob Brown had told him that the chance of the boys joining a cult was unlikely. But it was worth a shot.

Now here he was, dressed like a beach-going tourist, in swim trunks and a T-shirt, clean-cut with an intentionally naive look about him. Perfect fodder for a recruiting cult member. Almost immediately, the robed men idled up to Jeff and began asking him questions about his life.

"Are you really happy in this materialistic existence?" one of them asked.

"The way of life, the way of truth and happiness is by giving up all your belongings, living in a fellowship of brothers who are all under one law," the other said.

Jeff listened to them, at first enjoying the game of it. Then, so they wouldn't become suspicious, he acted doubtful about their organization. But after a while he agreed to follow them to a bus which would take him to some kind of home base.

In a matter of minutes Jeff was traveling fifty miles an hour in a run-down school bus with a dozen robed men, wondering if taking this job had been such a wise choice after all. Investigations had always seemed exciting, as if the investigator knew no rules and could spy on the lives of anyone he chose. But he hadn't figured he would feel this helpless. Here he was heading to some unknown "home base" and with no way to contact Bob Brown if there was a problem.

Bob had told him to infiltrate whichever cult responded the most aggressively in trying to recruit him. He would be paid one hundred dollars a day to go undercover as a new cult member and search for Jim and Daryl. If he found them, he was to leave the compound immediately and find the nearest pay phone where he would call for help.

Jeff knew these instructions by heart, but something about riding in the bus with the robed men made him feel very uneasy.

Suddenly, the bus stopped and turned off the highway onto a narrow dirt road. They made their way through a hundred yards of dense brush and when it cleared, Jeff could see a series of brick buildings spread out on several acres of flat land. It looked almost like a campus, but Jeff could see that everyone wore robes and all of them had shaved heads.

Jeff ran his fingers through his shoulder-length honey-colored hair. Going undercover was one thing, but there was no way he was going to let them cut *his* hair.

"No women out here, huh?" he asked the man who had brought him to the bus. There had been no conversation since the ride started and now the man stared at Jeff in confusion.

"Women?"

Jeff laughed nervously. "Yeah, you know, women. Girls, babes, chicks." He held up his hands and drew an invisible hour glass in the air.

Finally, the man nodded in understanding. "This is not a place for men and women. We are one in all things."

"So there's no women, then?"

"The females and males all look the same, all dress the same. Share everything and everything will be shared with you. This is our belief. It is the best way, the only way. You will see."

Jeff began to feel tiny beads of sweat breaking out on his hands and forehead. "Hey, man," he said. "I'm just checking this out. I'm not so sure it's for me."

"There is no other way. We are all one, all together. It is the only way to truly live. You will see."

Jeff stared at the man in horror. It was almost as if someone had systematically removed his brain and replaced it with a computer program. He sounded as if he no longer had the ability to think for himself. He shuddered. Whoever the missing teenagers were, he hoped they hadn't gotten involved with this group. If they had, there really might be no way out.

When the bus stopped, two men escorted Jeff into what appeared to be the main building. They walked into a room off a center hallway and inside were four other teens like himself. Their faces bore confused expressions, their eyes wide with concern. But they still wore beach clothes and so far each of them still had his hair, so Jeff knew they hadn't been at the compound for long.

Jeff was placed alongside the others and all five were directed to face the front of the room. At that instant, a dozen robed men walked into the room and began to stare at the newcomers. Finally, when ten minutes of uncomfortable silence had passed, a tall man with some kind of cloth hat walked into the room.

"I am your leader. You will repeat after me," he said. It was not a question and as he spoke, the other robed men moved closer to the new recruits. They broke into groups of two and three and surrounded the newcomers, staring directly into their eyes.

Suddenly, as if on cue, the robed people began whispering in unison, "You will obey, you will obey, you will obey."

While they continued this quiet chant, the tall man in the front of the room began to speak loudly. "I am nothing."

When the teenagers did not respond immediately, his voice rose several degrees. "Repeat after me! I am nothing."

Hesitantly, the boys responded. "I am nothing."

"I am nothing." His voice filled the room.

"I am nothing," they repeated.

"I own nothing."

"I own nothing."

After ten minutes of this, Jeff was feeling as if he might go berserk at any moment. While he was busy repeating the words of the leader, the other robed men continued to stare at him, their faces not more than ten inches from his. Their whispers had grown deafening. "You will obey, you will obey, you will obey."

It was one thing to play detective for a day. But Jeff was certain that this was something altogether different. He had the frightening feeling that these people did not mess around with new recruits. If one of the newcomers didn't agree with what was happening, Jeff suspected no one was going to hop in the bus and take dissenters back to the beach.

The whispers continued and Jeff was aware of what was happening. They were being brainwashed so that they would all think the same, act the same, and most of all, obey the leader.

"I own nothing." His voice boomed through the tiny, windowless room.

"I own nothing," they repeated. Already, Jeff could hear the voices of the newcomers changing. It was as if they could do nothing but go along with the tide of suggestion.

"I belong here."

"I belong here."

"I am nothing."

"I am nothing."

"I own nothing."

"I own nothing."

Jeff kept up with the others, repeating the words and appearing to be falling under the control of the leader. But he began to scan the eyes and faces of the dozen members who faced them. It was impossible to ignore their whispered commands. "You will obey, you will obey, you will obey."

He finished examining their faces and determined that none of them was Jim or Daryl.

Then, suddenly, the leader said something that Jeff did not understand. The robed members continued their whispers but they began to part to the side. Suddenly the leader came closer, standing directly in front of the newcomers.

"You will obey," he said, his voice clear and distinct over the constant whispers.

Each of the boys nodded in agreement. Then, the leader directed the boys into another room where there were separate changing areas. He handed them white robes and instructed them to remove all their clothing and personal belongings.

Jeff took the robe and went into a tiny curtained stall. *How did I get into this?* he asked himself. He decided to obey because he needed to get past this initiation phase if he was ever to mingle with the others and look for Jim and Daryl. He pulled off his clothes and put on the robe.

At about the same time, he and the others walked hesitantly out of the stalls. Then they were led into another room where they were told to sit in folding chairs. Suddenly, Jeff heard the distinct sound of an electric shaver.

Just as he was about to scream for them to stop, he felt the blades against his skull and saw thick clumps of his hair fall to the ground around him. There was no turning back now, Jeff knew. He was undercover.

For the next three hours the new recruits were forced to repeat basic sentences in what Jeff knew was more brainwashing. No wonder the man on the bus had sounded programmed. The cult leaders did not want new members to be able to think for themselves. It was a terrifying thing to watch and Jeff had to hold himself back from bolting out of the building and running for the highway.

Finally, at dinnertime, he and the others were led into a dining room. Jeff estimated there were more than two hundred teenagers and young adults seated at picnic tables. The man on the bus had been right. There seemed to be no males and no females. Everyone looked and acted and even sounded exactly the same.

"Eat for strength, eat for strength, eat for strength." The soft, seductive sound of a female voice was piped into the room stating the same three words again and again. Jeff forced himself to block out the sound as he took a plate of mushy food and began to search the eating area for Jim and Daryl.

No one seemed to be talking but across from him he overheard one teenager whispering to another.

"The ritual is next," he said. "The ritual is next."

Jeff's eyes widened in horror. He had heard enough. He needed to escape before the ritual took place, whatever it was. He finished scanning the room and decided that if any of the boys were Jim and Daryl, they had changed so much they were no longer the people they had once been. He stood up to take his plate back to the kitchen.

He approached the same robed hairless woman who had served him. "Where are the bathrooms?" he asked.

"Down the hall. Take a leader with you," she warned. Everything was said in a monotone and just the sound of her voice was enough to send fear coursing through Jeff's body.

"Yes." He wanted to appear as if he was going along with the program. "My leader is over there."

He turned around and walked in that direction until he was certain the woman was no longer watching him. Then he walked down the hallway toward the bathroom. He had lost his sense of direction, but he could see light in the distance. He knew if he followed the hallway he would probably wind up back in the main lobby of the building.

Walking quickly but not so fast as to attract attention, Jeff moved toward the light. Suddenly, a leader wearing a white robe and cloth hat turned the corner and stared him in the face.

"Where is your leader?" he asked, his eyes cold and calculating.

"I am running an errand. Getting information for my leader," he said, sounding as much like a robot as he could, considering his racing heart.

"Very well. Hurry." The man moved past Jeff and continued up the hallway.

Jeff began to sweat profusely. He needed to get out before something terrible happened. There was no telling what the ritual was and where it took place. He picked up his pace and turned the corner. There was the front door, just as he had hoped.

Ignoring the robed man at the front desk, Jeff pushed through the double doors and once outside, broke into a full-speed run. When he had gone fifty yards and was closing in on the dirt trail, he glanced over his shoulder. An army of robed people were walking toward him. Every one of them walking. Like robots. Jeff picked up his pace, running as fast as he could. He knew they were behind him, walking steadily toward him with that empty look in their eyes. But it seemed that no matter how fast he ran they were gaining ground on him.

He had only boxer shorts on underneath the white robe but the garment was beginning to trip him. He stopped only as long as it took to rip it off his body. Then, barefoot, bald headed, and wearing only lightweight boxer shorts, he entered the brush-covered trail. Running even faster than before, he headed for the highway. He had seen a gas station down the road a ways. If only he could get on the main highway he would be safe once again.

Finally, when his lungs felt as if they might burst, he saw the highway up ahead. He glanced over his shoulder once more but this time he couldn't see anyone. The brush was so dense alongside the trail that he did not have to worry about seeing white robes in the bushes. And since no one was directly behind him he slowed down so he could catch his breath.

Two minutes later he was on the highway. Although he received several strange looks from passersby, he jogged another fifteen minutes until he had reached the gas station and a telephone. He dialed Investigative Services.

"Bob?"

"Yes, is this Jeff?" Bob had been working weekends at the office since taking on the Michigan case. He was driven to solve it and the only way he could keep up with his other cases was by working seven days a week.

"It's me, Bob, I didn't find them." He was out of breath and his words came in short bursts as he gave Bob the address of the gas station.

"Are you okay?"

"Yeah, but I'll need you to bring me some clothes and a baseball cap," he said.

"You bald?"

"You guessed it."

Bob could only imagine what must have happened to Jeff inside the compound of a cult and he felt the urge to chuckle. But the young man wasn't laughing and he didn't want to make light of his ordeal.

"Sorry it didn't go so well."

Jeff ran his hand over his smooth head. "Well, look, Bob. I appreciate the job and all. But next time don't call me, okay?"

"Giving up so soon?" Bob smiled knowingly. Undercover work was never easy and infiltrating a cult was especially hard. But he had figured the young man should know what he was up against before devoting his life to being a private investigator.

"It's not my thing, man," Jeff said. "I've had enough excitement to last a lifetime."

"Well, in that case I have some good news for you."

"What?"

"The boys aren't in a cult after all. We got a big break in the case today. I'll tell you all about it when I pick you up."

CHAPTER 21

If it weren't for the speed limit, Bob would have flown to the Daytona Beach Police Department that Monday morning. This was the most exciting news he'd received since starting the investigation.

The break had come Sunday afternoon with Detective Mikelson's telephone call. Two days earlier, as soon as he'd purchased the information, Bob had notified Mikelson about Spider's real name. Thrilled that Bob was making headway on the case, the detective had promised to run Earl Smith's name in the computer and see if he had a record or if his whereabouts could be determined. Finally, by late Sunday afternoon Mikelson had found the information he was looking for.

"I ran his name, Bob," Mikelson had said. "You're not going to believe this. We've got him in the pen."

"What?"

"Spider Smith had a few too many weapons on him and just so happened to catch the attention of one of our officers. Seems he's sitting pretty over at the Volusia County Jail even as we speak."

"Let's get on it."

They had decided to meet at the police station Monday morning and go over a list of questions for Spider. Now, Bob couldn't drive fast enough. At just before nine o'clock, he pulled up in front of the station and hurried inside.

"Ready?" he asked as he took a chair near Mikelson's desk.

"Ready."

They decided that Mikelson would ask the questions and Brown would listen in. When they were no longer getting productive answers from Spider, they would show him pictures of the boys and watch for his reaction.

Over the years, both men had learned to rely a great deal on the reaction of suspects. Typically, when a person was a suspect in a felony case he or she was not a very good actor. When they were angry, they broke the law; when they were frightened, it showed in their faces. For that reason, it was fair to assume that if Spider responded strangely to their questions and especially to the pictures of the teenagers, there was a good chance he knew something about their disappearance.

This was their best chance yet at actually finding the missing boys. According to the trailer park couple Spider had once lived with Snake. Bob could only hope that Spider had seen the boys, too, and that he knew where they were now. The excitement had built throughout the morning, and now that they were at the jail, waiting to be ushered in to see Spider, Bob could hardly wait.

Finally, a bailiff motioned for the two men to follow him. They walked down a series of corridors until they came to a small room. Inside, with his hands cuffed behind his back, was a long-haired, tattooed man so thin his bones poked through his skin. Bob couldn't help but think the obvious. Earl Smith looked like a spider.

"Smith, we got some questions for you." Mikelson led the way, moving casually into the interview room and taking a chair on one side of Spider. Bob took the other and both men sat down. Spider remained silent.

"You ready?" Mikelson grinned at the inmate and Bob thought he looked much the way a chess player does just before he's about to announce, "Checkmate."

"What for?" Spider's voice was rebellious. "This about the weapons charge, man?" Spider's words spilled from the side of his mouth and he reeked of utter deceit. Bob felt his heart sink. Even if Spider talked he could never be sure he was telling the truth.

"This has nothing to do with the weapons charge, Smith. Now we're going to start with the easy questions." He paused a moment. "You know a man named Snake?"

Spider's eyes shifted nervously. "Yeah, I know Snake. What's it to you?"

"I'll ask the questions. You seen Snake lately?"

Moving his feet in small circles, Spider began to shift about in his seat. "Uhhhh ..." He found a spot on the ceiling and stared at it.

"I need an answer, Smith. You seen Snake lately?" Mikelson stood up and began to pace the room, making a tight trail around the chair where Spider sat.

"No." His answer was quick and to the point. "Ain't seen him since August sometime."

"August when?"

"I don't know, man." Spider was getting angry. "What's the difference."

"I should think you know the difference, Smith," Mikelson said, referring to the fact that inmates who answered police questions sometimes got a better deal in the long run. "You going to cooperate or not?"

Spider shrugged, his bony shoulders moving up close to his neck. "Maybe around the middle of the month. Something like that."

"Okay, now you remember Snake driving a red-and-black Chevy Nova?"

Suddenly Spider began swallowing nervously. It was as if he had choked on a cotton ball and now his throat was too dry to utter even a single sound.

"I'm waiting, Smith. Not like I have all day."

Spider swallowed again, this time forcefully. "A uh, red, uh, Nova?"

Mikelson nodded impatiently, his eyebrows raised in anticipation.

"Well, I think I remember seeing Snake with a red Nova."

"What about some traveler's checks, remember anything about that?"

Still swallowing every few seconds, Spider nodded his head emphatically. "Now that I do remember. Traveler's checks. Snake had lots of traveler's checks."

"Just a thought, here, Smith," Mikelson's voice rang with sarcasm. "But where would a nice guy like Snake get traveler's checks?"

"Well, hmmmm. That is a good question."

Mikelson stopped pacing and stared at Spider, moving his face close to the inmate's. Bob saw that Spider's face had grown pale. "I'm waiting, Smith," the detective shouted.

"Snake said he hit a heavy lick."

"Okay, now we're getting somewhere." Mikelson's voice returned to its normal level. "And what's that supposed to mean, Smith?"

"Well, you know, that's street talk." Spider was growing more uncomfortable by the minute. "Uhh, well, hit-tin' a heavy lick. Means he ripped someone off and, you know, just maybe someone mighta got hurt."

"Okay, so let me get this straight." Mikelson resumed his pacing. "You and Snake are friends—"

"Wait a minute, man," Spider interrupted. "I never said nothing 'bout us being friends. I know him. That's it."

"Sure, Smith." Mikelson was sarcastic as he waved off Spider's statement. "Now, you say Snake had a red Nova, lots of traveler's checks, and that he hit a heavy lick. But the last time you saw him was sometime in the middle of August. Is that right?"

Smith tilted his head slowly from side to side. Bob thought he appeared to be sorting the story through his mind, almost as if he was weighing its legitimacy. "Right," he said finally.

"Fine. Now, tell me where you were last time you saw Snake."

"The bars, man." Spider swallowed loudly. "Snake was taking off, man, heading for Mississippi."

"Mississippi?"

"Yeah, man. Mississippi."

Mikelson narrowed his eyes doubtfully. "Why would Snake head for Mississippi?"

"He has a wife there, man. In Biloxi or something."

"Was he going there by himself?"

Spider struggled to swallow, but after several unsuccessful attempts he appeared to give up. "When I saw him, he was by himself. I know that much."

"And what was he driving when you saw him?"

"The Nova."

Mikelson looked at Bob and saw him nod in a way that was barely perceptible. It was time to bring out the pictures. The detective pulled two photographs from his back pocket and thrust them in Spider's face.

"Ever seen these kids?"

Suddenly, Spider's eyes grew wide. He turned away from the photographs and glared at the detective. "No more questions."

"Fine. Just tell me if you've seen these kids before?"

"I said," Spider was shouting now, "no more questions! Get out of here and don't come back. I'm not answering no questions unless I have a lawyer or something. Just get outta' here."

Mikelson and Bob both were taken aback by Spider's reaction. "You think I can't see through this," Mikelson said, trying to trick Spider into answering his question. "You know these boys, don't you?"

"Listen, pig, I'm not answering no more questions. And that's final."

Mikelson glanced at Bob and sighed. "Well, looks like we have our answer," he said, ignoring Spider's demand that they leave immediately.

Bob nodded and Spider watched nervously. "What the heck is that supposed to mean, man?"

"Never mind," Mikelson said, his face filled with disgust and contempt for the scraggly inmate. He motioned for Bob and the two stood to leave. "You can have it your way. But we're not finished with you yet, Spider. Not by a long shot."

CHAPTER 22

By mid-November, the case of the missing Michigan teenagers had captured the attention of the very highest levels of the Michigan and Florida state governments. For the most part the chain reaction of outrage on the part of politicians was started by the efforts of Larry Burkhalter. But the chain of command did not fully become involved and underlings did not actually begin snapping into action until after Governor William G. Milliken of Michigan personally wrote this letter to Governor Reubin Askew of Florida:

Dear Reubin:

I am enclosing a letter which I received from the Honorable Larry E. Burkhalter, Michigan House of Representatives. In that letter Rep. Burkhalter outlines the cases of two young Michigan men who were last seen while vacationing in Daytona Beach, Florida.

I understand that the original missing persons reports were filed with the Michigan State Police which has been cooperating with the Florida authorities in investigating these disappearances.

As you can imagine, the distance between our states makes it especially difficult for the families of Messrs. Barber and Boucher since it is difficult for them to communicate with Florida law enforcement agencies. I would appreciate your help in obtaining information about these cases for the families. Warm personal regards.

Sincerely, Bill.

It was not often that, dealing on a first name basis, one governor asked another for his personal help in solving a missing persons case. And so Governor Askew decided that he would indeed give his personal assistance to solving the case. His efforts resulted in this letter addressed to the Honorable Edwin Duff II, sheriff of Volusia County:

Enclosed is a copy of a letter received by Governor Askew from Governor Milliken in Michigan regarding two young Michigan men who were last seen in Daytona Beach.

Governor Askew has asked that your department look into this matter and determine whether these two men may still be in the Daytona Beach area.

Your early attention to this request is appreciated.

Sincerely, Bruce C. Starling, General Counsel.

When Sheriff Duff received that letter he knew one thing for sure. His attention to the matter would be more than appreciated. It would be expected. A letter from his office was written November 14 informing Mr. Starling that the sheriff's department would begin an immediate investigation and promising that his department would notify the governor's office from time to time as to the progress they were making.

Later that week, on November 16, sheriff's deputy Joe Deemer was assigned the case and directed to put his full attention into the investigation.

At about the same time, a team of investigators from the Florida Drug and Law Enforcement (FDLE) agency was also contacted by the governor's office. Yes, they would be more than happy to check into this case, which, according to Mr. Starling, was of great personal interest to the governor.

So it was that Mikelson was sitting at his desk working on his ever-increasing workload when on Thursday afternoon—at the exact same time—he was visited by Deemer and two FDLE agents.

"Can I help you?" Mikelson was puzzled by their appearance.

"Yes, we've been asked by the governor to look into a certain missing persons case. We understand it's a case you're working on."

Mikelson was still not aware of what case they were talking about. "What case?"

Deemer glanced down at his notes. "The, uh, Barber-Boucher-case."

"Oh, yes." Mikelson rolled his eyes. "Actually, we are working on that case."

"Well, we've been asked to help speed up the investigation a bit," one of the FDLE agents said.

"We understand there were some traveler's checks cashed?" Deemer asked.

"Yes, but—" Mikelson was interrupted by one of the FDLE agents.

"We'd like copies of the checks, if you don't mind, and then we'll pay a visit to the places where they were cashed."

Mikelson laughed and held up his hand. "Look, officers, I'll give you whatever you need. But I have to tell you something first."

"What's that."

"Everything you men want to do has already been done. And then some."

"I thought your department was too busy to do much investigative work on missing persons cases," Deemer said.

"Our department had nothing to do with it. Everything we know about this case is the direct result of one of the best private investigators around."

The officers brushed off the comment and proceeded to copy the information from Mikelson's file.

"Don't worry about any private investigation at this point," one of the officers said. "We'll take care of everything from here."

And so the interest that the Barbers and Bouchers had tried so desperately to drum up was finally taking place. The governor himself had started the chain reaction and now it was only a matter of time before the various investigators found out what happened to the Michigan teenagers.

But of course, by then, it would be too late.

Bob Brown was weeks ahead of them, blazing a trail into an investigation that had seemed hopeless and making remarkable progress along the way. The morning after the officers visited the police station, Bob Brown was busy finding yet another lead.

One he'd been waiting weeks for.

Since Mikelson had been present the first time they questioned Spider, the detective had agreed to let Bob handle any further questioning by himself. Mikelson still had numerous cases he was working on and there simply wasn't enough time to be running the same questions by an inmate who had chosen to answer only the easy ones. Besides, Mikelson trusted Bob completely.

And so at ten o'clock that Friday morning the private investigator found himself sitting before Spider with virtually the same list of questions and as much time as it might take to get some real answers.

"Who are you, man?" Spider looked disgusted as he ran his eyes up and down the private investigator. He recognized him from the session earlier in the week. But he hadn't been able to understand who he was or why he had sat in on the questioning. "You some kind of narc or something?"

"No." Bob had decided to play on the fact that if Spider knew something about the boys and talked about it, he could very easily avoid a harsh prison sentence by cooperating.

"I'm a PI, hired to find these boys. Here, take a look." Bob took the photos of Jim and Daryl from his briefcase and showed them to Spider.

"Listen, man, I told that pig last time that I wasn't talking no more. Nothing's changed since then."

Bob pursed his lips and raised his eyebrows. "Well, of course that has to be your decision. If you're not willing to talk then there's nothing more to say." He paused long enough to capture Spider's attention.

"But there is something you should know."

Spider squirmed in his seat and again Bob was struck by the appropriateness of this man's nickname. "What's that, man?"

"Well, if you're involved somehow, and I'm only saying *if*, then you're only hurting yourself by not talking."

Spider seemed to think this over. Bob cleared his throat and continued.

"Let's just say you're involved or you know something about how come these boys haven't come home from their vacation yet. Eventually, someone's going to talk. And whoever talks first, well, that's the guy who gets the deal."

"Hey, I don't need no deal, man." Spider was defensive now, his body language showing his frustration.

"That's fine. But if you cooperate, you're always better off in the long run."

For five minutes, neither man spoke. Bob sat perfectly still, his eyes trained on Spider's as he waited calmly for the man to break. Bob could read that much in Spider's face: the man would break eventually. This was where Bob excelled as an investigator. He could almost always get someone to talk. Even if it was merely a matter of waiting until the subject would break down—just as a means of ending the silence—and tell him everything.

When five minutes had passed, Spider began to swallow loudly, much as he'd done the day before when his nerves had gotten the better of him.

"Okay, I've seen them before," he admitted, pointing to the pictures that now lay on the table beside Bob's briefcase.

Bob raised an eyebrow. "All right, now we're getting somewhere. Where did you see them?"

"Snake's trailer."

"Let's back up a bit here. How did the boys get to Snake's trailer?"

Spider shrugged.

"Look, this is your ball, Smith," Bob said. "It's up to you what you want to do. You talk, and you get the best deal possible. You make us find Snake and we'll get him to do the talking. We'll get the truth one way or another."

More time passed and finally Spider coughed loudly. "Snake met the boys at the Thunderbird Motel. He asked them back to his place for a pot party, you know."

"No, I don't know anything about it. You'll have to tell me everything you can."

Spider sighed and seemed to slouch over as if he was dejected by what was happening. Bob guessed that Spider was regretting having said anything at all.

"All right, Snake's a party guy, you know? He does dope, has people around who smoke and buy and sell. Understand?"

Bob nodded.

"Okay, well, he meets these two pigeons—"

"Pigeons?"

"You know, tourists. Fresh in from some backward state like Michigan."

"So Snake meets the pigeons and then what?"

"Well, he brings 'em to his trailer. That's where I saw 'em. I went to the trailer for the party and we all smoked a little pot there."

"The boys smoked, too?"

"Oh, yeah. They was big smokers. We was all getting high and stuff and then later on everyone left."

"Where'd everyone go?"

"I went home."

Bob's patience was being severely tested and he took a deep breath. "Where did Snake and the kids go?"

"Oh, they went to Mississippi, like I said."

"You also said Snake went to Mississippi by himself, if I remember correctly."

"Yeah, well, you know, man. I guess I forgot about the boys."

"If you know anything else, now's the time to talk about it, Smith. Any day now we're going to find other people who are more than willing to talk. And then all the deals anyone might ever make with you about this case will be called off. We only need one guy to spill his guts. Know what I mean?"

Spider nodded. "Wish I could help you, man," he said, his eyes drifting off in space. "But that's it. That's all I know."

Bob was satisfied. He stood up to leave and gathered his belongings.

"I'll be back Smith. See if you can't rack your brains and try to jar your memory a bit. I'm sure you can remember a few more details if you really try."

"Whatever, man." Spider had tuned out and was no longer paying attention.

As Bob left the jail, he decided that all in all it had been a productive week. In a matter of days he had pieced together the fact that Snake and Spider were the last people seen with the boys before they disappeared. He could always come back and spend more time with Spider.

For now he had another lead to check—the Thunderbird Motel.

CHAPTER 23

Armed with the information from Spider Smith, Brown set out late Friday afternoon for the Thunder-bird Motel. He knew that even if Jim and Daryl had stayed at the motel, they were not there any longer. But perhaps there was someone who had spoken with them or who knew where they had gone. At least he could verify part of what Spider was saying and in doing so lend credence to the rest of his story.

Bob arrived at the motel sometime after three that afternoon and went immediately to the manager's office.

"May I help you?" A big man walked out from a smaller back room and came up behind the desk.

Bob flashed his identification card. "Bob Brown, private investigator," he said curtly. "I need to see your register book for the week of August twelfth."

"Well, I'm Stanley Robinson, manager here," he said, sounding as if there was a great deal of prestige in such a position. "I'm afraid those books are private property."

Bob smiled patiently. "I can be back with a police warrant in thirty minutes," he said politely. "Shall I do that, or would you mind just getting the books and letting me take a look?"

Robinson was a solid man with an unruly mustache and thinning hair that curled awkwardly about his head. His image rather fit that of the Thunderbird Motel, which while not run down was certainly not considered one of the finer places to stay at Daytona Beach. Robinson appeared to be agonizing over the choices Bob had given him. Finally he dramatically tossed up his hands in the air.

"What's this country coming to, anyway," he mumbled as he went into the back room. Bob could hear him from where he sat waiting in the lobby. "People just walk in here like they own the place and think they can look at someone else's books. I thought this was America."

When he returned, he opened the book to August 12 and handed it roughly to Bob. "There. Enjoy." Then he walked away in a huff of indignation.

Bob scanned the entries carefully and was surprised that there had been so few guests the night of August 12. Mid-August was usually a time when every motel along the beach would be bursting at the seams. But according to Robinson's book, the Thunderbird had only filled six rooms that night and none of the guests was Jim Boucher or Daryl Barber. He flipped through the pages one at a time, slowly reading each entry. The shortage of customers at the Thunderbird seemed to continue consistently throughout the week. Bob continued to search the book but finally he closed it and rang the bell for Robinson. The boys' names had not appeared at any time during the week.

"You done nosing through my books?" There was a cigar hanging lazily from Robinson's mouth and a trail of smoke that followed him into the lobby.

"Yes." Bob smiled cordially. "Thanks so much for your trouble." Bob turned to leave and then stopped.

"By the way," Bob said as he stared the manager in the eye. "You must be worried about the business."

Robinson looked suddenly suspicious. "What's that supposed to mean?"

"One of the busiest weeks of summer and you hardly had any guests at all," Bob said and Robinson detected more than a little sarcasm in his voice.

"Times ain't easy, Mr. Brown." Robinson smiled wryly.

"And I doubt if they'll be getting any easier." Bob winked and then turned around to leave.

The most obvious reason why Jim and Daryl's names hadn't been in the book was because Spider, in all his depth of character, hadn't been telling the truth.

But Bob wondered if perhaps the motel hadn't been quite as empty as the books suggested. If that were the case, Bob knew he would find out eventually. And then he would be more than happy to share whatever missing information there might have been with the Internal Revenue Service. Bob knew what the IRS would do with someone if he was cheating the books, and it wasn't pleasant. In fact, if Robinson wasn't doing honest business, times would indeed be getting tougher.

For now, though, until he knew differently, Bob had to believe that Robinson was telling the truth and Spider was lying. And if Spider was lying about which motel the boys had stayed at, he was probably lying about everything else, too.

That same afternoon, in Metamora, Michigan, Roy Boucher had finally decided to make the dreaded trip to the bank. He had put it off for days but the time had come to withdraw Jim's money. They had run out of alternatives.

As Roy drove to the bank, he gazed at the rows of maple trees that lined the streets. It was late fall and the leaves had turned brilliant colors: oranges, reds, and yellows. Winter would be here soon and with it the holidays. Usually, the excitement Roy felt for the Christmas season had started by now. But this year was different. Everything was different. Jim was gone and in all likelihood he wasn't coming home. For the hundredth time Roy wondered why they were throwing their money away trying to find the boys. Especially Jim's money. Obviously something had happened to them. If they were still alive, they would have called.

But each time Roy asked himself the question, he instinctively knew the answer. No matter how slim, there was a chance that the boys had been abducted or that they were trapped somewhere. In that case, obviously any amount of money they might spend to find them would be worth the expense.

James Byrd, the Michigan investigator, needed the next installment by Monday morning and Roy had waited until the last possible moment before making this trip. Earlier in the day he had contacted the Chevrolet dealer from which Jim had ordered his brand new Camaro. The salesman had questioned his reason for canceling the order, offering a better price and a finance plan to change Roy's mind. But Roy had declined and even been short with the man.

"I just want to cancel it, all right?" he had said angrily.

The salesman paused a moment. "Is there a problem with the product, sir?"

"No! It's a personal thing. We just won't be needing the car."

Now, Roy wondered if that was true. What if Jim came home? Wouldn't he be angry that his money was gone and that his car no longer was on order?

Roy shook his head, disgusted with himself for thinking that Jim would be angry. The boys had been missing for three months and he and the other parents had run out of ways to fund the investigation. This was their only remaining option.

He pulled into the bank parking lot and turned off the engine. For a long moment, he sat in the car and leaned his head on the steering wheel. Jim had been so proud of himself for winning that bowling contest. The prize money had been unheard of. Ten thousand dollars. There were professional bowlers who didn't make that much money after bowling an entire year of tournaments.

They had celebrated at home the night he found out about winning the grand prize. Faye had taken a picture of Jim in front of the trophy and then they had all shared cake and ice cream. Roy rested a moment longer, savoring the memory and willing himself to be back in that moment once again: when everyone was safe and home and Jim was sitting on top of the world.

Roy sighed. He knew he had to get out of the car, go inside the bank, and make the withdrawal. Jim had wanted his father's name on the account since he was a minor when he opened it. Now Roy knew the bank would not have a problem with him taking the money, if only he could summon the strength to leave the car. All he wanted to do was stay there and keep remembering, pretending he didn't have to use Jim's money to pay a private investigator. There was something so final about reaching this point.

He took a deep breath, and summoning every bit of his remaining resolve, Roy climbed out of the car and headed for the bank. It was the darkest day he could remember ever having.

When Bob got back to the office at five o'clock there was a message for him to call Mike or Rob. His two assistants had agreed to go back up and down Interstate 10 with a new description—this one of Snake Cox. Naturally no one had seen two nice-looking boys from Michigan driving the red Nova. But perhaps someone had seen Snake. It was worth a try.

Bob picked up the phone and dialed Mike's number.

"It's Bob, what've you got?"

"Got a lead, Bob."

Bob grabbed a pen and paper. "Shoot."

"Okay. Rob and I found a tow truck driver near Biloxi who remembers working on the battery cable of a red Chevy Nova, Michigan plates, sometime between August eighteenth and August twentieth."

"You tell him about Snake?"

"Sure did. According to the tow truck driver, Snake was the one driving the car."

"Bingo." Bob was thrilled with this information. "What else?"

"Nothing really. Just that after he fixed the car, the guy headed south."

"Great," Bob grinned. "Hey, thanks, Mike. Keep it up. We're going to find those boys yet. I'm getting that feeling."

Mike laughed. When Bob had a feeling about a case, it was usually solved in a matter of days.

"I'll be in touch."

"Right."

Bob hung up the phone and pondered this new information. Spider had said that the boys went with Snake to Mississippi. Same story the trailer park couple gave. But not once had Bob believed that to be the truth. Why would the boys drive north to Mississippi with a shady guy like Snake when they were supposed to be headed for Disneyworld?

Now he knew that even if the boys had driven north to Mississippi with Snake, they apparently hadn't returned with him. Bob loved a good lead, and this one more than qualified. It meant that if the boys had come to harm, the web of evidence surrounding Snake—and probably Spider—was finally starting to take shape.

CHAPTER 24

By Saturday morning, Brown had finally gotten a photograph of Snake. He had thick, greasy, shoulder-length brown hair which he wore brushed back off his head. His face was thin and pockmarked and his dark bushy mustache curved down around the edges of his thin lips. But it was his eyes that one first noticed. They were brown and beady and flat, like pictures Bob had seen of killer sharks.

Mikelson had asked that the FDLE send a copy of their file photo on Cox and they had done so by mail. It had arrived late Friday afternoon. Bob looked closely at the photograph. Definitely not like any of the pictures he'd used in previous investigations. This was not an average cheating spouse or a parent who had denied a former spouse custodial rights to their child. In Bob's opinion of such people he thought Snake looked downright evil. The idea of him carrying not one, but two loaded guns was purely terrifying.

Bob sat at his Orlando desk staring at the picture.

He had reached a crossroads.

For the first time in his career as an investigator he was looking at the face of a person he wasn't sure he could find. Not only that, but he wasn't sure he wanted to find him. John Snake Cox was a hardened, dangerous, heavily armed criminal who was wanted by a number of law enforcement agencies. And what experience did he, Bob Brown, a private investigator of domestic cases, have with such people? Bob knew the answer.

He had none.

For nearly an hour Bob sat at his desk considering his options. He was not going to give up. He would find Snake somehow and he would find the missing teenagers. By now their parents must be beyond worry. They had probably realized that their sons were dead but because they could not be positive, they had been denied the chance even to grieve. They deserved answers and Bob wasn't going to stop the investigation until he had some.

One option, Bob knew, was for him to continue walking the Daytona Beach bars, flashing hundred dollar bills until someone said something about Snake's whereabouts. Of course, he might just as easily get himself killed by doing that. The bikers did not like him. He was not one of their kind and even the rival gang members hadn't approved of his presence. If he couldn't gain the confidence of the bikers, he didn't stand a chance of finding Snake.

He could push Detective Mikelson, beg him to start asking questions about Snake. But if bikers weren't willing to be paid for information, they certainly weren't going to give it away free to the police.

Suddenly, he knew what he had to do. He would have to hire a new employee, a special kind of temporary operative who could infiltrate the biker bars and somehow learn the whereabouts of Snake. This person would have to appear to be a biker but he must be neither a Pagan nor an Outlaw. Someone with no affiliation to either group would have the best chance of getting information. Whatever he looked like, he would have to be menacing with the kind of intimidating size that would increase his chances of getting a favorable response. Now, it was a matter of finding such an employee.

As with other stages of the investigation, Bob knew of only one way to locate the person he was looking to hire. He bowed his head on his desk and prayed. For thirty minutes he spoke with God, asking him to further assist him in the investigation and to continue sending him leads he could work with. Especially, he asked for guidance in finding that certain employee who could lead him to Snake. When he was finished, he humbly thanked God for all he'd done so far and again asked for protection.

Then he hit the Orlando bars.

The best way of finding a biker who belonged to neither the Pagans nor the Outlaws, he figured, was by looking in the Orlando area. But by eight o'clock that evening, he was beginning to give up hope. He had checked seventeen bars, most of them with a heavy biker clientele. Still, he hadn't found anyone like the man he wanted to hire.

He went back to his car and decided to try one more bar. After that, he was going to go home. He could try again Monday. Before he got out of his car he said another brief prayer.

As he climbed out of his car, he looked toward the front door of the Hillside Saloon and suddenly he saw the silhouette of a man who could easily have been mistaken for a grizzly bear. Bob stood motionless, quietly watching the man.

He appeared to be a patron, and he seemed to be having a conversation with the bouncer. Bob was taken aback by the immensity of the man. He looked like a mountain with wild, fiery red hair and a full beard. His arms bulged against his black leather jacket and he held his head and eyes in a way that would strike fear in all but the most foolish people. Bob smiled. God willing, he had found his employee.

He walked up to the man and introduced himself. "Bob Brown, private investigator. You got a minute?"

The man looked Bob up and down and grinned as if he found something humorous about Bob's question. He shrugged, looking at the bouncer and then back toward Bob. "All right."

Bob motioned toward the front of the bar, outside and away from other people. "Listen, I need to know if you belong to a biker gang?"

The man laughed out loud. "I am a biker gang, man."

Bob nodded as if that was the answer he had expected all along. "Well, I've got a job for you if you're interested."

The man sneered. "What makes you think I'd be interested?"

Bob pulled a hundred dollar bill from his pocket and the man raised an eyebrow. "You interested?"

"Talk."

"I need to know where I can find a biker named Snake," Bob began. He pulled out the black and white photograph of John Cox. "This is him. He hangs out at the Boot Hill Saloon in Daytona Beach."

"What's in it for me?"

"One hundred now. One hundred when you get the information. By the way, what's your name?"

"Larry." The man took the picture from Bob and stared at it a moment. "Two hundred bucks, huh?"

"Two hundred." Bob looked him in the eyes. "Deal?"

"Deal."

There was a stillness in the air, a humidity that was unusual for mid-November. Bob sat in his sedan looking for the man he had hired the night before. They had agreed to meet at eleven o'clock that morning and it was already a quarter past. Only one other time had Bob ever been taken by a potential informant. And even now he didn't believe Larry had stood him up. The man would appear at any time. He had to.

Two more minutes passed and suddenly there was a hard knock on Bob's back window. Immediately, Bob pulled his gun and turned around. It was Larry, grinning and motioning him to roll down his window.

"Don't do that, Larry." Bob released a long sigh and slowly replaced the revolver under his suit jacket. "Let's make a plan."

"I'm going into the saloon. Time to start asking questions," Larry said. He was definitely not afraid of this assignment. "What are you gonna' do?"

"I'll cover you." Bob pointed to the old cemetery down the street across from the saloon. "I'll walk in there like I'm visiting my old grandma and once I'm in I'll hide behind a tombstone. The gun's loaded, so don't worry."

"Do I look worried, Bob?" Larry grinned. He had every intention of enjoying the job ahead of him.

"Either way, I'll be there. You got the picture of Snake?"

"Won't need it."

"You might need it, Larry."

The hulking man pointed knowingly to his right temple. "It's up here, Bob. All safe and secure. I'll find the guy for you, don't you worry."

He started to cross the street. "Be careful!" Bob whispered. Larry waved him off and continued toward the saloon.

Walking boldly through the front door, Larry strode to the center of the bar and looked around. "Listen up!" he shouted.

Every eye in the place was instantly on him.

A ripple of tension coursed through the bar and several bikers rose to their feet in anticipation of trouble. Larry waited until he had their undivided attention.

"Anybody know where Snake is?" Each syllable boomed through the saloon and bounced off the walls. Larry looked around waiting for a response but there was none. Moving slowly in a small circle and snorting like a caged Brahma, Larry glared at the bikers who surrounded him. He walked to the bar and stood perfectly still. Then, in a sudden whir of raging anger, he brought his fist down. A spiderweb of tiny cracks appeared in the bar.

"I said," he bellowed, "does anybody here know where Snake is?"

Although no one attempted to physically kick him out of the bar, not a person responded to his question. Larry waited what he considered a fair amount of time and when no one answered he began once more walking slowly, this time over to a pool table where a handful of bikers had interrupted their game to see what the red-haired giant wanted.

With a swipe of his paw, he erased their game, sending balls spewing across the table and onto the floor. He lowered his face menacingly.

"Does anybody here"—at this point he paused, glaring at the faces around him, detonating each word like a hand grenade—"does anybody here know where Snake is?"

This time when no one said anything, Larry turned around and marched out the front door. Out on the sidewalk he looked at the line of shiny, well-cared-for Harley-Davidson bikes parked neatly one alongside the other. They covered the entire length of the saloon and their chrome fenders shone in the sun.

Across the street, Bob had positioned himself behind a gray, ceramic tombstone. His gun was drawn and he watched nervously as Larry came out from the bar and stood in front of the row of bikes. He watched as suddenly Larry lifted his booted foot and kicked the first bike over. One by one the polished choppers fell on top of each other, collapsing and crashing to the ground like a row of two-wheeled dominoes.

"Goodness," Bob whispered.

Instantly, dozens of angry bikers poured from the bar and appeared ready to charge Larry. Bob aimed his gun and waited.

Larry saw the mob and, grinning madly, he pulled out a cigarette lighter from his pocket and ignited it. Then he bent down and held the flame inches from the gas tank of the first bike.

"They're all going up in one big bang unless someone tells me where Snake is," Larry announced calmly.

Across the street Bob had no idea what Larry was saying. But suddenly the bikers stood perfectly still as if they were afraid to move another inch.

Larry laughed again and the bikers watched him helplessly, terrified of what he might do. At that instant one of the men stepped forward and cleared his throat.

"Look, man, we don't know where Snake is. Honest." The biker was in his forties and had a thick gray beard. His eyes held fear and Larry smiled. What a sham, these gangster bikers, he thought.

"Speak!" Larry ordered.

"But Fat Man knows. You ask Fat Man, he can tell you."

Another biker stepped forward. "Yeah," he said. "Fat Man knows the truth."

"And where might I find Mr. Fat Man?" Larry asked, his demeanor suddenly calm and gentle as he straightened and put his lighter back in his pocket.

The bikers visibly relaxed while from behind the tombstone Bob remained frozen in place, his revolver cocked and ready to fire.

The man who had spoken first pointed down the street. "He hangs out at the bar down there," he said. "About six feet tall, real thin, narrow face and long blond hair. That's Fat Man. Likes one of the dancers down there, you know what I mean, man?"

Larry did not answer. Instead, he turned around and walked away, heading directly for the bar down the street. Back in the cemetery, Bob took a deep breath, placing his revolver back into his jacket. He took out his handkerchief and wiped the perspiration that had broken out across his forehead. Making his way among the tombstones, Bob moved along the length of the cemetery until he had once again positioned himself across the street from the bar where Larry had disappeared.

Once again, Larry moved into the center of the bar and demanded silence. "Where's Fat Man?" he asked.

This time he got a response. "He's not here, man. Says he'll be in later."

Larry did not thank the man or even pause to acknowledge him. He turned around and left the bar, walking quickly across the street and leaning with his back against the cemetery wall. He stood there casually as if intent on watching the passing traffic. Bob waited a moment and then crept up behind him.

"What's up?" he whispered.

"No one at the first place knew where Snake was," Larry said, still looking straight ahead so as to not give away Bob's hiding place. "Fat Man knows where he is."

Fat Man! Bob hadn't been asking about Fat Man much any more because no one had seen him near the boys. But it made sense that he might know where Snake was. After all, the two had been roommates at one time. He listened for Larry to continue.

"He's not in there. But he'll be back. If he knows where Snake is, I'll get him to talk. Don't worry."

Bob smiled to himself. What a wonderful choice Larry had turned out to be. He was not only reliable, he was brilliant. The perfect man for the job. "I'm going back to Orlando. You have my number. Call if you hear anything at all."

"Two hundred bucks, right?"

"Two hundred bucks."

Crouched low to the ground, Bob wound his way toward the entrance of the cemetery and then remained on his knees for a moment in front of a specific tombstone. He read the words and bowed his head respectfully. Then, as if saddened by a great loss, Bob stood up and walked slowly back to his car. When he drove away he was laughing. They were about to catch a snake.

Larry waited outside the bar until a man who fit Fat Man's description sauntered into the bar. A tightly clothed woman hung on his arm and the two seemed oblivious of anyone but themselves. Larry walked purposefully toward the couple and firmly took Fat Man by the arm, prying him away from the woman.

"Hey!" she cried out.

Larry lowered his head and smiled at the woman. "I'm just going to borrow him for a minute. Don't you worry your pretty head none, you hear?"

The woman looked terrified of Larry but she nodded, moving quickly into the bar and ignoring the pained look on the face of the skinny blond-haired man.

"You Fat Man?" Larry asked as they moved away from the bar and across the street to a full-size pickup truck.

The man struggled to pull free from Larry but the man's strength was phenomenal. "Yeah, so what? What's this about, man?"

Larry opened the passenger door to the truck and shoved Fat Man inside. "We're going for a little drive, Fat Man. Sit tight."

The truck peeled away from the curb and Larry turned the wheel hard, forcing it into a U-turn. They headed toward the beach, driving until they found an isolated spot along the strip. Larry turned off the engine, walked around, to the passenger side of the truck, and removed Fat Man with one hand. Twisting the frightened man's arm behind his back, Larry forced Fat Man onto the ground until his pinched pale face was inches from the sand. Larry could feel him shaking with fear.

"You're going to tell me where Snake is," Larry said.

"Hey, man, I don't know where … aahhhh." Larry turned Fat Man's arm another several degrees until the man's eyes filled with tears from the pain.

"I'll say it again in case you didn't hear me." Larry spoke in a calm, quiet voice. Something in his gentle tone scared Fat Man to death. "You're going to tell me where Snake is."

Fat Man released a string of profanity, his voice little more than a high-pitched whine. "He's in Tampa, man, really."

Larry kept his hold on Fat Man and moved closer to the quaking biker. "Where in Tampa?"

"He's living with his wife … in a trailer park." The pain was causing Fat Man to speak in short, broken phrases. "He's driving a truck … for a Tampa trucking company."

"More," Larry demanded. Fat Man winced in pain.

"All right, all right. What do you want?"

"He driving a red Chevy Nova?"

"He's got the Nova. Gave it to his wife for her birthday, couple of months ago. Sold the stereo for fifty bucks."

"You know where the trailer park is?"

"I think so."

Larry twisted Fat Man's arm just a bit more. "You better know so, you hear me?"

"What's in it for me?"

Larry couldn't believe the man's nerve, asking such a question while in such an uncompromising position. He chuckled. "Look, I can get you a hundred bucks, but you darn well better have the information."

"I've got it, man. I do."

Larry yanked Fat Man back onto his feet and shoved him into the truck. Without saying a word to the biker, Larry drove back onto the highway and in utter silence returned to Orlando. Once inside the city limits he drove to the nearest phone booth and dialed Bob's home number.

"Hello?"

"Two hundred bucks, right?"

It was Larry. Bob felt his heart skip a beat in anticipation. "What'd you find?"

"I'm back in Orlando. I've got Fat Man with me."

Bob cringed. "Did he come on his own or did you convince him?"

Larry laughed. "Yeah, he needed a little convincing. That's a good way to put it."

"That's a good way to go to jail, Larry. That's called kidnapping, taking a hostage." Bob rubbed his temples with his thumb and forefinger. Great, he thought. Now he was hiring operatives who were committing criminal acts in exchange for information.

"Don't sweat it, Bob. Everything's under control. Fat Man here knows where Snake is. But he wants a hundred bucks for the information."

Suddenly Bob was grinning like a kid at a birthday party.

"Get the address first. Pay him and get him on a bus, then meet me at my office with the information. I'll pay you back and give you your money as soon as I verify that Snake is where you say he is."

What seemed like hours later, Bob was sitting in his office when he heard a knock at the door. It was early Sunday evening and Bob knew there was only one person who would come to his office at that hour. He opened the door and Larry walked inside.

"Here you go." He handed Bob a slip of paper, then sat down to wait for his money.

Bob held the paper up and read the information. According to Fat Man, Snake was at the Bay Front Trailer Park, 108 South 28th Street, Lot 40. Bob moved to the telephone and dialed the phone number.

"Yes," Bob said when a woman answered the phone. "I need to know if a John Cox lives in Lot forty. Can you help me?"

"Sure." The woman at the other end sounded groggy, as if she'd been awakened by the call. "Just a minute." There was a moment of silence and then she returned.

"You bet. John Cox is over in Lot forty."

Bob thanked her, hung up the phone and let out the loudest victory shout of his life. He peeled off two hundred dollars for Larry, sent him on his way, and in five minutes was back in his car headed for the Interstate.

Some time later he was in Tampa.

CHAPTER 25

The Bay Front Trailer Park was located on the far east side of the city and quite a long distance from the general population of Tampa. It was past seven o'clock and already dark when Bob pulled his car into the parking lot and got out to walk. He did not know what he was going to encounter, but he wasn't about to give himself away by driving up to Lot 40 and ringing the doorbell.

He would sneak around quietly, see what he could find out, and then decide what to do next. Still, he made certain he had his gun with him and that it was fully loaded. He was on a Snake hunt and there was no telling what dangers might lie ahead.

The trailer park was exceptionally still, with only the sound of muted television voices coming from a scattered number of trailers. Dense Florida scrub brush covered the grounds surrounding the park, and cypress trees filled in the spaces between the trailers. But even with its privacy, the park appeared to be the home of low-income transients. Clothing hung from tree branches, and rusted gas cans and car pieces lay scattered about. The trailers were old and run-down and some of them had boarded-up windows.

Bob was not surprised that Snake had chosen this as a place to live. He looked up the dirt road that ran through the center of the park and saw that the lot numbers got successively higher in that direction. Moving through the trees, he made a path parallel to the road and began looking for Snake's lot number. Lot 37, Lot 38, Lot 39. There it was. Lot 40.

With experienced patience and expert care Bob silently positioned himself between two reedy thin trees so that his body was hidden completely by a palmetto bush. Then he watched.

The trailer was very narrow and covered with a dingy white coat of paint that for the most part had long since begun to chip away. The windows were dark and no one appeared to be home. Then Bob saw the car. Parked alongside the trailer was a red Chevy Nova, with no license plates.

It was Daryl's car, for sure, but Bob wanted to be absolutely certain. He pulled a slip of paper from his pocket upon which was scribbled the serial number of Daryl's car: "1X27F2W194878." If Bob could find that same number on the inside of the car's engine, then there was no denying the fact that this was indeed Daryl's car.

Moving on his knees so as not to be seen, Bob crept silently toward the car. He would be able to hear any car that might drive up and he felt there would be enough time to hide. Soundlessly, he lifted the car's hood and stood up just long enough to read the engraved numbers inside. He looked at them, closely matching each one with those on the slip of paper: "1X27F2W194878."

It was Daryl's car.

Bob shut the hood and quickly moved back to his hiding spot. He decided that since the serial number matched he now had enough evidence to call the police. At the very least, Snake was in possession of stolen property and possibly guilty of grand theft. Certainly, there was enough here to make an arrest.

Moving as quietly as he could, Bob crawled through the brush and returned to his car. Bob drove to a convenience store pay phone just a few hundred yards from the trailer park's entrance and telephoned the Tampa Police. He identified himself and explained the situation.

"Oh, and one more thing," he added. "You might want to be careful. Cox is supposed to be heavily armed and dangerous."

Then he returned to his spot outside Snake's trailer and waited. Within ten minutes, five police cars had pulled into the trailer park and surrounded Lot 40, lights flashing and police radios echoing through the area.

Bob shook his head in disgust as he made his way to the nearest car. "Get these cars out of here!" he ordered.

"Listen, Mr. Brown, we'll take over from here," the officer said.

Bob sighed. This was the trouble with private investigations. You could solve an entire case and still not gain the respect of the authorities. He lowered his voice and pleaded with the officer.

"Cox isn't here. Now what do you think he's going to do when he finally comes home and sees this sort of welcome committee outside his front door?"

The officer considered this and nodded. "You're right. Good point," he said. Then he picked up his radio and notified the chief that they were going to pull their cars back until someone came home. A trio of officers joined Bob in his hiding spot and waited.

At ten thirty that evening, less than an hour after the police had set up the stakeout, a car pulled up outside Lot 40. A man and woman, arms draped around each other, fell out of the car and for several seconds were unsuccessful at numerous attempts to stand up.

"Oooo!" the woman whined, drawing the word out as if it were several syllables long. Then she began to giggle.

"Stone drunk," Bob whispered to the officers, who nodded in agreement. At once they stood up from their hiding place, guns drawn, and ordered the couple up against the car they'd arrived in.

"Watsis all about?" the man shouted. His speech was severely slurred. As Bob and the officers drew near they were assaulted by the heavy smell of sweat and alcohol.

"Just move back and put your hands up!" Sergeant Joe Williams of the Tampa Police Department was in charge of this scene and he moved forward toward the couple.

The man and woman obeyed the orders, struggling to keep their hands over their heads without falling down.

Sergeant Williams shone his flashlight at the man and saw that his clothing was partially undone. "You John Cox?"

The man shook his head vehemently and laughed. Then he looked at the woman. "Nah, I'm much better looking, right baby?" He burped loudly.

"Besides, he ain't coming home for a few days yet, is he, baby?" He tried to twirl a strand of her hair but missed and nearly lost his balance.

"Hands up!" Williams ordered.

"Lissen ossifers." The woman was barely understandable. "I'm Sandra Cox. Snake's wife. Can I help you?"

"Snake?" Williams asked.

"That's Cox," Brown interjected.

Williams nodded. "We're looking for Snake, ma'am. Is he inside?"

The woman's eyes grew wide and she covered her mouth like a schoolgirl with a juicy secret. Then she began to giggle. "I hope not!" She turned and blew a kiss toward the man who had brought her home.

"Listen, Mrs. Cox, this is a serious matter. We need to know when your husband will be home."

"Lesseee," she mumbled to herself. "Well, not before my friend, here, leaves. Right, baby?"

"Right, baby." The man winked at Sandra.

"Where is Snake now?" Williams was not getting anywhere with this line of questioning and he wanted to find out all he could before the woman passed out. The Tampa Police had agreed to come to the trailer park and if possible impound the vehicle and arrest John Cox for his outstanding warrants. But now that he wasn't here, this was a simple matter of getting the car. He'd had enough of this drunk woman and her illicit boyfriend. The woman was ignoring his last question.

"Mrs. Cox, I need to know where Snake is now?"

"Work." She smiled lazily. "Good man, that Snake. Got a job and everything."

"Ma'am, I'm going to need to know a little information about that car over there," Williams said, pointing to the Nova. "That your car?"

"Sure is!"

"When did you get it?"

"Well, it don't have a stereo no more. Darn Snake sold it for his bike or some silly thing. Best stereo you ever wanted to hear. You know what I mean, ossifers? It was real nice, lots of music, too, and then last week we were talking about—"

"Ma'am!"

Sandra was suddenly silent. "What was the question?"

"When did you get it?"

Bob was frustrated as he stood in the background watching this exchange. He hoped Williams would get to the point of the matter soon—before the woman realized who she was talking to and wisely refused to answer any more questions.

"Lesseee," she whined. "Hmmmmm. Oh, yeah! My birthday. Snake gave it to me for my birthday. Brought it to me up in Biloxi. Then we drove on back to Daytona Beach and, oh, lessee. That's right, after a while we moved it on over here to Tampa." She turned toward her companion and gave him a cutesy wave. "Right near my sweet lil' old friend, here."

"Ma'am, I need a date. When did all that happen?"

"Now, if you're asking me when my birthday is, then I hope you're going to get me a present. Are you gettin' me a present or something, huh? Sure could use a new stereo! A black one with those tiny, eensy, weensy, little knobs and—"

"What's the date, ma'am?"

"Okay, okay." Sandra sounded like a petulant child with a speech disorder. "August thirteenth."

Bob was disgusted. Snake had given his wife a car that in all likelihood was stolen from a couple of dead kids and had had the nerve to call it a birthday present.

Williams scribbled some notes. "All right, now when did you move to Tampa?"

"Ohhh," Sandra said. She was drifting off, starting to sway from side to side, and Bob prayed she wouldn't pass out before the questions were finished. "Beginning of September. Something like that. Not at Chrismis' time. I know that much."

"Where did he get the car, ma'am?"

"Well." she held up her thumb and forefinger and pinched them together. "It was a teensy, weensy little deally-type thing. He worked it out fair and square and, hey, I got the papers. You wanna' see papers or what?"

Sandra had started to lurch forward and Williams raised his gun. "Back up and keep your hands in the air, ma'am. We're not finished."

Williams removed from his pocket the photographs of Jim and Daryl that Bob had given him. "Ever see these boys, ma'am?"

Sandra moved her face dramatically closer to the pictures and opened her eyes wider. "Hey, that one there's pretty cute!" She burst into laughter and then turned once more and blew a kiss toward her boyfriend. "Just kidding, baby!"

Williams was nearing the end of his patience. "Ma'am, I need an answer or I'll have to take you down to jail."

"For what?" Sandra shouted back in defiance.

"Grand theft. We think this car may have been stolen."

"What! My little Snake wouldn't never do nothing like that!" She tried to look serious but then she erupted into a burst of laughter. She seemed to think this was perhaps the funniest thing she'd heard in a long time. "You hear that? Snake wouldn't do nothing like that, right, baby?"

"Ma'am!"

Sandra turned toward the sergeant and gradually stopped laughing. "What?"

"Have you ever seen these boys?"

"Nah, never seen 'em in my life."

"Okay. Now I want you to listen up. I'm going to need to know where I can find your husband."

"Maybe if you try the ole truckin' company down the way! Could be there, maybe. Maybe not." She giggled again.

"Ma'am, I need a straight answer about where I can find Mr. Cox. If I don't get one, you and your sweet little old friend over there will be spending the rest of the evening in jail."

Sandra stuck her tongue out at Sergeant Williams. "Spoil sport!" she yelled. "All right. I'll tell. But lemme tell you something else, too. Snake won't be happy about it. Not, one bit."

"Where is he?"

"Works over at the Commercial Vehicle Trucking Company. Or maybe it's the Trucking Commercial Vehicle Company. Something like that."

"Fine. You can put your hands down. Both of you." The couple did as they were told and Sandra moved up close to the man.

"We've got business to take care of, ossifers," she mumbled happily, gazing suggestively into her boyfriend's eyes.

"We're done. You can go inside if you want."

"What about my car?" Sandra looked slightly concerned as she turned back toward the Nova.

"We'll be taking the car. If we don't find anything, we'll bring it back in a few days."

Bob laughed softly to himself. If his suspicions were correct, the next time Sandra Cox would see that car again would be in photographs. Large photographs pinned up on an evidence board in superior court.

Williams moved to his squad car and ordered a police tow truck to the scene. An hour later, the Chevy Nova was hooked up and on its way to the Tampa Police crime lab for a thorough analysis.

"Nothing we can do about Cox for the time being," Williams told Bob once the Nova was gone. "Not until the morning."

Bob nodded. "Then what?"

"Well, we really don't have much to go on. I mean, they're just a couple of missing teenage boys. They could have *given* the car away for all we know."

Williams paused a moment and saw that Bob expected more of an answer.

"I guess we could call over to the trucking company and see if Snake really works there," Williams conceded. "If so, we'll pay him a little visit. Or maybe the Daytona Police should check into all this. It's actually their case, right?"

"Actually," Bob emphasized the word, "there's a bunch of people working this case. Everyone from Daytona to the FDLE. But so far only the privately paid people have found out any information."

"Yeah. That's how it is around here. These missing persons cases don't draw a lot of attention unless something big happens."

"Well, from where I stand this thing is very big and growing bigger by the minute." Bob nodded to the sergeant and began heading toward his car. "I'll be seeing you." He turned around and headed toward his car.

"Hey, Brown," Williams shouted. "Where you going?"

"I'll give you one guess."

"The trucking company?"

"You guessed it."

Williams thought about this a moment. "Call us if he's there, will you? We'll leave it to you."

"Sure thing, Williams," Bob said. "You'll hear from me."

He turned away, shaking his head in frustration. Even now, with a car that was quite possibly stolen sitting in police custody, he couldn't interest a single officer to commit to the case. He had heard from Mikelson that the sheriffs department and the FDLE were working the case now. Something about it being of special interest to the governor.

But Bob hadn't run across any of them in the course of his investigation. So either they were forging a completely new trail or they were still weeks behind anything Bob and his operatives had accomplished. Either way, the boys were still missing and at this point all the agencies in the state of Florida weren't making a bit of difference to change that fact.

Bob remembered the sergeant's words. *Just a couple of missing teenage boys.*

But what if they were dead? Wasn't that a possibility now that they'd found the car and still had received no word from the boys. If there was even a chance that the teens had been killed, there should have been a dozen officers frantic to solve the case. The way Bob interpreted the law, there was enough existing evidence to at least *suspect* Snake Cox of murder. After all, it was a felony to kill.

Even if the victims were just a couple of missing teenage boys.

CHAPTER 26

On the way to the trucking company, Bob used his car radio phone to call his assistant, Mike Black. It was after midnight, but Mike could hear the urgency in Bob's voice and he agreed to meet his boss at the trucking company.

"You get the first shift," Mike said, his voice still groggy. "I've got about six hours of sleep to catch up on."

Bob laughed. "With any luck, neither of us will be sleeping."

Bob liked to have backup assistance whenever he had to stake out a certain location. That way if one of them needed a break, the other could continue the watch without taking the chance of missing the subject.

The men met at the Commercial Vehicle Trucking Company outside of Tampa at 2 A.M. and parked alongside each other so as to clearly see the traffic going in and out of the main building.

They waited throughout the night and into the morning and, finally, when Bob was certain that the company was open for business, he straightened his rumpled suit and walked inside. He could only imagine how he looked, having had no sleep for nearly two days. He took a deep breath.

"I'm looking for John Cox," he said politely. "I understand he's a driver for you."

The receptionist nodded. "Yes, Mr. Cox is one of our newer drivers."

"Will he be back today?"

"Oh, no," she said, shaking her head. She was a middle-aged woman with a squarelike shape. "He's on a cross-country run and won't be back for at least three weeks. Is there something I can help you with?"

Bob was visibly disappointed but he shook his head. "No, that's all right. Can you give me the approximate date he might return?"

The woman turned toward a work schedule posted on the wall behind her and studied it a moment. "Looks like he won't be back until maybe Monday, December eleventh."

Bob nodded his appreciation. "Much obliged, ma'am."

When he got back to the cars he stuck his head through Mike's passenger window. "Bad news, Mike. Our man Snake's gone on a three-week run."

"Great."

"Really. Now, Mike, let me ask you something. If Mr. Snake is responsible for the boys' disappearance and gets wind of our investigations, and right now he's off somewhere in Southern California lying in the sun, what do you think the chances are he'll come back to Florida in three weeks?"

"Slim to none?"

"Yeah. And that's if we're lucky."

CHAPTER 27

Bob did not intend to sit idly by and wait for Snake's return. Instead, he would get to know Snake the same way he had gotten to know the missing teenagers. And the one person who knew more about Snake and his recent actions than any biker in Daytona Beach was his wife. The next morning Bob set out for the Bay Front Trailer Park in Tampa. He intended to catch Sandra in something less than an inebriated state. As he made the drive he wondered if he was wasting his time. The woman was under no obligation to answer his questions. Still, he prayed intently that she would talk.

At eleven o'clock that morning he pulled up in front of the trailer, climbed out of the car, and knocked on the door. After several minutes the door opened slightly.

"What?" Her voice was raspy and hard. Bob thought she still sounded slightly drunk.

"You alone?"

"Yeah. So, what's it to you?"

"Got a few questions for you, ma'am. Mind if I come in?"

Sandra opened the door slowly and squinted as the light hit her eyes.

"You got a warrant or something?"

"No, ma'am. Just a couple of teenage boys been missing for a few months now. Parents are worried sick."

"What's that got to do with me?"

"I think Snake's involved."

Sandra shook her head and started to close the door. "No, sir. Ain't nothing I'm going to say about Snake."

"Wait." Bob was desperate. He wanted so badly for the woman to trust him. "What?"

"You don't have to tell me anything bad about Snake. Just tell me what happened. Tell me how he got the car, that kind of thing."

Sandra was silent a moment.

"Well?" Bob was hopeful. "Can I come in?"

She sighed loudly and opened the door. "Oh, all right. But I ain't saying nothing bad about him. You got that?"

"Fine." Bob followed her into the dark trailer and waited until she sat down before sitting across from her on the worn sofa. "Okay," he said, "now why don't you tell me how you got the red car."

Sandra ran her fingers through her uncombed hair and sighed. "He ain't gonna' be mad at me for this, is he?"

Bob shook his head. "You can't say anything to hurt him, Mrs. Cox. All you're going to do is help us understand what happened to those kids."

She nodded and began to talk, drifting back in time to recall the specifics of August 13, 1978—her twenty-third birthday and the first time she'd seen Snake with the Chevy Nova.

That day Sandra had been up north in Biloxi, Mississippi, lounging on the living room sofa at her mother's house. She had been restless and bored without Snake. And the television, with its string of lusty soap operas, did little to fill the afternoon's emptiness. It had been her birthday, and she hadn't heard a word from her husband in days.

The trouble had started a month before that, back in July, she told Bob. The investigator nodded, allowing her to talk uninterrupted.

July was when Snake began having money troubles. As their finances grew more and more scarce, Snake began yelling at her and pushing her around their mobile home. Finally, things got so bad she put her things together and left for her mother's house. But after a while that had grown old, too. By the time her birthday arrived, she was wondering how much longer she could live with her mother and she thought about Snake constantly. Despite his faults, Sandra believed that life with him was better than being alone.

That afternoon she had been missing Snake badly when suddenly, the telephone rang. Sandra stood up and reached for the receiver.

"Hello?"

"Hey, babe." The voice at the other end was silky-soft and seductive in a way that sent shivers through Sandra's body.

"Snake!" She did nothing to hide the excitement in her voice. There was something dangerous about Snake, something she couldn't quite put her finger on. In her opinion he was the ultimate challenge and she could never get enough of him. Even when he treated her badly.

"Where are you, baby?"

"I thought you didn't care where I was?" He was teasing her and she groaned.

"I didn't," she said. "But I changed my mind. You miss me, baby?"

"You don't know how much," he said, his voice dropping several levels. "Hey, I got a surprise for you!"

"A surprise!"

"Well, it's your birthday, isn't it?"

"Snake, you remembered!" Sandra was thrilled, all her ill feelings toward Snake gone in an instant.

" 'Course I remembered, love. Got you a little surprise."

"Well …" Her Southern drawl was more dramatic as she played along. "When do I get it?"

Snake laughed. "A few hours."

She gasped. "You mean you're on your way here?"

"You bet. Be there by three o'clock."

"Oh, Snake. I missed you so much!"

Snake paused a moment. "Hey, baby. Your momma home?"

Sandra giggled. "Gone till six."

Snake howled into the phone. "Yee-hah! I'll be there by two thirty."

"Hurry, Snake," she whispered. "I'll be waiting."

Sandra paused a moment and explained to Bob that since Snake had remembered her birthday, she had planned to make it an afternoon he wouldn't forget.

Bob ignored the statement. "Then what happened?"

Sandra continued.

At two forty-five that afternoon, Snake had pulled up in front of his mother-in-law's house in Biloxi. Inside the house, Sandra heard his car outside. She ran quickly to the door and opened it. Snake was walking up the sidewalk and he held out his arms.

"Snake!" She ran to him and then they kissed for a long time until finally she pulled away breathlessly. "Where's my surprise?"

Snake turned his body and made a sweeping, gallant gesture toward the car parked out front. "Ta-daa," he said.

Sandra stared at the car in confusion.

"I don't get it, Snake."

"There it is," he said. "That's your present."

She gasped and ran toward the car. "This?" she asked in shock.

"Yes. I got you a car for your birthday. Like it?"

"Like it? Snake! I love it. It's gorgeous."

She opened the driver's door and slid into the bucket seat. Quickly she turned the key and flipped on the radio.

"I can't believe it, Snake," she said. "It's really mine?"

"All yours. Let's go inside and you can thank me proper like."

Sandra fiddled with the car's gadgets for several seconds and then suddenly turned to her husband warily. "Snake," she said, doubt filling her voice.

"What?" he asked defensively.

"Snake, where'd you get this here car?" she asked. "You didn't steal it or nothing, did you?"

"Baby!" he said, indignant at her suggestion.

"Well, where'd you get it?"

Snake's face grew serious. "Got it for a kilo."

"Snake! You got my birthday present from a drug deal?"

"It was all on the up-and-up, real fair-like, understand?" His temper had risen at that point. "Coupla guys bought a kilo of prime weed. I got some money and the car. Fair and square."

Sandra thought a moment.

"Hey, don't worry! I got the papers on it. It's all legal and everything."

Slowly Sandra's face broke into a smile. She couldn't be angry with her husband. At least he had remembered her birthday. She looked over the inside of the car and could feel her excitement rising. She had never had such a nice car. She got out of the sporty-looking Chevy Nova and ran her hand over the paint. Besides, it was her favorite colors. Bright red with a nice-looking black vinyl top.

"How could I complain about a birthday present like that?" she asked Bob, her story complete.

Bob paused a moment. "What's the next thing you remember? You came back to Daytona Beach with him, right?"

"Right."

"Then what? What made him leave?"

"Well, I can tell you about all that, I guess. Ain't no harm in telling a little story."

Bob nodded and leaned back. "Go ahead, ma'am. I'm listening."

Then Sandra began talking.

After they had returned to Dayton Beach driving the red Chevy Nova, Snake began acting strange. Sandra watched her husband for days, puzzled by his behavior. He was constantly looking out the window, always checking to see if the Nova was still parked outside and nervous about leaving the trailer. Something was definitely wrong.

All his life Snake had been the personification of cockiness, she told Bob. He had ruled the beaches for years, stirring terror in the eyes and hearts of people of all ages, especially anyone who interfered with his beach-side business dealings. He was a Pagan biker who knew no fear.

But suddenly, for reasons Sandra could not explain, Snake seemed to have grown afraid.

There was something else that seemed unusual. Spider hadn't been by at all. Normally, Snake and Spider were nearly inseparable. They worked the beach side by side, and afterward they would crash at Snake's trailer. There they would smoke marijuana and sit about the room for hours at a time, their eyes barely open, discussing significant subjects.

"Such as the color of the sky," Bob piped in, "or the contents of milk?"

Sandra wrinkled her forehead. "What?"

"Never mind. Go ahead. Tell me what happened."

Well, Sandra said, another thing that seemed strange was how often Snake seemed to talk about moving to Tampa. Snake had never wanted to move before. He loved Daytona Beach, where he could have everything right when he wanted it. There was the beach, the biker bars, and the best customers around.

But suddenly he wanted to move to Tampa, of all places. And even more out of character, he wanted to work. A real job, with a boss and scheduled hours and a steady paycheck. Sandra hadn't been sure if she should be thankful or concerned.

Then one afternoon, when it seemed as if Snake's anxiety level would push him over the edge of his definition of sanity, some really strange things began to happen. Snake had walked into the sitting room of the trailer with a handful of tools.

"Where you going?" Sandra had asked, looking up from her magazine.

"The car," came his curt response. His eyes were narrowed angrily and he didn't attempt to look at his wife. He seemed like he was about to explode.

Sandra decided not to force the issue. Instead, she watched as he burst through the trailer door and moved with determination toward the Chevy Nova. He slid into the driver's seat and began dismantling the car stereo. Suddenly Sandra no longer cared about Snake's bad attitude. That was her car, after all, and her stereo. She stormed outside, hands on her hips and glared at her husband.

"What are you doing?" she shrieked.

"Shhh!" Snake hissed. "Shut your mouth, woman!"

"No, Snake," Sandra whined, intentionally keeping her voice at a high level. "That's my car and I want to know what you're doing to my stereo?"

"Taking it out," he said. "Now shut up!" Snake rose to his feet and moved menacingly toward his wife. But Sandra ignored his implied threats, even if she did lower her voice considerably.

"Snake!" She sounded exasperated. "I don't want it out. I like that stereo."

"Yeah, well, I'm selling it."

"What?" Sandra raised her voice again.

"Listen," Snake moved as close to Sandra as he could without touching her. He was so angry he was shaking. "Don't raise your voice at me again or I'll lower it myself."

"Why are you selling my stereo?" she asked, her own anger evident despite the fact that she maintained a much quieter voice than at first.

"I got the darn car," he said between clenched teeth. "I can sell the darn stereo if I want to. Understand, woman?"

"But why, Snake?"

"I'm getting a front end for my bike, that's why," he whispered.

"A front end? You don't need your bike fixed. You can use the Nova any time you want," she whined again, and Snake had grown more irritated by the minute.

"I don't want to drive your old Nova!" He glared at Sandra and then perhaps before he might do something he would regret—especially in broad daylight and at the trailer park where everyone knew him—he turned around and resumed his efforts at removing the stereo.

Sandra did not give up. She walked up to the car and peered inside.

"What you want that rusty bike fixed for anyway?" she whispered loudly. "Where you going?"

Snake sat up and stared at her. "I'm leaving for Tampa. Gotta find a job. Any more questions or will you get out of my hair?"

Sandra had thought about that a moment. "No more questions," she said, maintaining the whisper. "But you better get me a new stereo for my car. You hear, Snake? I mean it!"

Snake had ignored her last comment and continued working. Not until Sandra got back inside the trailer had she considered how strangely her husband had acted. The strangeness wasn't so much in the fact that he wanted to sell the stereo. What was really odd was how he had wanted to keep so quiet about it. Snake was a loud person, probably part of the biker image he so enjoyed. Why, then, in the middle of the afternoon, would Snake want to keep quiet about taking a stereo out of the Chevy Nova.

"It wasn't like we had anything to hide," she explained to Bob. "We owned the car, understand?"

Bob nodded and waited as she continued.

That afternoon Snake had taken the stereo to the bike shop and come home happier than he had been in weeks. His Harley-Davidson had a new front end and he had fifty dollars spending money in his pocket.

"I believe that's my money, Snake," Sandra had said when Snake pulled the cash out in front of her and counted it.

"What?"

"You got the money for selling my stereo," she said defiantly. "It's my money!"

Snake looked at her in disgust and for a moment it seemed he might even spit at his wife. Then he turned around, mumbling a string of profanities, and walked out the door. In a matter of minutes he had started up the bike and disappeared.

"Fine," Sandra had said out loud as she watched him disappear. "But don't expect me to sit around waiting for you to come home, Snake. You'll be sorry."

Sandra had paced the empty trailer trying to decide what to do now that Snake had most likely left for Tampa. If she wanted to meet men, she couldn't go to any of the biker bars where the Pagans and the Outlaws hung out. The gangs might have been rivals, but they knew who their women belonged to. Sandra belonged to Snake, and even if she found someone willing to take her home, Snake would hear about it as soon as he got back in town. The way the gangs worked, someone could lose their life over using another member's woman.

Most of the time, Sandra explained to Bob, she liked being married to a Pagan biker. It made her feel important. But there were times, like that August afternoon when Snake left for Tampa, that she wished they had a more private life, without the involvement of an entire motorcycle gang. Especially one as potentially vicious as the Pagans.

"Anything else?" Bob asked quietly. She had already told him far more than he had hoped to hear, but perhaps there was more.

"What do you want to know?"

"What happened in Tampa?"

"Oh. Right. I guess I could tell you that."

Surprisingly, she told Bob, Snake's month-long trip to Tampa paid off. He had ridden his motorcycle home at the beginning of September and informed Sandra that he had been hired by a trucking company. He would be responsible for driving medium-size trucks across the country and back, making product deliveries along the way.

"Get your things together," Snake had announced when he walked in the door.

Sandra had stared at him blankly. He had been gone for such a long time that she doubted if he would ever return. Not that she hadn't enjoyed herself while he was away. But Tampa? What was there to do in Tampa?

"Snake, have you flipped?"

"Listen, old lady." Snake was suddenly angry. "I got me a job in Tampa and we're leaving today. Starting a new life. Right now. You hear?"

Sandra threw up her hands and moved toward their bedroom, muttering as she went. "I just don't know about you, Snake, up and leaving like this with no warning and all and here I am supposed to just pack up and move." She talked mostly to herself as she threw her clothing into a suitcase.

"Just like that," she told Bob, shaking her head in disbelief. "Move to Tampa. I mean, I didn't know what to think."

"Go ahead, Mrs. Cox." Bob didn't want her to stop now.

Sandra nodded and continued. After she had complained about the move for several minutes, Snake burst into the bedroom in a fit of anger.

"Ah, shut up, woman," he shouted. "I want outta here in fifteen minutes and you better be ready."

"Oh, sure, Snake. Thanks for all the time."

"I said," Snake raised his voice even louder, "shut up! Get to work!"

Sandra had been silent then. Whatever was happening to their lives she didn't like it one bit. Especially when all her friends were here in Daytona Beach. And why would Snake have gotten a job? Sandra couldn't figure it out.

Nearly an hour later they had emptied the trailer and packed their things into the Chevy Nova. The trailer was furnished when they rented it so they took none of the furniture. Snake also tied several items to the back of his Harley-Davidson, which he was going to ride while Sandra followed in the Nova. When they were ready to go, Snake ordered Sandra into the car.

"What about the manager?" she had asked. "Aren't we going to check out or something."

"None of his darn business where we're moving." Snake's forehead was covered with perspiration from loading up their belongings and he was short of breath and angry. "Now let's get out of here!"

"You sure are acting weird, Snake," she said as she slipped into the driver's seat of the red and black Nova. She leaned her head out and stared at her husband. "Hey, Snake," she said sarcastically. "Now'd be a good time to have a car stereo, don't you think? First you give me the car, then you take the stereo. Nice guy, Snake. Real nice."

"Listen, I've had enough talk about that. Don't bring it up again. I got rid of the stereo. Period. Shut up and drive."

"Sure, sure." She had slammed the door shut then. "Whatever you say, my loving Snake."

And with that, Sandra concluded, she and Snake had started off on a new life in Tampa, leaving Daytona Beach—and whatever it represented—behind them.

"Anything else?" Bob asked.

Sandra shook her head. "Not that I can think of."

Bob stood up slowly and reached out to shake Sandra's hand.

"Thank you, Mrs. Cox. I think your stories will be a great help for us."

Sandra rose, wiping her sweaty hands on her jeans. "I ain't said nothin' bad about Snake, now, understand?"

"Right," Bob said as he left the trailer. "Nothing bad at all."

That evening Bob pondered all that he had learned about Snake and his actions. There was a common thread that ran through the stories Sandra Cox had told him. Snake was guilty. Now Bob had to find out why.

CHAPTER 28

Later that week, back at his Orlando office, Bob Brown spent a great deal of time thinking.

The boys had last been seen the evening of August twelfth, sometime after making the phone call to their parents. During that time, they had apparently driven to Snake's trailer, where they had spent at least some time in the company of Spider. After that, the boys had disappeared. A few days later Snake had wound up with Jim's traveler's checks and Daryl's Chevy Nova, which he had then cheerfully given to his wife for her birthday.

Bob thought about the scenarios that were not likely given these certainties. First, it was not very likely that Jim and Daryl had sold the car and the traveler's checks to Snake in exchange for a kilo of marijuana, as his wife had suggested. Even if the boys had decided to do something completely out of character like purchase drugs from Snake Cox, they would not pay for them with their single mode of transportation.

Second, even if they had sold the car, they would at least need money in order to get through the weekend. They had money, of course: Jim's ten thousand dollars sitting back in Metamora. But the boys hadn't touched that money and they hadn't contacted any of their friends for assistance. Therefore, Bob didn't see any possible way that the boys had sold their car to Snake.

If, then, they had not willingly given away their possessions, there was the other option. Snake had stolen them. If that was the Case, Bob believed the boys were probably dead. Long ago there might have been a chance that they were being held hostage. But since Snake had moved to Tampa, there would have been no one to watch the boys, no one to make sure they had proper food and water.

Only Snake knew what had really happened to the boys. And it was completely possible, Bob reasoned, that Snake wouldn't return to Tampa in three weeks. It was possible he might never return.

Bob decided he needed another type of employee. Not a biker or a young man willing to shave his head for a hundred dollars. Someone with intelligence and weapons, and clout. Someone with a reason to arrest John Cox. Someone whose authority would cross state lines, if necessary. Bob needed to hire the FDLE.

In the past Bob had never even considered hiring a law enforcement officer. For one thing, no one in the agency's higher levels of authority would approve of officers taking private money in return for investigative services. But at the same time, since Bob was neither a criminal suspect nor a potential witness, there was nothing explicitly illegal about taking such an offer of pay.

The more Bob thought about the situation the more he thought that the idea might just work. Of course, technically the agents were already working the case. Special favor for the governor and all. Bob knew that nothing had actually been done to further the investigation since the FDLE's involvement. However, if he was able to kindle their interest with the offer of cash, it was possible that something might get done. He picked up the phone and dialed.

An hour later, he had successfully placed two special agents on his payroll. They would be reimbursed by funds still coming in from Michigan. The deal was that the agents would notify Bob of anything they learned about Snake and in doing so they would receive two hundred dollars per tidbit.

With that added incentive, Bob found it remarkable how quickly the next piece of information turned up. That afternoon, he took a call from the agents stating that they had spoken with a Mississippi highway patrolman who had seen Cox cash a check in Pascagoula under the name of James Boucher. The officer had recognized Cox as a Pagan biker named Snake who rode a Harley-Davidson chopper.

The information was wonderful news for those in Bob Brown's camp and well worth the two hundred dollars. Because now in addition to the outstanding warrants, which might only hold Cox in prison for twenty-four hours, the FDLE could arrest him for possible forgery. No judge would set bail for a man with outstanding warrants. So with Snake sitting safely in jail the authorities would have plenty of time to ask him about the mysterious disappearance of two Michigan teenagers and how it was that he had wound up with the boys' car.

"I do believe this is a wonderful working relationship," one of the agents said after informing Bob of the newest lead and after Bob had promised to wire him the money.

"My thoughts exactly. Stay in touch."

And so while the special agents tried to dig up information on Snake, Bob devoted the next few weeks to a number of cases.

Since there seemed to be nothing to do except wait for Snake's return, he made up new flyers with the boys' pictures. This time there was a five hundred dollar reward and the phone number listed was that of Bob Brown, Investigator. The flyer read:

> Subjects last seen in Daytona Beach area on August 12, and were alleged to have
> been in the company of another man, John Carter Cox, Jr. Street name: "Snake."
> All calls are strictly confidential.

By November 24, Bob called Rob and Mike into his office and handed them a stack of hundreds of flyers.

"Here you go," he said.

"Where do you want them, boss?" Mike expected Bob to list a handful of places.
"You know those open spots around Daytona Beach?" Bob said.

"Open spots?"

"Spots. On the walls, on the sand, on the boardwalk, in the arcades."

"Okay, what about them?"

"Cover them. If someone goes to Daytona Beach this week and doesn't see our posters we've done something wrong."

As is often the case when money is offered, the reward posters brought in a bevy of calls.

On November 25, Bob received a call from an anonymous source stating that quite possibly the boys were living in the upstairs apartment of a duplex just off the beach. The caller swore he had seen two young men who fit the description of Jim and Daryl heading into that apartment just one week earlier. A man who owned that apartment, the caller said, often allowed young male runaways to live in his home for free. The caller left an address of the apartment and a phone number where he could be reached in case he earned the reward money.

Bob sent Mike to check out the apartment and in a matter of hours he returned. It had been a bad lead. The only boys living there had been doing so for more than a year. They looked nothing like Jim and Daryl.

Then, on November 26 a woman called saying that a teenager who "looked a lot like the photograph of James Boucher" had been seen at the Bellair Bowling Lanes in Daytona Beach. She said she would stay at the bowling alley every day until she saw him again and when she did, she would call back. Then, she asked, could she receive the reward money or would she have to wait until the boys were safely home?

At times Bob wondered if the telephone would ever stop ringing. Each day he took dozens of calls from people who had not actually seen the boys but were willing to look. Especially if it meant getting a piece of the reward. But while the flyers were not turning up any real leads, Bob was happy about one thing. Time was passing. And eventually, unless he'd gotten wind of the police impounding the car, Snake was bound to return home. When he did, Bob and at least one arresting officer from the FDLE would be waiting for him.

Bob Brown wasn't the only one receiving bad tips about the case of the two missing teenagers.

The Tampa Police Department had also been the recipient of a rather sick bit of information only days after impounding the Chevy Nova. But if they hadn't determined anything else, by the end of November the department's crime lab technicians knew one thing for sure. The strange tip had thankfully been nothing but a cruel hoax.

The bad information had come Tuesday morning, November 21, when the department received a letter from a young man in Philadelphia, Pennsylvania, stating that he had been in Daytona Beach recently and spoken with a man named Spider. According to the letter, the man had reason to believe that Spider was now living in Tampa.

That of course, was not true, since Spider was still sitting in the Volusia County Jail. But that alone was not what interested the Tampa police. The man also wrote that Spider had told him something the letter-writer thought needed repeating. Spider had told him that he and his friend, Snake, had killed two men in Daytona Beach and dumped them in the trunk of an automobile.

At that point, no one had yet begun the examination of the Chevy Nova. But with letter in hand, Sergeant Williams himself walked to the crime lab and ordered that the trunk be opened immediately.

"The examination isn't scheduled until the end of the week," one of the technicians explained.

"I don't care." Williams was horrified at the possibility of there being dead bodies in the trunk of the Chevy Nova. Worse, that they might have sat in the crime lab for nearly three days, decaying under their very noses. He shuddered at the thought.

"Open it up," he shouted. "Now."

"Okay, boss, your call." The technician grabbed a report sheet and a pair of latex rubber gloves. He opened the door carefully and pulled a lever which then popped the trunk open. Williams held his breath as the technician walked around to the back of the car and opened the trunk.

It was empty.

CHAPTER 29

Thanksgiving came and went with little more than an obligatory dinner at the Barbers and the Bouchers. Both families spent the holiday with their remaining children and in both homes there was one very obvious, very empty seat.

But the pain of spending the holidays without their missing sons was nothing to remembering their birthdays without them. The hardest day since the boys had disappeared came on Thursday, November 30, Jim's eighteenth birthday.

Faye was up before the others, wandering quietly about the house staring at pictures of her oldest son. Where had the time gone? And when would anyone find her son. She wondered if anything could be worse than not knowing where your child was, whether he was dead or alive, trapped or in need of help.

She thought about going into Kristi's room, the place where she had found comfort so many times over the past fourteen weeks. But not even the cuddly little girl could take away the ache she felt today. This was Jim's birthday—a day when he should have been home having his favorite breakfast and opening a roomful of presents. He should have been picking up the car he'd ordered and getting ready for his final semester of high school. There should have been talk of proms and graduation and college education and scholarships.

But instead there was nothing to talk about. They couldn't openly grieve for Jim because they still did not know if he was dead. They didn't know anything. And they could hardly talk about the investigation. So there was absolutely nothing to talk about. All they knew was there was one man in jail who seemed to know something but wouldn't talk. And another man who had somehow gotten Daryl's car and Jim's traveler's checks. That man, Snake, hadn't even been questioned yet.

The Barbers and Bouchers had discussed these elements of the sixty-thousand-dollar private investigation nearly every night and now, on Jim's birthday, Faye didn't want to talk about it. All she wanted to do was remember Jim and pray for him.

She was surprised that her faith had remained so strong since Jim's disappearance. In some ways, she might have resented God for not answering her prayers that Jim would be brought home safely. But instead she believed that whatever had happened to Jim was not something caused by God. It was, instead, the result of evil in the world. Indeed, God had not let her down. He had provided them with a way to afford the investigation and he had given them friends who had surrounded them with love and support.

Even if Jim was dead, Faye knew she could not blame God. After all, if her son was dead then while they worried and prayed and wasted away, he was feeling no pain or sadness. He was in Heaven. Still, Faye believed that prayer made a difference. And she continued to pray daily that someone would find the boys soon. Roy couldn't take much more of the waiting.

As the day wore on, there was little conversation around the Boucher household. No cake, no presents, no celebration. Marian Barber called early in the afternoon to let them know she and Ron were thinking about them.

"Daryl's birthday is just ten days away," Marian said softly. "I just keep praying we'll know something by then."

Faye was silent a moment. "You won't know until the actual day of his birthday how terrible it is to remember his birth and his life while constantly being consumed with his death."

Tears filled Marian's eyes. "We're with you, Faye. Call us if you need us."

As it turned out, by the end of the day, Faye and Roy decided that they did need the Barbers. They needed to talk with them about a plan they'd devised.

What if the families offered to pay for the defense of Spider, the man being held at Volusia County Jail. In exchange Spider would have to tell the entire truth. Maybe he didn't know anything more than he was saying. But if he did, and if he was in any way responsible, he certainly had no way to hire a defense attorney.

Marian and Ron talked the plan over. It was hard to imagine paying money for the defense of someone who might possibly have had something to do with the disappearance or even the murder of their son. But at this point, the need to find Daryl had exceeded their desire for vengeance. They were willing to do anything to find him, even if it meant lending financial support to a creepy drug peddler like Spider Smith.

Once they had made the decision, Faye contacted James Byrd, who in turn, as he had done every day since the investigation started, contacted Bob Brown. Bob couldn't believe the desperation of parents who would be willing to pay for the defense costs of someone like Spider. But it gave him a reason to see Spider again. And maybe this time, with the offer of a free defense attorney, Spider just might be able to remember something else.

The interview was scheduled for the next day, December 1, and Bob arrived ten minutes early. He was sitting in the interview room when the bailiff ushered Spider inside.

Bob stared at the man, wondering if indeed he might know more information. In the two weeks that had passed since the last time they'd spoken, Bob thought Spider had grown thinner and more despondent. He seemed completely shut off from the outside world as if everything about him was dead and only a mechanical shell remained.

"Smith, I've got a few more questions for you." Bob sat across the table from Spider and spoke in a calm, gentle voice. His notes were casually pushed aside and he tried to make Spider feel at ease about the interview.

"Nothing to say, man." Spider leaned back against his handcuffed hands, kicked his feet out in front of him defiantly, and gazed into space. "Nothing to say."

"Well, Smith, I got a little something to say to you." Bob raised his voice a bit in an effort to capture Spider's attention. "I got word yesterday that the parents of those missing boys are willing to pay your defense costs, but there's a catch."

Spider glared at Bob. "What's the catch?"

"You tell us everything."

"Hey, man, I don't need no defense attorney. I ain't guilty a' nothing."

"Okay, that's fine. We can leave it like that if you want."

"What's that supposed to mean, man?"

"I can leave you alone and wait for someone else to talk." Bob stood up and began to straighten his file. "Eventually someone's going to do some talking. And when it happens, don't say I didn't give you a chance. Your loss, Smith."

Spider moved uncomfortably. "Wait a minute." He seemed suddenly anxious and Bob wondered if he had changed his mind. "What's the deal again?"

"You talk, tell me everything you know. Everything." Bob spoke each word slowly. "And if, after telling me everything you know, you find yourself needing an attorney, the boys' parents are willing to pay the costs."

Spider seemed to ponder the possibility. "You sure about that?"

"Positive." Bob hid his excitement. Spider must know more information if he was willing to consider the parents' proposition. "Not only that, but I promise you you'll get some kind of deal from the state, too."

"Like what?"

"I will personally go to the state attorney's office and see that you get the best deal available. Whatever that is. But you have to tell me everything."

"And what if I don't know anything, man?"

"You and I both know there's more to the story. So far, you haven't been talking much. But Smith, I promise you one of these days someone's going to start talking. And the way things work, the first one to talk is the one who gets the deal."

"What do you wanna know, man?" Spider fixed his gaze on his feet and refused to look Bob in the eyes.

"Everything."

"I need questions, man. I already told you everything."

"Tell me where the boys were staying."

"The Thunderbird."

"You lying to me, Smith?"

"No, man, it's the truth. The Thunderbird." Spider looked up now and focused his hateful eyes on Bob. "You calling me a liar?"

"How do you know it was the Thunderbird?"

"Saw the room key. Room one-oh-nine. Thunderbird."

"How'd you see the key, Smith?"

"Lying right out in the open, man, right on the dashboard."

"Whose dashboard?"

"The Nova." Spider seemed frustrated as if the answer should be obvious. "The boys' car. The keys were on the dashboard."

Bob paused a moment. Whether Spider realized it or not he had just placed himself inside the boys' car. He stared at the scraggly man before him and slowly sat down. Now they were getting somewhere.

"Don't sit down, man. I ain't got nothing else to say."

Bob stood up to leave again. "Fine. But I didn't get anything today that helps us find those boys. So don't expect any favors." Bob turned around and headed for the door.

"Wait!"

Bob turned around.

"Don't look too hard for them boys." Spider spat the words.

"Why not?"

" 'Cause, man."

Bob stood motionless, waiting for him to continue. Spider moved restlessly in his seat and then took a deep breath.

"'Cause." He looked once more at Bob and spoke with a voice that was utterly indifferent. "The boys are dead."

CHAPTER 30

By Monday, December 4, the pressure on Sheriff Duff from Governor Askew's office to find the Michigan teenagers was becoming a force to reckon with. Despite his promise to personally see the case solved, by the beginning of December Duff had been forced to give the governor three reports showing that his department had made no progress whatsoever.

And so on the previous Friday, in addition to Deputy Joe Deemer, Duff assigned homicide investigator Murray Ziegler to the case. Until then, Deemer had been doing his best to reconstruct the boys' vacation by means of the canceled traveler's checks. But neither he nor anyone of any official status had been investigating the boys' disappearance as if it might possibly be a homicide.

Ziegler was a twenty-year man with the department, a small but gutsy detective with a big voice and a bad attitude toward lawbreakers. Around the sheriff's office they liked to say that Ziegler had solved more homicides by pure instinct than all his peers combined. He had thinning hair, a full mustache, and a reputation for getting the job done.

Daytona Beach being what it was, Ziegler was a busy man. Never in two decades had he spent valuable investigative hours working a missing persons case. So when he got word from the department's head honcho, Sheriff Duff himself, that he was to begin immediately treating the disappearance of two Michigan teenagers with top priority, he felt it necessary to take a few hours and examine the facts.

Since his days were so busy, Ziegler took the case home with him Friday night, and by one o'clock in the morning the next day he was still reading. He had gone over the details of the boys' disappearance ten times until his instincts had taken hold. So that after memorizing the specifics he was instinctively convinced of one thing. The boys were not merely taking the long way home. The boys were dead.

His file included information about Snake Cox and how the boys' car had been impounded from the trailer park in Tampa. Also the fact that Spider Smith was sitting in Volusia County Jail playing head games with a private investigator named Bob Brown, who apparently had worked miracles in finding out the existing information.

Ziegler had heard of Brown and knew of his professional reputation. But he wondered if Bob knew what he was up against with these two characters. Ziegler was not a slow study and he had seen enough Snakes and Spiders to know the poisonous ones from those who were harmless. And in Ziegler's opinion Cox and Smith were the type that were flat-out deadly. He decided to call Brown

Monday morning. Maybe they could join forces and pay yet another visit to that insect of a man. And if they posed the questions just right, maybe this time they could get down to the truth.

Silence echoed through the jailhouse interview room.

"They're dead.?"

"Yeah, man. That's what I said."

Bob tried not to react too dramatically. He took a deep breath and moved away from the door toward Spider. "What happened?"

Spider laughed. "Listen, man. I'm not gettin' into details here. Didn't say I had nothing to do with it, did I?"

"Are you talking to me or not, Smith?"

"I told you what I know. They're dead. And I ain't saying nothing else. It wasn't nothing to do with me, man. That's the truth. Just that I don't want you wastin' your time lookin' for guys that are dead."

"Where are they?"

"No more!" Spider shouted. "I'm done. I told you all I know, man. Now get outta here!"

Bob had replayed the scene over in his head a hundred times since Friday and now he knew what he had to do next. If Spider knew that the boys were dead, he knew more than that. It was time to bring in the law and now, with Spider claiming to know that the boys had been killed, Bob figured the detectives would be climbing over each other looking for a chance to get in on what was no longer a missing persons case. Now it was a homicide investigation.

Bob had planned to call Mikelson first thing Monday morning, but before he had the time, he took a call from Murray Ziegler.

"Been going over the details of that case you're working on," Ziegler said after explaining that he had been assigned to the case and given orders to make it a priority. "I think you're right. There's more to it."

Bob chuckled in a way that held not even a trace of humor. "You haven't heard anything, yet."

And for the next fifteen minutes Bob told the well-known detective what he hadn't heard. He told him about Spider seeming interested in making a deal and about his shocking statement Friday that the missing boys were actually dead.

"Tell me this, Brown," Ziegler said. "You believe the guy?"

Bob considered the question for a moment. "You know, I've wondered if maybe I'm not dealing with a psychopath when I talk to Spider. Maybe he's just taking me for a ride. Maybe he's looking for attention."

Bob was quiet. "But then I look him in the eyes and what I see there scares me to death," he said.

"He knew about the boys' car, right?"

"He knew more than that. He knew that the boys' motel keys were on their dashboard."

"That puts him in their car," Ziegler added, "even if everything else he says is a flat-out lie. We still know he was with the kids before they disappeared."

Bob was quiet a moment. "You ever been in someone's car, Ziegler?"

"Sure, why?"

"You pay attention to every little detail?" Bob asked. "You know, noticing what kind of items might be hanging on the rearview mirror, what kind of junk might be on the dashboard. That kind of thing?"

"Not usually that close."

"Me either. And you're a hotshot detective."

"What's your point?"

"Well," Bob said, "our friend Spider was so good at catching details that he managed to notice not only the keys on the dashboard but the name of the motel and the room number on the keys."

There was silence as Ziegler pondered this detail.

"You thinking what I'm thinking?" Bob asked.

"That Mr. Spider just might have done a bit more than soak in the atmosphere while he was sitting in the boys' Nova?"

"That's what I'm thinking."

"Yeah." Ziegler grunted in disgust. "Like scour every inch of the car after the boys were dead and gone."

The detectives decided to meet at county jail at noon and see if they couldn't persuade Spider to share the rest of the story. He obviously knew something. Now it was merely a matter of getting him to talk.

The men had taken seats at opposite ends of the interview table when Spider was ushered in. From the beginning, he looked defiant and rebellious as if he despised breathing the same air as the two detectives.

Seeing Spider in person did nothing to change Ziegler's original opinion of him. He looked like the kind of parasitical human being who for even a few bucks wouldn't think twice about killing someone.

"What's the deal, man?" Spider glared angrily at Bob. "Thought I told you I was done talking."

"Mr. Smith," Ziegler interrupted, smiling sarcastically at Spider. "I'm here from the sheriff's office and I want you to know a thing or two before we get started." Ziegler stood up and, despite his lack of size, appeared to tower over the handcuffed Spider.

"First," he began to lower his face close to Spider's, "you should know what you're looking at." Spider turned away, refusing to acknowledge the investigator.

"That's fine," Ziegler said. "You don't have to watch. But you have to listen." He moved his face still closer to Spider's. "Now here's the deal. The way I see it, you've gotten yourself involved in something pretty messy. Probably a double homicide."

He straightened up and began pacing slowly in front of the inmate so that Spider was forced to turn his head from one side to the other in order to avoid looking at him.

"How do I know that?" Ziegler continued. "Because Friday you told Mr. Brown, here, that you believe the boys are dead. Right now, you're the only person on the planet who's told us anything even close to that. And that, Mr. Spider, makes you a prime-time murder suspect."

Ziegler moved close to Spider once again and stared at the man. "You have any idea what that means in the state of Florida?"

Spider was silent.

"I'll tell you what it means. You get yourself involved in a double murder involving even a tiny little bit of robbery or grand theft or anything else along that line and you wind up in the electric chair." Ziegler watched for a reaction and noticed that Spider's hand had begun to twitch nervously. He stood up and resumed his pacing.

"Now, the electric chair isn't some sort of Club Med vacation, Mr. Spider. It's a very serious place, the kind of place where every last living cell in a person's body becomes fried meat in front of a room of witnesses."

"Enough, man!" Spider shouted suddenly, looking up at Ziegler with hateful eyes. "I don't wanna hear that. I ain't done nothing wrong."

Ziegler shrugged indifferently. "Not my problem, Smith. You're the one who's playing games—a piece of the story here, another piece there." He stopped and stared at Spider.

"What's the truth, Smith?" His voice exploded throughout the room, echoing off the walls. He had Spider's attention now, and when Ziegler spoke again his voice was barely more than a whisper. "Because just like Mr. Brown told you, we're going to get the truth one way or the other. And by the time that happens, you'll be headed for the chair."

"Don't threaten me, man!"

Ziegler moved his face inches from Spider's. "That, Mr. Spider, is not a threat. It is a promise."

Spider squirmed uncomfortably in his seat. "What about the deal?"

Ziegler laughed. "No deal for a guy like you, Smith. You aren't talking truth, you aren't talking the whole story. We only make deals with people who tell it like it is."

"I never said I wasn't interested in making a deal, man."

"The question is whether we're interested in making a deal with you."

Bob stood up at this point and moved to the other side of Spider. He was enjoying this questioning immensely, almost like having a front row seat at a very exciting movie. None of his past cases had involved anything close to murder and his heart was racing with the intensity of the situation. He cleared his throat.

"Like I said, Smith," Bob spoke in his usual calm voice, "we need to know everything. And if we happen to find out that you're not telling us the whole story, any deal we might make would be off."

"Okay, man, I understand." Spider stared at his feet. "I want the deal. 'Cause ain't no way I deserve the chair for this, man. Ain't no way. I didn't do nothin' wrong."

Ziegler leaned back against the table and Bob pulled a chair up in front of Spider. "Okay," Ziegler said. "Let's talk."

"Tell us about the boys," Bob said. "They're dead, right?"

Spider shook his head wildly as if he had suddenly remembered something. "No, no, I never said nothing like that, man. I said they might be dead. Might be alive, might be dead."

Bob shot a disgusted glance at Ziegler and then turned toward Spider again. "That's a lie, Smith, and you know it."

"No, man, you just didn't understand me. I don't know what happened to the boys. But I just thought you should know they might be dead."

"What else might have happened, Smith?" Brown said. "If they're dead, how did they die?"

"Oh, man." Spider leaned back in his chair and gazed at the ceiling. "Maybe they were gassed."

"You're putting me on." Bob wanted Spider to know that he was skeptical at best.

"No, man, they were probably put in a tomb and then they were gassed."

"And if this was the case," Bob began, "did they suffer?"

"No, they were probably asleep when it happened."

Bob took a deep breath. "You know, Smith, you sure sound like you're keeping an awful lot of the story to yourself."

Spider was silent.

"You know what happened to those boys, don't you?" Ziegler cut in.

"All right, man," Spider said. "I know what happened. But listen, man. I want to know if I'm guilty of something before I go spillin' my guts. Understand?"

Bob's pulse quickened and he reached for a pen and paper.

"You tell us what happened and we'll tell you if you're in trouble," Ziegler said. "That's the best we can do."

"Well ..." Spider seemed to be searching for the right words. "Let's say there were two people in a boat. You know, the water is real deep." Spider glanced up to see if the detectives were listening. When he saw that Bob was taking notes he continued.

"Okay, and let's say that these two people are locked up down in the bottom of the boat, in the hold somewhere. And let's say the boat catches fire. Now, is it a crime to stand by and watch 'em die. Is a person guilty for that even though they didn't do nothin' wrong?"

Bob looked at Ziegler and put down his pen. Then he turned toward Spider once again. Bob was a patient man but he was nearing his limit. "Is this what happened to the boys?"

"Let's say it is," Spider said, tilting his head back in a cocky manner.

"If you want to know about guilt," Ziegler said, standing up straight and moving closer to Spider, "yes. A person who stood by and watched something like that would be guilty. No doubt about it."

Spider seemed discouraged by Ziegler's words. He hung his head and appeared to be thinking. "Okay," he said, lifting his head after nearly a minute. "Let's say a person watched two boys being locked into a tomb and then that same person simply stood by and allowed those boys to be gassed. Is that a crime?"

Ziegler shook his head angrily and picked up his things. "Listen, Spider, I've heard enough. I'm through playing games here. You aren't getting anywhere with these scenarios and I've got better things to do than sit here and play make-believe with a scummy, no-good loser like yourself." He turned around and headed toward the door, motioning for Bob to join him.

Bob looked once more at Spider. "You know, Smith, when this is all over with, don't say you didn't get a chance."

Then the two detectives left the room and conferred in the hallway.

"He's lying," Ziegler said.

"About some things."

"Yes. But until he's ready to tell the whole story we're wasting our time."

"He's closer than he was before, Ziegler. Believe me. I think your little word picture about the electric chair really got him thinking."

Ziegler shook his head in frustration. "It's not enough, Brown. He's got to tell us everything. All that garbage about what if this and what if that. Just a bunch of lies. Nothing we can go on."

"Might be worth checking into." Bob wanted desperately to remain hopeful. There had to be something, some workable lead, that could come from everything Spider had said.

"Well ..." Ziegler looked at his watch. "I've got four other cases that need my attention. What we really need is Spider's charming associate, Mr. Snake. Then we'll get to the bottom of this."

"You think they're dead, don't you?" Bob asked softly. Even though he had figured as much weeks ago, he tried to cling to a glimmer of hope that somehow the boys might be alive.

"Listen, Brown," Ziegler said, a softness showing in his eyes, "Sheriff Duff asked me if I would personally make this case a priority. Now, Brown, I'm a homicide detective. And someone like Sheriff Duff doesn't give me a case unless there's a body involved." He paused a moment. "To answer your question, yes, I think they're dead. But that weasel in there isn't doing one thing to help us put the pieces together."

Bob nodded. For the time being he was on his own again. "Keep in touch?"

"Every day." Ziegler paused. "Hey, Brown. I read the file, stayed up late Friday going over all the work you've done." He shook his head in awe. "You're one heck of an investigator. You ever want a job at the department, let me know."

"Thanks. But you can keep your office job, Ziegler." Bob laughed. "We private investigators don't do too well working by your rules."

Ziegler raised one eyebrow and held up the file. "Obviously."

CHAPTER 31

While the Barbers and the Bouchers spent yet another day in the fog of not knowing the whereabouts of their sons and Snake Cox spent the day touring about the country making product deliveries as if he wasn't perhaps the prime suspect in what had now become a homicide investigation, Bob climbed into his white sedan and drove toward the beach. There were still four hours of daylight left and he wanted to know one way or another if there was any truth to the bizarre scenarios Spider had suggested.

His first goal was to check the docks. Along Daytona Beach there were only a handful of places where one might even find boats, let alone dock them. If he moved quickly, Bob knew he could check each of those places.

"You know the docks around here?" Bob would ask once he found someone who seemed familiar with the area.

"Yeah. Why?"

"I need to know if there's been any fires here in the past four months."

"Fires? On the docks?"

"In the boats. As far as you know have any of the boats burned up in the past four months?"

"Not around here they haven't."

"Fine, thanks anyway."

Then Bob would find ten more people and ask the same question. When he was reasonably certain that there had not been a fire he would leave and head for the next dock. Then he would ask the same questions of at least ten people there.

No one had heard of a boat fire anywhere near Daytona Beach until he reached his final location. He approached a teenage boy who was selling bait at a concession stand near the docks.

"Any boats around here catch fire in the past four months?" he asked.

The boy's eyes lit up. "Yeah, pretty bad fire, too," he said.

Bob felt his heart skip a beat. Could Spider have been telling the truth? Could the boys have died out here in a fire without anyone even having known they were aboard the boat?

"Listen, young man, I need to find out more about the fire. Who can I talk to?"

The boy searched the water where dozens of speedboats and sailboats were anchored. "There," he said, pointing to an older man with a red baseball cap. "It was his boat. He can tell you everything you need to know." The boy looked at Bob curiously. "You with the insurance company or something?"

"Something," Bob said. He thanked the boy and headed toward the man in the red cap.

"Bob Brown, private investigator," he said, offering his hand.

The man was fishing and he smiled kindly in return. "Joe Greenwald," he said. "What can I do for you?"

"I need to ask a few questions about that boat of yours. The one that burned down."

The man looked puzzled. "The *Berkeley Bear?* Why, she didn't burn down."

Now it was Bob who looked puzzled. He pointed toward the concession stand where the teenager was working. "The boy there said your boat burned down."

The man laughed. "Youth," he said. "Make a mountain out of a molehill. The *Bear* didn't burn down, sir. She had a little engine fire a few weeks ago but we fixed her up nice and sound." He pointed toward a blue-and-gold yacht anchored a few feet from where he was sitting. "That's her, right there. A beauty, eh?"

Bob felt his body slump with the letdown. "Yes, sir," he said. "Beautiful. Sorry about the trouble."

By four o'clock he had ample reason to believe that there had not been a boat destroyed by fire anywhere in the vicinity of Daytona Beach for at least the past year. Bob looked at the sun. It was setting fast but there were still two hours of daylight left. He walked back to his car and headed for the old cemetery. It was time to check out the tombs.

As Bob drove he replayed Spider's words in his head:

"Let's say a person watched two boys being locked into a tomb... ."

Bob thought about all the places around Daytona Beach that might serve as a tomb. It was possible Spider was referring to an underground cavity in the sand somewhere, or perhaps the closet of a house. But the most obvious tombs in town were those that were right out in the open, in the old cemetery across the street from the Boot Hill Saloon: the place where—until Jim Boucher and Daryl Barber came to town—Snake and Spider spent most of their spare time.

Was it possible, Bob wondered, that Snake and Spider had met up with the boys, stolen their car and traveler's checks, and then taken them to the cemetery to kill them? Bob shuddered at the thought. Maybe they had found an old grave site and forced the boys inside. And maybe that's where the boys had been gassed and left to die.

Bob drove as quickly as he could and then parked the car. Of course, he told himself as he climbed out of the car, the whole idea of the boys dying in a tomb might just have been the first thing out of Spider's mouth. In all likelihood there was probably nothing more truthful about it than there'd been about the boating-fire story.

Either way, Bob had to find out the truth. He made his way up a small dirt hill toward the field of tombstones. The cemetery grounds formed a perfect square. Starting at the top right corner of the square, Bob knelt down and read the tombstone.

THE SNAKE AND THE SPIDER

MARTHA D. JOHNSTON
1845–1923
LOVING WIFE AND MOTHER

Bob took a deep breath and pushed on the tombstone, trying to see if it would move or give way. It didn't budge. Then he stood up and walked around the stone looking for soft areas in the dirt, places where there might have been a cavity in the earth—somewhere someone like Snake and Spider might have buried two teenage boys moments before gassing them. The ground was solid.

Meticulously, Bob moved to the next stone and did the same thing. He continued on this way, picking up speed as he went. Darkness was beginning to cover the cemetery and he wanted to complete his search while he could still see what he was doing.

About midway through the grounds, Bob pushed on a large stone and lost his balance as it lurched unevenly and toppled over. Bob gasped.

Under the stone was an area of dirt that had given way, leaving behind a sizable hole. Bob looked inside, unsure of what he would find. Placing his head partway in the hole, he reached down into the hole and felt the soft outer wood of a well-polished coffin. He moved his hand around the hole until he was convinced there was nothing, and no one, inside. Then he replaced the fallen tombstone and read the inscription.

BENTSON HODGE
JANUARY 2, 1911–NOVEMBER 30, 1978
IN LOVING MEMORY

Bob backed away in disgust. The man had just died a few days ago and his burial had probably taken place over the weekend. Now here he was digging his way toward dead people who'd only just been buried. Bob steadied the tombstone and shook his head. He would have to talk to the cemetery grounds people about doing a better job filling in the holes when people were buried.

He finished the final two rows of grave sites and then headed back toward his car. If Spider had been referring to a tomb in that cemetery, he had been lying. At the end of his tiring search late that afternoon Bob was certain of the fact.

Throughout the evening, even after his wife, Lois, cooked a mouthwatering roast beef dinner, Bob could not stop thinking about Spider's words. The burning boat and the tomb. Trapped by fire, death by gas. He longed for the days when his cases didn't haunt him as this one did. But at the same time he was driven to solve the case. He was getting closer. He could feel it.

That night Bob dreamt he was trapped in an underwater tomb which was slowly being filled with poisonous gas and fireballs.

145

* * *

That same evening, Snake was having a celebration dinner in Barstow, California. He had successfully delivered all of his product loads and now was about to make the trip back to Florida.

The man next to him was smoking a cigarette and asking questions. This was something Snake had not enjoyed about being on the road: the way the truckers all seemed to nose around in other truckers' business.

But tonight he was feeling especially good and he was midway through his fourth beer. Maybe there was something to this trucking business. Maybe he could be a law-abiding citizen now and make a legal living this way. Maybe not. But at least he could make a living even if he couldn't quite manage to be law-abiding.

Snake was probably thinking these things over when the man next to him looked his way.

"You been on the road long?"

"Yeah, pushing three weeks now," Snake said, sounding proud as if it was something of an accomplishment just to have held the job that long.

"Where you from, man?" The other trucker was several years younger than Snake, and in some ways he reminded him of his good friend, Spider. Wherever he'd disappeared to.

"Tampa," Snake said flatly. Maybe a conversation would be good now, what with the beer and the empty truck and the whole country spread out before him like a life-size atlas. Why not make a little time for a bar-side chat?

"Got a long drive ahead of you, man."

"That's the truth."

The younger man snuffed out his cigarette and took a swig of beer. "My name's Fred. Truckin' for ten years now. How 'bout you?"

"Snake. And this here's my first run."

The other man looked surprised. "What'd you used to do?"

Snake laughed out loud. If only Fred knew. "You really want to know?"

The man nodded and Snake felt his importance growing. There were times when people like Snake bragged about things that other people might just as soon keep to themselves. Not that it mattered much. Most people didn't believe the things that people like Snake bragged about. And even if they did, they never got enough information to do anything about the tall tales. Besides, there was something almost enjoyable in watching the surprise on people's faces when they heard some of the stories Snake liked to tell.

He looked at the younger man, still waiting for an answer. This would be a wonderful opportunity to tell such stories. Snake turned his stool a bit to face the other trucker.

"You wouldn't believe me if I told you, man," he said, lighting a cigarette and taking a deep drag.

"Go on." The other man laughed. "Can't be that bad."

Snake raised an eye and ran his hand over his long, uncombed hair. "Don't bet the farm on it," he said.

"Well," the young trucker urged, "I'm listening."

Snake picked up his beer and guzzled it until it was gone. "I was into a lot of bad stuff, man," he said. When he saw that the man was listening intently he continued. "Drugs, deals, death. All kinds of bad stuff."

The man looked surprised and more than a little doubtful. "Death?"

"Just part of the game, man," Snake said. "That's how I got my old lady her birthday present."

"What'd you get her?"

"A car." Snake motioned for the bartender to pour him another beer. "Nice little car, too."

The young man narrowed his eyes. "You killed someone for the car?"

Snake laughed. "Now, don't go calling me a killer, Freddy, boy. These nice respectable people wouldn't want to serve me beer if they thought I was some kind of crazy killer, now would they?"

"Hey, man, you said it." Fred looked uncomfortable as if he was thinking about ending the conversation and leaving the bar altogether.

"Nah." Snake laughed again. "I said there was death involved. Someone had to die so I could get the car. You know, what with it being my wife's birthday and all."

"Who died?"

"Ah, just a coupla pigeons."

"Pigeons?"

"Yeah, no big deal."

"Who killed 'em?"

"Well, we big-time former troublemakers don't go giving away all our secrets." Snake chuckled.

The other trucker laughed nervously. "But someone died?"

Snake shook his finger as if he were reprimanding the younger man. "Not someone. Just a coupla pigeons."

The other man watched as Snake began to laugh. Then, thinking that Snake must have been talking about birds and not people, Fred joined in until both men were laughing so hard they were crying.

"Just a coupla pigeons?" he asked Snake, wiping at the tears and trying to catch his breath.

"You bet," Snake said, finishing yet another beer and slurring his words as he spoke. "Jus' a coupla pigeons."

CHAPTER 32

Sheriff's homicide detective Murray Ziegler contacted Bob early Tuesday morning and listened while Bob talked about his investigation the day before. He said nothing while Bob described his search throughout the Daytona Beach docks and the old cemetery across the street from the Boot Hill Saloon.

Because he was a man who operated largely by instincts, he could understand Bob being driven to prove Spider's stories true or false. He, too, felt strangely about Spider and believed that the man knew something about the disappearance and probably the death of the boys. There was even a possibility that some of what Spider had said regarding the boys being trapped in a tomb before their death was true.

And so that morning he agreed to go with Bob to the state attorney's office. If this had really become a homicide investigation, they would have to talk to the state attorney before they could offer Spider any specific immunity.

They drove together to the Daytona Beach courthouse located on City Island and went immediately to State Attorney Jack Watson's office.

Watson, a man in his mid-forties with a knack for winning cases, had been brought in by the governor two years earlier as part of the push toward eliminating crime in the area, and so far Watson was proving to be just the man for the job. He was handsome with dark blond hair and a fullback's physique. He looked at Ziegler and Bob Brown and motioned them into his office.

"What can I do for you gentlemen this fine day?" he asked, leaning back in his chair and folding his hands behind his head. Behind his desk was a panoramic view of a clean stretch of sandy white beach and the vast, green-blue Atlantic Ocean. In Florida there was little or no humidity in December and that day was one of those that typically caused tourists to send for their furniture and never go home.

Watson knew Ziegler quite well, even though he'd only been working the state attorney's position a short time. Ziegler was oftentimes the hard-hitting force behind the cases he won and the two men were friends outside of work as well.

"We got this one particular case," Ziegler started. This was always how Ziegler presented his cases and Watson couldn't help but smile. By the time Ziegler brought a case to his attention it was usually almost solved. Ziegler didn't bark up many wrong trees.

"Tell me about it," Watson said.

"Couple of Michigan teenagers come here in mid-August, make a phone call to mom and dad back home, and then disappear. Later we find people who saw one of the locals, Snake Cox, with the boys' car. Snake's a bad guy, wanted by the FDLE, known to be armed and dangerous.

"Then we find out that Snake's friend, another local, Spider Smith, was also with the boys the night they disappeared. As it turns out, Spider's sitting over at County on another charge and Mr. Brown, here, gets the chance to talk with him at length."

"Let me guess." Watson said. "He knows something about the boys' disappearance."

"Good guess. Spider tells us that the only way he's doing any talking is if he gets a deal from us."

"And that's why you're here."

"Right." Ziegler smiled. "You're so quick, Watson."

Watson leaned forward and straightened the papers on his desk, seeming to be deep in thought. Suddenly he looked up.

"Ziegler, between you and me and Mr. Brown, I can tell you one thing. I've heard about those boys. The governor's hot on the trail and wants to take care of it personally. If Spider Smith can lead us to the boys we'll work out something for him. But the fact is I can't make any kind of written offer, no formal deals, until I know for sure that a crime's been committed and that he's involved."

Ziegler nodded.

"Obviously the answer is yes," Watson continued. "There was a crime and he is involved. But we need to hear it from him. Then you'll get your deal."

Bob Brown and Deputy Ziegler were back in the interview room, back in the company of Spider. It was late Tuesday afternoon and this time they kept the conversation short. Ziegler did most of the talking.

"This is your last chance, Smith," Ziegler said. He did not hide the fact that he was bored with the idea of spending more time in an interview room with Spider.

"I told you everything, man," Spider said. He had dark circles under his eyes and he looked as if he hadn't showered in days.

"Just shut up and listen!" Ziegler barked the command and Bob forced himself to keep a straight face. He enjoyed watching Spider suffer under the intense questioning of Deputy Ziegler. Now Spider was visibly shaking in the wake of Ziegler's opening command. It was as if he knew the detectives were through playing games and that it was finally time to come clean.

"Now, this is the way it works," Ziegler said. His words were sharp and clipped, like a drill sergeant having a particularly bad day. "We're ready to offer you a deal. But we need to know two things for sure. Then we'll leave you alone."

Ziegler moved a few steps closer to Spider until the inmate could smell the onions on Ziegler's breath. "First," the detective barked angrily, "you tell us if those kids were killed or not."

He allowed a few seconds for Spider to answer. When he didn't, Ziegler's face grew red. "Answer me, Smith!" he shouted.

Spider jumped visibly. "Okay, man. All right. The answer is yes. They're dead."

Ziegler tilted his head and stared into Spider's eyes. "Second, I need to know if you had something to do with their deaths."

Spider thought about this a moment but then before Ziegler could yell at him again he spoke. "Yes! All right? Now you know. The answer's yes. We killed 'em and got rid of the bodies."

Bob felt his heart sink. There was something different about the way he was talking today, and this time Bob was certain Spider was telling the truth. Jim and Daryl were dead.

Ziegler stood up and looked at Spider as if he was a piece of moldy food. "Now. Those two answers mean that we'll make a deal with you. I'll get it taken care of tomorrow morning. But just because I get the state attorney to promise you a deal doesn't mean you'll get one."

"What's that mean, man?" Spider looked suddenly betrayed.

"It means that if you don't tell us the whole story, the deal is off. Completely." Ziegler turned to Bob. "You got any more questions?"

Bob nodded. "Just one." It was something that had been bothering him for a long time. Each time Spider spoke of where the boys stayed he always said it was the Thunderbird Motel. But the motel records had only shown a few visitors that week, none of them from Michigan, none of them named Jim or Daryl. Bob wanted to know for sure where the boys had stayed so he could make contact with any possible witnesses. He straightened his suit coat and looked at Spider.

"Where were the boys staying, Smith? I want the truth."

"That's right," Ziegler interjected. "From this point on, don't even bother telling us those lies from the other day. We want the truth or don't waste our time."

"Man, you two don't believe me anyway," Spider whined.

"Look, Smith, you're not drumming up any sympathy here. Either answer the question or keep your mouth shut so we can get out of here."

Spider shook his head as if he was being treated very poorly. "I told you. The Thunderbird Motel. Room one-oh-nine."

"Fine." The detectives stood up to leave. "We'll be in touch."

The next morning, Wednesday, December 6. Brown joined up with Ziegler and Deputy Joe Deemer and followed them to the Thunderbird Motel. The time had come to get to the bottom of the mysterious motel records which showed the place half empty during the busiest time of the year.

This time the men bypassed the front office altogether. Instead, they walked around the perimeter of the motel searching for the maids. Most of the cleaning crews who worked the motels along the strip used people from Puerto Rico or

Mexico. Bob did not speak Spanish and neither did the sheriff's deputies. But he hoped he could find one member of the cleaning crew who might be able to clear up a little of the confusion.

Her name was Zelzah and they found her in Room 110. She looked frightened as the three men dressed in suits peered into the room at her.

"Can I help you?" she squeaked. She had brown skin and long black hair. Bob guessed she was Persian but she seemed to be able to speak English.

"Yes, I was wondering if you've worked here very long." Bob asked.

The woman looked even more nervous. "Yes. Is something wrong?"

Ziegler shook his head. For all his tough-guy image, he could be especially kind when it came to talking with women. He was one of those guys who could almost always charm a member of the opposite sex into cooperating. This was no exception.

"No, there's nothing wrong." His voice hummed as he spoke and he smiled warmly. "We're just trying to find someone who has a lot of experience here."

The woman smiled proudly, no longer afraid. "Yes, I've been working here four years."

"Right," Ziegler said. "That's just what we're looking for. Now, can you tell us if you remember who stayed in that room next door, room 109, back in the middle of August?" Ziegler pulled two pictures from his pocket of Jim and Daryl and showed them to the woman.

She stared at the photographs and wrinkled her nose daintily. "I can't remember," she said. It was obvious that she was trying to be helpful. "The boys don't look familiar."

Ziegler nodded. "That's okay. But tell me something. Did your boss cut your hours that month?"

The woman laughed. "No, of course not."

"Well ..." Ziegler was still moving gently through the area he wanted to cover. "We understand half the rooms were empty that month." Ziegler sounded sympathetic. "Must have been pretty slow."

Now the woman laughed out loud. "You must have heard wrong, sir," she said.

"Why's that, ma'am?"

"August? We were filled every day."

"Every room?"

"Every room."

Just at that moment, the motel manager, Stanley Robinson, entered the room. When he recognized Bob and saw that he and the men with him were questioning his cleaning woman, he became furious.

Robinson stood staring at the men, his eyes wide with rage. "What do you think you're doing?" he demanded. "This is private property!"

"Sir, we just had a few questions for your cleaning woman, here," Bob said.

"Well, you men are trespassing and that's a crime," Robinson said. "I'm calling the police."

"Sir," Deemer interrupted, pulling out his badge. "We are the police."

"Yes," Ziegler added, whipping out his badge and waving it in Robinson's face. "But don't worry about us. We're leaving. Of course, you may expect a little telephone call from the IRS, Mr. Robinson. And that's a phone call you have every right to worry about."

CHAPTER 33

The call came into Bob's office early Thursday morning.

"Hello?" Bob's primary assistant, Mike Black, answered the telephone on the first ring.

"Yeah, uh, listen." The man at the other end seemed to be nervous and he spoke in a voice that was barely above a whisper.

"Who is this?" Mike reached for a pen and some paper.

"Well, see, I don't really want to give my name. Not yet. Let's just say I'm Dolphin, all right?"

Mike rolled his eyes. He was used to people like this who called the office with what they believed was a hot tip. They tended to get caught up in the idea that Bob was a private investigator and even when it wasn't necessary they sometimes talked in codes. "Go ahead, Dolphin," he said, casually doodling on the paper.

"Well, I think I found the boys."

Mike sat up straighter and began paying attention. "What boys?"

"You know," he whispered. "The boys. On the poster. The missing kids from Metamora, Michigan."

"Okay, Dolphin. I'm listening," Mike said. "Tell me where they are?"

"Well, I only saw one of 'em. Saw a man that looked exactly like that Daryl Barber."

"Where'd you see him?" Mike began writing notes. They hadn't had a call on the Barber-Boucher case in a few days and this man sounded very serious.

"At the Texan Motel. Right there in Daytona Beach." He paused a moment. "Man, I'm sure it was him."

"Listen, Dolphin, let me get your number and I'll check this out. Anything comes of it I'll call you back."

"Hey, I don't even care about the money, man. But there was some kind of weird-looking guy following this kid, Barber. Looked like he might be a hostage. Something like that."

"Gotcha' Dolphin."

"Hey, I don't want no trouble or nothing. Just thought someone should know."

"You bet. We'll be in touch."

Mike had planned to work on other cases that day. But this was a lead worth checking into. Usually, he would let Bob know before checking into such a lead. But if, by some miracle, the boys really were alive and being held hostage at a

Daytona Beach motel, there was no time to waste. Besides, by now Bob would be at the courthouse and he could be tied up there for hours.

Ziegler met Brown at the City Island courthouse at nine o'clock that morning. Armed with Spider's admission that, yes, there had been a crime committed involving the boys, and, yes, he had been involved, they were now ready to obtain formal immunity from State Attorney Jack Watson.

Of course, there was obviously much more to the story and both detectives were convinced that Spider knew more than he was saying. But perhaps when they presented him with the official document promising immunity in exchange for the entire truth, he would talk. Then they might finally have the facts as they really were and enough information to find the boys.

Bob was feeling almost festive as they walked into the courthouse. This had been the biggest, most important case of his career and they were closer than ever to solving it. The way Bob saw it, the Michigan teenagers had been guilty of one thing: they were too naive. And now, if Spider was telling the truth, they were dead. The idea of getting the truth and seeing the responsible parties punished for such a ruthless crime would be something akin to a celebration as far as Bob was concerned.

"You know, Ziegler," he said, "this is going to be a good day. I can feel it."

Ziegler cast him a wary eye. "You think so, huh?"

"When Spider sees that official paper he's going to open up his mouth, and you know what's going to come out?"

"What?"

"The entire story. Beginning to end."

"What if he doesn't talk?"

Bob thought a moment. "We offer immunity to Snake instead."

Ziegler smiled. "You're mighty optimistic, Mr. Private Eye."

"What do you mean?"

"First we have to find Snake."

Watson's door was open and they walked in.

"You're back." Watson looked up from a file he was reading and smiled warmly. "Find what you needed?"

Ziegler looked proud of himself. "Did you doubt us?"

Watson laughed and motioned for the men to sit down. "Well, let's have it. What'd he say?"

Bob kept quiet while Ziegler pulled out the interview notes from the previous day. "Seems our friend Spider Smith knows for certain that the boys are dead. That takes care of the first criteria. Right?"

"Right. A crime's been committed."

"Next, he tells us he was involved in the murder. And that's the second issue."

Suddenly Watson's face grew worried. "Involved?"

"Yeah, involved. Why?"

Watson sighed loudly and stood up from his desk. He turned around, staring out his window at the ocean. "Well, boys, that presents a problem."

Now it was Ziegler who looked confused. "You said he needed to admit to being involved in the crime before we could officially offer immunity."

"But you know how it is. If the crime is murder, and if the person is a conspirator, everything's very uncomplicated. But if it's murder and the person is actually involved in the killing, a participant to the murder, everything gets a little sticky."

"Look, we've wasted a lot of time on this thing, Jack," Ziegler said. He was frustrated and not afraid to hide the fact. "What's the bottom line?"

Watson turned around and faced the detective. "We can offer immunity, but I need to clear it through the judge."

"Fine. What's the problem?"

"The problem is the judge will most likely assign Spider a public defender. And if that happens, you and Mr. Brown won't be allowed back in for any questioning."

Ziegler slumped backward in his chair. "I get it," he said. "And if we can't talk to Spider, good luck finding the boys. Right?"

"Right."

So much for feeling festive, Bob thought to himself. Out loud he said, "Let's say the judge assigns him an attorney. Can't we continue to ask questions as long as the attorney is present?"

"You can try," Watson said. "But in a possible double murder? Where the state's witness is personally involved? I sure wouldn't bank on it."

A hour later, Circuit Court Judge Warren H. Cobb of the Seventh Judicial Court in Volusia County was provided information regarding the request to grant partial immunity to Earl Lee Smith regarding his role in a possible double murder.

Judge Cobb signed the request and without hesitation issued an order stating that Spider Smith receive immediate public counsel.

Deputy Ziegler and Bob Brown were still waiting in the courthouse when Watson found them and gave them the news.

"He'll be represented by Dick Kane," Watson said. Bob could tell from his tone of voice that what he was about to say was not good news. "Kane's a no-nonsense kind of guy. Needless to say, he doesn't want his client to undergo any more questioning until further notice."

And with that, the unofficial questioning of Spider Smith came to a complete and sudden end.

That afternoon, after Ziegler had temporarily his entire emphasis to other cases and after Bob had returned to his office, Mike was finishing a preliminary investigation into the lead he had received earlier that day. Now, he was at the Texan Motel about to find out the truth.

A kind-looking elderly man had been sitting behind the front desk reading a book when Mike walked in. "Can I help you?" he said, smiling as he stood to greet the tall, young man.

"Yes, I'm looking for a couple of missing teenagers," Mike said. He spoke with a gentle voice that had come from years of working with Bob Brown. He pulled out the pictures of the teens and placed them on the counter.

The man stared at the pictures and raised his eyes in surprise. "Why, that picture looks just like one of the boys staying here!" He picked up the photograph of Daryl Barber and stared at it closely.

Mike felt his heart beat faster. "We took an anonymous call this morning from a man who said he saw someone who looked like Daryl Barber staying at this motel. He thought there might be some kind of problem." Mike searched for the right words. "Maybe the boy was being held against his will."

The man looked puzzled and he shook his head. "I don't think it's anything like that, son," he said. "The boy I'm thinking of goes by the name Jeff Houser. He stays here, but he's not a guest. Works for me, in fact."

Mike listened carefully. "How long has he been working for you, sir?"

"Oh, about three months. Something like that. But like I said, his name's Jeff Houser."

Mike nodded. If the boy had only been at the motel for three months there was still a chance he might actually be Daryl Barber. "Would it be possible for me to meet Jeff Houser. Maybe that way I could clear this whole thing up and be on my way."

The man smiled amicably. "Why, certainly," he said. "Follow me. He should be out back washing down the patio chairs."

The two men walked through the office and onto a cement patio behind the motel where a small swimming pool was surrounded by a cement brick fence. They could see the back of a teenage boy who was washing chairs as if his life depended on it.

"Jeff, there, doesn't have any family," the elderly man whispered. "He takes his job here real serious-like. Does a great job and always treats the customers with respect. Not like a lot of those long-hair teenagers on the beach. You know the type."

Mike nodded. He was anxious to stop the conversation and talk with the boy. "Can we talk to him a minute?"

"Sure." The man raised his voice. "Jeff! Come here a minute."

The boy turned around and Mike was stunned. He was the mirror image of Daryl Barber.

"Howdy," the boy said, coming up quickly and tipping his head politely. "Y'all have more work for me, sir?"

Mike's heart sank. The boy's southern accent was so obvious there was no way he could be from Michigan.

The owner smiled at Mike. "See what I mean. All manners, this one." He turned to the teenager. "This man has a few questions for you."

Instantly, the boy's face clouded with fear. "Somethin' wrong?"

Mike shook his head quickly. "No, no. Just wanted to ask you a few questions. That all right?"

"Sure." The boy shrugged and again Mike was struck by how much he looked like Daryl.

"First I'll need your name."

"Jeff. Jeff Houser."

Mike looked up and stared into the boy's eyes. "That your real name, Jeff?"

"Why, yes, sir. Sure is."

"Okay, then. How old are you?"

"Nineteen."

"And where'd you live before you started working here at the Texan Motel."

"Louisiana, sir. Shreveport."

Mike looked up again. This line of questioning seemed pointless unless there was something the boy was hiding. "Just one more question, Jeff. Ever heard of a guy named Daryl Barber?"

"No, sir. Never hearda him."

"You sure about that?"

The boy shrugged. "Never hearda him."

Mike watched the boy's face, looking for any signs that he was nervous or uneasy. Like Bob, Mike prided himself on being able to tell if a person was lying. There was always something: a twitch or an inability to make eye contact. He stared at the boy now, almost hoping he would see some sort of sign.

There was none.

He thanked the teenager and his boss and headed back for Orlando.

Two days later, amidst tears and phone calls from family and friends, Ron and Marian Barber remembered Daryl's twentieth birthday. By the end of the day, Marian knew that Faye had been right. There was no way to describe the pain of living through the birthday of a son with no idea whether that son was even alive. It was something a person had to go through to understand. And although the detectives and Bob Brown knew the boys were very likely dead they were waiting for concrete facts before telling the boys' parents.

Before they went to bed that night, Marian began to cry and Ron pulled her into a hug.

"We've got to have some answers soon," Marian said. "I can't take this, Ron."

"I know, Marian." Ron smoothed his wife's hair. "None of us can."

That night, like others before it, Marian had nightmares about her missing son. But this time they were more vivid, more terrifying. And sometime in the wee hours of the morning she sat straight up in bed and screamed the words that were on her mind day and night—the words she could never quite rise above, no matter how hard she tried. That night the words echoed through the silence of the morning, shattering any image of peace in the home.

"Daryl!" she screamed. "Where are you?"

Driven by the same question, Bob Brown spent Daryl's birthday in an entirely different manner. After waiting three very long, very frustrating weeks, the time had come to visit the trucking company again. Snake was on his way back to Tampa. And Bob was willing to wait days if necessary to see that he got a proper welcome home.

CHAPTER 34

The stakeout had been going on for thirty-six hours and Bob was beginning to lose track of what day it was. He and Mike had parked in the trucking company parking lot late Saturday, December 9—Daryl's birthday. There they had set up their watch from two separate cars and already each had taken several sleeping shifts.

In the past week Bob had not only talked to Snake's wife but had also compiled every bit of information he could about Snake and Spider from arrest records, paid informants, and interviews with Spider. Now, as he sat waiting for Snake's return, he was more familiar with the men than he'd ever hoped to be. And while their childhood and teenage years had been anything but ideal, Bob did not feel sorry for them. They had made their own choices, and if somehow they had harmed those boys, then they deserved to be punished to the full extent of the law.

Bob opened the file that contained the background information on Snake and Spider and read through it once more.

Earl Lee Smith had been conceived twenty-two years earlier in a violent manner which now seemed less than surprising. When his mother was only a teenager, she had been out late one night, as she often was, with friends nearly twice her age. After midnight, when the fun was over, she walked home by herself through a tenement section of town known for its violence. Suddenly she turned a corner and at once was grabbed by a masked man who shoved a gun into her ribs.

"Get down or I'll kill you." He seethed the words, hatred spewing from every part of his face.

Terrified for her life, she had no choice but to obey.

"Get over there," the man said, kicking the young girl behind a Dumpster. When she followed his orders, he ripped her clothes off and raped her again and again, leaving her unconscious and naked body tossed in a heap like a discarded piece of trash. Passersby found her the next morning and called police, who ordered an ambulance for the young woman and rushed her to the hospital.

Three weeks later the doctor who had treated her in the emergency room gave her a pregnancy test. The result was positive.

The teenage girl believed in her heart that the child was not at fault for the horrible crime committed against her. And so she decided to carry the baby to term and make a home for the baby. Naturally, her parents were mortified over their daughter's predicament and were unable to accept her decision and the idea of having a rapist's child in their home. Angry with their attitude, the girl ran away, deciding she would have to survive on her own.

KAREN KINGSBURY

But all of her well-meaning ideas about raising the baby and forgetting about how the child had been conceived disappeared as soon as she went into labor. She had never felt such pain before and could compare the experience to just one thing—her violent rape. She named the little boy Earl and when the nurse tried to set the child in her arms she turned away, appearing to be suddenly nauseous.

"I don't want to hold him," she said, sounding as if something inside her had died. "Just take him away. Please."

The nurses were puzzled, not having known her background or the way in which the pregnancy had come to be. But they took the child away as the young woman had asked and for the next three days the nurses took turns playing mother to him. When the time came for the mother and child to go home, each of the nurses whispered her fears about what kind of life the little boy would have living with a mother who seemed to have no ability to love.

The nurses' fears had been founded.

Earl Smith's existence was meager, the love he received next to nothing. His mother got married not long afterward and her husband became the only father Earl would ever know. But from his earliest memories the man was an abusive alcoholic who treated Earl and eventually his younger brother as if they were unwanted and more trouble than they were worth.

It seemed to Earl that the man wanted a lifestyle that did not involve small children. But as cruel a blow as that might be to most children, Earl never seemed to care. He never seemed to feel anything at all. Not even about his mother, whose attitude toward him grew over the years from indifference to obvious dislike.

Perhaps living with such an abusive man caused her to grow increasingly angry over a number of aspects involving her life. Because she must have had no other place to take out her anger, she took it out on her son. One day, when she had berated him at length over a relatively minor issue, she suddenly turned toward him, fire blazing in her eyes, and said the one thing she had sworn she would never say.

"You're no better than your father, the piece of trash," she shouted at her six-year-old son. "Do you hear me? You're no better than the man who raped me. If he hadn't raped me you wouldn't be here and I wouldn't have to deal with you!"

"What's rape?" Earl asked, showing no signs of being hurt by his mother's comments.

"Rape!" she screamed at him. "Don't you understand? Your father was a dirty old dog who beat me up and forced himself on me. He left me in the streets for dead. I don't even know his name."

After that, Earl wrestled with what his mother said to him that afternoon. He never forgot her words. And if he didn't quite grasp their meaning as a six-year-old, then he certainly understood the truth about his conception as he grew older.

The single place where Earl received love was in the home of his grandparents. Although they had been upset about their daughter's situation, they grew to love

160

their brown-haired grandson as if he were their own. They cared for him much of the time when his mother or stepfather were either too uninterested or too caught up in their own troubles to spend any time with him. Earl's grandparents enjoyed being with the boy and did all they could to steer the child right.

But whether it was the boy's upbringing or something bred in him during his violent conception, Earl never once responded to his grandparents' love. He showed no emotion whatsoever, whether he was being loved or ignored, helped or beaten. It didn't matter. The child had flinty eyes from the time he could talk, and by the time he was twelve years old he began doing what seemed absolutely natural to those who knew him. He began breaking the law.

At age twelve, Earl Smith had finally found the group where he fit in. It was a group many people feared and others tried desperately to eliminate from society. His place was among the city's youthful delinquents. By then Earl had allowed his hair to grow long and scraggly. He had a mustache and a face that never smiled or even looked somewhat happy. If the way Earl walked—shoulders stooped, feet dragging—didn't tell a person something about his character, his cold eyes did. Earl had dead eyes, black and hard with no life whatsoever behind them. He wore the same lifeless look that year, the winter of 1968, when he stole his first car and his grandparents tried to bail him out of jail.

"Oh, Earl, honey, how could you have gotten yourself into this trouble?" his grandmother cried that evening.

But Earl only looked at her with those cold, dead eyes. No remorse whatsoever, no anger. Nothing. And because he seemed to own no emotions, he was unable to understand hers. Why was she upset? He had no car of his own so he had taken one that belonged to someone else. No big deal. Nothing to get upset over.

By then Earl's soul and spirit were apparently dead because of more than his upbringing or his innate nature. He was also well on his way to becoming a drug addict. In his circle of friends marijuana was easily available. So were the mind-altering drugs which everyone knew could burn a person's brain up after only three or four uses. Earl didn't care about that bit of information any more than he cared about anything else. He did drugs to pass the time. And the only people he ever interacted with were people he wanted something from. Drugs, money, sex. Once his needs were met he discarded the people who met them much the same way his mother had been tossed aside after her rape years earlier.

After the car theft, there were other crimes: felony thefts and charges of possessing drugs or deadly weapons. Each time, Earl continued to show no emotion and nothing even close to remorse about his actions.

Naturally, some people, especially court-appointed defense attorneys, blamed Earl's actions on his childhood. But no one could ever really be certain if Earl was truly a product of a disastrous upbringing. More likely, some people reasoned, Earl was just a very, very bad seed, someone who would inevitably spend his adult years in a state prison somewhere.

By the time he was eighteen, Earl moved to Daytona Beach and immediately decided to stay. Everywhere he looked there were teenagers hungry for adventure and thrills they could purchase. Earl figured most of them were probably looking for something that could be smoked or snorted or popped. And not long after arriving in Daytona Beach, he hooked up with someone so like himself it was uncanny.

John Carter Cox, Jr.

If it were possible, John was even more unfeeling, more sociopathic than Earl. At the age of twelve he had left home and moved to Daytona Beach where he took up residence at a group flophouse. In those days there were fewer such houses but those that existed did so under the leadership of local drug dealers. Largely, their illegal efforts went unabated by police, who, although aware of what was happening at the houses, were unable to catch the occupants publicly breaking the law. Police were careful to watch for young runaways during school hours, hoping to pick some of them up for truancy. But for the most part the runaways were careful to stay inside until the afternoon and evenings. And John was even more careful than most.

By the end of that first year, John was running drug deals for the house leader and establishing himself as the "candy-man" of the beach. He made a tidy profit for the work he did and in turn developed a heavy addiction to several drugs.

And if that wasn't enough, when he was seventeen he joined the Pagans. Prior to that point he had caused harm only to those who bought his drugs and to himself. But once he became an official motorcycle gang member, a Pagan, no less, he probably felt free to hurt anyone who got in his way. Even some who didn't.

For the next fifteen years John lived this lifestyle, dealing drugs, doing drugs, and wreaking havoc on his Harley-Davidson. Rumor had it that John was involved in even more heinous acts. If no one had ever proven the rumor, certainly John's actions on Daytona Beach did nothing to dispel it. Together Earl and John made a tidy living selling drugs to kids along the beach and apparently caring very little about who got hurt in the process.

Bob Brown had heard stories that once in a while John or Earl would rough up a customer. Maybe John and Earl figured the ability to hurt a person came with the territory and it wasn't something that bothered either man. Since both John and Earl rode motorcycles and associated themselves with the biker gang, Pagans, the rough way in which they may have treated some of their customers only added to their hardened image.

In fact, by 1978 Earl and John had all but dropped their given names. Instead, they went by their nicknames, names that were by far more appropriate. So that by the time Jim Boucher and Daryl Barber landed on Daytona Beach everyone knew them only as Snake and Spider.

But for as much as Bob knew about Snake and Spider, he still did not know the specifics of how they had met up with Jim and Daryl. Spider had been alone on the beach that evening when he had spotted the Michigan teenagers. Business had been slow along the beach since summer was nearly over. He was hurting for money and Snake had been pushing him to get something going. He had smiled as he watched the boys set up their towels.

"Coupla pigeons," he muttered to himself.

Pigeons, at least along Daytona Beach, meant tourists who could be taken for all they had with very little effort. Satisfied with himself for spotting them, Spider had walked out of the shadows from beneath the boardwalk and headed their way.

After telling Jim and Daryl about the beach party, Spider had offered the boys the marijuana cigarette he was smoking. When both boys shook their head, Spider had laughed.

"What?" Spider had taken another long drag, and a hollow laugh mingled with the marijuana smoke that escaped from deep in his throat. "Don't you smoke?"

"Sure, man," Daryl had quickly lied and Jim turned and looked at him, his eyebrows raised.

Bob figured the boys had lied to impress Spider and so as not to appear naive in their new environment. After all, they might not have been interested in smoking marijuana but they still wanted to find a beach party.

"Yeah," Jim broke in, probably doing his best to appear confident before the stranger. "Yeah, we both smoke now and then. Just not right now."

Spider had shrugged in disinterest.

"Hey, you local around here?" Daryl asked. Bob could imagine Jim grinning, impressed at how casual his best friend sounded. Just as if he hung out on Daytona Beach every day.

"Sure," Spider had replied, finishing the cigarette and burying the tiny piece of paper that remained in the white sand.

"Do you know of any parties around?" Daryl asked.

"There's one over at the Days Inn down the beach."

Spider had been laying a trap for the teens, but both boys were completely unaware of the fact. Spider had seen the way they lied about smoking pot and he probably sensed their nervousness. A deep sense of satisfaction probably began to build in Spider. The boys were even more naive than he had guessed. They were perfect for a hit.

"Where is it? I mean, is it close?" Jim had asked then. He was pleased with himself, convinced that he sounded just as experienced as Daryl had.

"Sure, just down the beach a mile or so." Spider pointed vaguely toward the strip.

"We talking about an open party?" Daryl had said.

Spider nodded slowly, his eyes barely open as his body reacted to the effect of the marijuana cigarette. He took out another and lit it, inhaling and then holding his breath as the smoke worked its way into his blood-stream. Finally he exhaled and then looked at the boys. "It's open. Most of the guys are pretty cool about newcomers, you know?"

Daryl nodded. "What room is it?"

Spider shrugged. "I could take you there, man. I'm going myself. It's up to you."

Daryl did not hesitate.

"Hey, sounds great," he said. He thought a moment and then added. "I'll drive, Okay?"

Spider shrugged again. "Sure, man. Your gas."

Standing up slowly and stretching, Spider flicked what remained of his cigarette onto the sand. "That's some good weed, man," he said again.

As Daryl and Jim had stood up Spider pulled out a plastic bag of marijuana and began sifting through it with his fingers.

"Let me know if I can be of service, understand?"

"Yeah, man," Daryl said. "We'll let you know. Hey, we have to get some things from our room before we go. You want to come?"

"Right behind you, man," Spider said, stuffing the bag back into his shorts pocket.

"Hey," Daryl said, stopping suddenly. "I'm Daryl and this is Jim. What's your name?"

Spider pointed to a vivid tattoo on his left arm and Daryl leaned closer to see it.

"It's a spider, man," he said. "That's me. Spider."

"Cool."

Bob doubted whether Jim or Daryl had ever met anyone named Spider. Somehow it probably seemed an exciting name, a fitting name for someone who knew everything there was to know about Daytona Beach.

The trio had walked back toward the Thunderbird where Spider followed the boys up to their room. Jim and Daryl changed into jeans and fresh T-shirts while Spider sat on one of the beds and looked around. He noticed their suitcases and the clothes they contained and the expensive camera sitting on the dresser. That's when it occurred to him that the teens probably had cash on them. And lots of it. Snake would be thrilled.

"Let's go," Daryl said, grabbing his car keys and patting his wallet to make sure it was in his jeans pocket.

They walked out to the car and Spider could probably feel his excitement level rise. Michigan plates. That meant the boys were on vacation far from home. Not only were they pigeons. They were wealthy pigeons. Wealthy, dumb pigeons.

Next Spider had climbed into the backseat and waited for both teens to get in and close the doors. Once they were all inside, he began to speak. From everything he knew, Bob guessed that was the moment Spider began to set the plan in motion.

"Hey, I've got a buddy of mine, not too far from here," Spider had said, leaning forward so Daryl and Jim could hear him. "What do you say we pick him up and take him to the party, too?"

Daryl glanced at Jim. Both boys seemed comfortable with the idea and Daryl shrugged casually. "Sure. Just tell us where to find him."

"Toward the boardwalk at McDonald's," Spider said. As he spoke he pulled out another marijuana cigarette and lit it. This had probably bothered Daryl somewhat because he didn't want his car to smell like marijuana smoke and because if they were pulled over they could be in big trouble if an officer found drugs in the car. But it was a short drive and everyone was in good spirits. Most likely Daryl didn't want to dampen the mood so he kept quiet and did as he was told, carefully following the speed limit as he drove to McDonald's.

"Wait here," Spider said, flicking the cigarette butt out the car window and waiting while Daryl moved his seat so he could climb out of the Nova.

At that point Spider was very satisfied.

The setup was ideal and Snake would presumably be anxious to get in on the hit. He walked into McDonald's and spotted Snake immediately.

Like a deadly reptile, Snake had sat by himself in the fast-food restaurant that night, his thick brown hair hanging in greasy clumps. There was a look of utter indifference in Snake's eyes that set him apart from the younger set which commonly populated the beach-side hangout. Everyone knew they could find Snake at McDonald's. If he wasn't there, he was at one of the nearby arcades. Snake made his living selling drugs, and the only way he knew to be successful was to be available. Snake saw Spider approaching him and he rose to meet him.

"Hey, what's up?" he asked and the two sat down at the nearest table.

"Got a coupla pigeons outside." Spider hissed the words, glancing about nervously to be sure that no one nearby could hear him.

Snake shrugged. "Let 'em go. It's too late tonight."

Spider shook his head. "Hey, man," he said, his tone of voice more urgent. "These are a coupla rich pigeons, man. I mean it. They're from out of town and they want to find a beach party."

"Rich?" Snake asked, raising one eyebrow skeptically.

"Yeah, man. I saw their wallets," he lied. "Real rich."

Snake thought a minute and then grinned. "Okay, let's go get 'em."

Snake had led the way and the two men walked out toward the boys' car where they slipped into the backseat.

"This here's Snake," Spider said, making the introduction brief. "This is Daryl and Jim."

Snake was at least ten years older than Spider and Bob guessed Jim and Daryl probably wondered why the older man would be interested in a teenage beach party. But no one discussed the point, probably because there were more pressing matters at hand. Daryl's car was running on empty.

"Where's the nearest gas station?" Daryl asked, pulling back onto Atlantic.

"Next corner," Snake said. "Broadway and Atlantic."

Daryl had steered the car across two lanes of traffic and pulled into the station. After pumping ten gallons of gas, he pulled out his wallet and took out a fistful of bills. From where they were alertly watching from the backseat,

Snake and Spider could see that Daryl had a sizable wad of what appeared to be twenty-dollar bills.

"Uh," Snake said once Daryl was back inside the car. He cleared his throat as if he hadn't quite decided what he wanted to say. "Hey, maybe we can go back by my place for a minute."

Daryl glanced in his rearview mirror at the two men in his backseat. "Where do you live?"

"Just about a block or so from here. Gotta pick up some things for the party." He nudged Spider as he spoke. "Okay with you guys?"

Jim looked at Daryl and then at his watch. "It's getting late. How long will the party go?"

"Hey, man, it's early," Snake said. "Those parties last forever. Besides, it'll just take a minute."

Daryl shrugged again. "Sure. Tell me how to get there."

Snake then directed Daryl to turn right and head into the city. A few streets up they turned left and then made a quick right into a run-down trailer park.

"My place is up there on the left," Snake said as they pulled up and Daryl parked the car. "I'll be right back."

In only a few minutes Snake returned to the car carrying a brown bag.

"What's that, man?" Daryl asked.

"Just a few party goods," Snake replied and then he started to laugh. For several seconds he laughed while Spider sat motionless beside him and Daryl and Jim focused on the road ahead. There was nothing humorous about Snake's laughter and Daryl seemed suddenly anxious to get to the party. Whoever this Snake was, Daryl didn't like the idea of spending time with him.

"Which way to the party?" Daryl asked, his voice sounding strangely irritated.

At that point there had been the rustling sound of the brown paper bag and in the backseat Snake pulled out two guns. He handed a .25 caliber automatic blue-steel pistol to Spider and kept for himself a .38 revolver. He grinned evilly at Spider.

"No party tonight, boys," Snake had said, and hatred seemed to fill his voice.

Jim turned around and stared into the backseat. As he did, he spotted both guns. Snake laughed again and held up the .38, jamming the point of the barrel into the back of Jim's head.

For a moment, Jim probably thought it was some kind of joke. But then instantly he knew he was wrong. Bob bet that at that moment the boys understood the severity of their situation. There had never been any party or any party goods. They had been set up. Right from the beginning.

"Daryl," he had said, keeping his head very still and wincing as Snake pushed the gun harder against his head. "They've got guns."

Daryl turned quickly and saw the two revolvers. As he did, Spider held his gun up and placed it against the back of Daryl's head. The blood must have drained from Daryl's face. Despite his inexperience with such things he was certain that they were in deep trouble. He began to worry about the money he and Jim were carrying. In all likelihood, these guys would rob them of everything they had.

"That's right, boys. Guns," Snake said, laughing once more. "Now do what I tell you and no one'll get hurt. Just keep driving."

He had directed the teens onto Highway 92, a deserted stretch of two-lane road that crosses vast swampland and scrub brush and eventually leads into Orlando.

The boys had been silent as they drove, too terrified to do anything but obey Snake's commands. The only sound at all other than the car's engine was the occasional sound of Snake laughing. A mean, cold laugh which must have sent chills down the boys' spines.

"Where are we going?" Daryl finally asked; his face was white with fear, his skin tight around the tense edges of his mouth. Jim clutched the door handle tightly, listening for Snake's answer. The night was pitch-dark and they were heading farther and farther from the beach.

"Just keep driving."

Bob sighed as he scanned the final pages of his notes, which so far included none of those specific details. He guessed that at that moment, Jim and Daryl must have stopped worrying about the money they might lose and started worrying about their lives.

Bob closed the file.

That much of the story he knew, and it was enough to tell him that in all likelihood the Michigan teenagers had not survived their encounter with Snake and Spider. Bob narrowed his eyes and looked toward the roadway. He was glad he had decided to bring Mike along for the stakeout. If Snake was going to return on schedule, he would do it soon and it was crucial that one of them be watching when he did. Bob had his plan mapped out perfectly.

He and Mike, working shifts from their separate cars, would watch for Snake, knowing that he would have to return sometime in the next few days if he wanted to be paid for his three weeks of deliveries. Then they would radio the FDLE. Bob had not received any further information from the agents, despite his financial agreement with them. He knew the reason. The investigation was at a standstill. Everyone—from police officer Mikelson to sheriff's deputies Ziegler and Deemer to the FDLE agents—was waiting for Snake to return.

Once Bob had spotted him and radioed the FDLE, he and Mike would follow him. Then, at some point the FDLE would catch up to them and make the arrest.

Bob could hardly wait.

Of course, there was the chance that Snake wouldn't show up. But Bob didn't think it very likely, since Snake would have to forego his paycheck by dumping the truck and failing to return to the shop. There was only one reason why someone like Snake would do that, Bob figured. And that was if he knew for sure the legal trap that faced him back home.

The wait had continued through Saturday night and Sunday. Finally, it was Monday morning and Bob motioned for Mike to roll his window down. Mike had just sat up after taking a four-hour sleeping break. According to the schedule they'd worked out, now it was Bob's turn to sleep.

"Today's the day, Mike," Bob said, looking more alert than Mike despite his lack of sleep.

"Okay, boss." Mike was too tired to be enthusiastic. "You going to get some sleep or what?"

Bob looked outside his car window at the bright blue sky. There was an unusually cool breeze in the air and Bob had been savoring the weather before Mike woke up. "No, not now. I'm not tired. He's coming home today, Mike. I have that feeling."

"You know, boss, that feeling of yours has been wrong a time or two."

Bob grinned. Mike was right. Especially when it came to this case. "This is different, Mike. Feels like it does before the big bang. Just before everything finally comes together. It's going to happen, Mike. Today's the day."

Mike held up his hand and nodded his head. "Sure, Bob, whatever you say. Care if I sleep since you're so perky this morning?"

Bob looked at Mike in mock amazement. "Oh, sure, go ahead. Go to sleep and let me sit here by myself. No one to talk to. Of course, you'll miss the big moment. Just don't say I didn't warn you."

Mike shook his head and laughed. "All right, all right," he said. "I'll stay awake."

An hour passed and then two and Mike was yawning. "Still have that feeling, boss?"

Bob nodded. He was sitting straight up, his eyes alert and his face full of suspense.

Suddenly, they heard the sound of a truck pulling into the parking lot.

Immediately both men sank lower in their seats and watched as the truck positioned itself in front of a company stall and parked. They still could not make out the driver, but the description of the truck fit that of the one Snake was supposed to be driving.

The truck door swung open and they watched a man climb out. He shut the door and for the first time Bob could see his face. He knew instantly that it was Snake Cox. The man had tattoos on his arms and brown hair that was slicked back. They sat perfectly still while Snake walked into the shop. He hadn't seen them.

"Turn your engine on," Bob whispered to Mike. "Let's be ready."

He turned the key in his ignition and when the engine was running he picked up his citizens band radio and found the frequency he needed. In a matter of seconds he was connected to the FDLE.

"I've got him," Bob said, taking care to keep his head down.

"We're on our way. What's your location?"

"I'm at the trucking company in Tampa. How quick can you get here?"

"Not quick enough. We'll send one of the local guys. Fifteen minutes."

"Get it lined up and then let me call you first. No telling which way Snake will go when he gets out."

Bob hung up the phone and waited. Seven minutes passed and then Snake walked out of the office, folding a white envelope. He slid the envelope into his back pocket and pulled out a set of keys. Oblivious to Bob and Mike, he walked toward a Harley-Davidson chopper, climbed on top and started the engine. In a matter of seconds, he had pulled away.

There's an art to following someone without being detected. And Bob had perfected the art long ago. Many detectives made the mistake of following a subject too closely. The chase went much more successfully if the pursuer followed at a greater distance, anticipating the subject's next move. Most drivers were fairly predictable. They drove at a steady pace and when they made a turn it was usually preceded by a blinker. The key was having enough patience to maintain a significant distance from the subject being followed.

Bob waited for Snake to pull onto the highway. Then, after several seconds, first Bob and then Mike pulled out after him.

As he drove, Bob picked up the radio and once again dialed the FDLE.

"It's Bob Brown. We're traveling south on the old highway near the trucking company. Roll the units."

Then Bob hung up the phone and concentrated on the task ahead of him. For the next five minutes they followed Snake without incident. Bob began to look in his rearview mirror, praying that the FDLE would catch up to them soon. If they didn't, and if for some reason they were unable to make the arrest, Bob was not sure what he would do. He was armed but he was not sure if he was capable of apprehending someone like Snake Cox.

"Hurry," he whispered out loud. "Please hurry."

Just then, he saw flashing lights behind him.

"Thank God," he said.

He and Mike were positioned between the squad cars and Snake, and Bob hoped that Snake would be unable to see their lights until they were nearly on top of him. Bob picked up speed, closing the gap between himself and Snake. When he was only a car length behind him, the FDLE agents sped past him and turned on their sirens.

Snake looked up, startled by the sudden commotion. The agents waved him toward the edge of the road and he pulled over. As his bike came to a complete stop, the two squad cars pulled up alongside, at either end of the motorcycle.

Snake was shouting a litany of profanity as the officers approached him. Bob and Mike pulled over a few feet away and climbed out of their cars to watch.

"What's this all about, man?"

"You John Cox, Jr.?" one of the uniformed agents asked.

"Yeah, so what? I ain't done nothin' wrong."

All four agents at the scene had their guns drawn and directed in the vicinity of Snake's face. They had decided to go with the forgery charges and not warrants for past crimes since the forgery charge was directly related to the disappearance of the boys.

"We have a warrant for your arrest." One of the agents moved close to Cox. "Put your hands behind your back, Cox."

Cox angrily followed the officer's command and began spewing hateful four-letter words at everyone around him. He turned toward the arresting officer.

"What's the charge, man?" he shouted.

"Forgery." He placed the handcuffs on Snake's wrists. "John Cox, you have the right to remain silent. Anything you say or do can and will be used against you in a court of law... ."

Snake shook his head furiously while the officer continued to read his rights. "This is a bunch of lies," he said, his eyes seething with anger.

From the distance, Bob Brown and his assistant watched in satisfaction. *Finally,* Bob thought. *We're going to get to the bottom of this mess.*

CHAPTER 35

By that afternoon, Snake had been booked into Volusia County Jail, just a few corridors away from his good friend, Spider. He had been charged with eight counts of forgery in connection with the signing of Jim Boucher's traveler's checks and—although Bob had hoped there would be no bail set—the judge had set bail at forty-two thousand dollars.

Mikelson had been notified and had agreed to allow Ziegler and the sheriff's department further pursuit of the matter. The FDLE officers had also decided to back down from the case. Ziegler and the sheriff's department would be the official investigative agency from this point on.

Of course, by then Snake knew that something had gone terribly wrong regarding the ordeal involving the Michigan teenagers. Everything had seemed so perfect, like it had gone without a hitch. After all, what happened had taken place months ago.

But, if he saw Jim Boucher's name on the written charge against him, he must have known there was trouble. In fact, he probably realized that when the law enforcement agency of Florida state was through with him, paying the penalty for eight counts of forgery would be equivalent to a day in the park.

By eight o'clock, several contacts had been made regarding the turn of events that day. First, the state had assigned Snake a public defender. By that night the two had made initial contact and were working on a plan involving Cox's defense should the case go to trial. Even at that early stage when no one had mentioned that murder charges might be pending, the defense they were working on had nothing to do with forgery. It had to do with a double homicide.

Second, James Byrd (the Michigan investigator who had in the past six weeks made a tidy profit without ever leaving his desk) contacted the Barbers who in turn contacted the Bouchers.

It was the best news they'd had in weeks.

Snake Cox, the man who had somehow gotten hold of Daryl's Nova, had finally been caught.

The couples met at the Barbers' house that evening and tried to contain their nervousness.

"You know what this means, don't you?" Faye was saying to the others. "It means they might find the boys in the next few days."

No one said a word. Even after all the time that had passed, the emotions surrounding the possibility that the boys might be found were utterly mixed. There was a sense of relief, that just maybe the nightmare might soon be over.

But just as strong was the feeling of heartbreaking fear that with the discovery of the boys would come the truth. The boys were probably dead. Still, it would be better to know. It was the not knowing, the unanswered questions, the inability to go on with life that was killing all of them. And now the answers were closer than ever before.

The parents considered the time that had passed since the boys' disappearance. As long as their sons were missing, as difficult as the past six weeks had been on the families, there was hope that the boys were still alive. But once they were found, if they were indeed dead, then even their hope would have to die. Even that, they agreed, would be better than not knowing.

And so, since there was nothing any of them could say to lessen any of these emotions, they spent that night each comforted by the presence of the others in virtual silence. Mostly, that evening gave them time to prepare for the worst. Because unless the boys were miraculously alive somewhere, the truth was going to be a severe blow for all of them. Even after weeks of guessing that the boys were dead, none of them were prepared to hear the news spoken as fact.

CHAPTER 36

Dick Kane was a bright young attorney with a potentially brilliant future in defense. He was tall and thin with a knack for dressing tastefully. And he had a soothing voice which had a way of convincing juries he was telling the truth. Even if the facts didn't quite add up. One of the first rules of thumb Kane followed was that when someone was offering his client a deal, it was worth checking into.

Of course, if his client was not guilty, they would turn down the deal and fight the charges tooth and nail. But if, as was quite often the case, his client was guilty, then usually a deal would be the best way to go.

And so when Spider Smith mentioned in the early part of his conversation with the lawyer that the state attorney's office had offered him a nonspecific deal in exchange for the truth, Kane knew which questions needed to be asked next.

"Smith, we're going to have a talk here and it's going to be strictly confidential," Kane began. "But you need to tell me the truth. Understand?"

Spider had swallowed one or two times with some difficulty and then nodded. For the next two hours they discussed what really happened to Jim and Daryl and whether it was necessary for Spider to tell the state what he knew in exchange for some kind of immunity.

When Spider was finished talking, Kane must have known they were in particularly bad shape. So bad was his client's situation that if, for instance, the state was willing to bargain, he probably would have been ecstatic if his client received merely a life sentence in prison. Because according to Spider's version of the story, what he probably deserved was the death penalty.

So it was that on Tuesday morning, December 12, Kane placed a phone call to State Attorney Watson, who in turn telephoned Ziegler and Brown. The news was, Spider wanted to talk. As soon as possible and in the presence of his attorney.

In itself, this would have been wonderful news if it hadn't been for one small detail. By then Cox had entered the picture. Cox—being quite a bit more experienced at criminal activity and quite a bit more intelligent than Spider—had assured his attorney that he, too, wanted to talk about what happened. Whether his attorney was present or not.

"Okay, then who gets the deal?" Bob asked when he arrived and conferred with Ziegler over the turn of events.

"Whoever talks first," Ziegler said.

"I think Spider wants to wait for his attorney to show up."

"Well, Snake doesn't care about that detail. He wants to talk now."

"So you're saying we give Spider the same chance."

"Exactly."

"And if he won't talk because he doesn't have his attorney present?"

"Then he can fry."

Bob looked confused. "I don't understand."

Ziegler smiled wickedly. "We got both of them here, right?"

"Right?"

"Okay. Now I say we put 'em in rooms, side by side. You take Spider and I'll take Snake. And I bet one thing for sure. I bet before the hour's through we have the case solved and at least one scumbag headed for the chair. And if that scumbag happens to be Spider, then as far as I'm concerned, he can fry."

Bob nodded. Ziegler's mention of the electric chair reminded him that he must have been crazy to take on this case. He was used to cases involving late alimony payments, not death by the electric chair. He took a deep breath and mentally rehearsed the questions Spider would need to answer. "When do we start?" he asked.

Ziegler had been busy filling out paperwork and at that moment he set down his pen. "Right now."

The sheriff's deputy summoned two bailiffs and asked them to get Smith and Cox. Then the two detectives walked down the hall toward two adjacent interview rooms.

"The trick is," Ziegler said grinning, "to bring them in at the same time so that they see each other."

Bob didn't need an explanation to understand the reasons why. He laughed. Snake and Spider had made his life miserable for six weeks, not to mention what they'd done to the lives of the boys and their families. The idea that now they might have to suffer a bit did not bother Bob at all.

At that moment, the bailiffs appeared, each at different ends of the hall. Suddenly, Snake and Spider recognized each other, and for the first time they became aware that the other was being questioned. Bob watched the faces of the men and thought that Snake looked far meaner than Spider. He decided if anyone had been the motivating force behind what had happened that August night, it had to have been Snake.

The men glared at each other and then the bailiffs moved them into the separate interview rooms.

"Good luck," Bob said cordially, nodding his head to Ziegler, who laughed out loud.

"Yeah, you, too. First one to speak is the winner."

The men separated and went into their respective interview rooms, Bob with Spider, Ziegler with Snake.

"Well, Smith," Bob said, "I guess you'll want to wait for your attorney."

"Darn right, man," Spider said, "I said I'd talk, but not without the lawyer."

Bob shrugged. "Like I said, first one to talk gets the deal. And you saw your good buddy Snake next door. It's just possible that Mr. Snake isn't going to wait for his lawyer to arrive before he starts talking. Know what I mean?"

Spider squirmed in his seat. He was not having a good time with this, having seen for himself that Snake was indeed headed for an interview room much like the one he was now sitting in. And so at about that time, Spider began to cry.

"Listen, man," he sobbed. "I'm scared. I don't know what to do! I need my lawyer or I can't say nothin'."

"Sounds like you rehearsed that line, Smith. That what you've been doing in that cell all this time. Rehearsing a bunch of garbage like that."

"Stop it, man! That's what I'm supposed to say if anyone asks me anything before he gets here. So get off my back, man. I'm scared to death, here."

Bob thought the sight of Spider Smith blubbering about being afraid was nothing short of pathetic. Especially after he had played a part in killing two people. He wondered how anyone could represent a person like Spider and still sleep at night.

"Well, suit yourself, Smith," Bob said.

Spider twisted and turned in his seat and Bob wondered if he was anticipating how the electric chair might feel.

"Wait!" he shouted suddenly. "I want the deal! Really, man," he said. His nose had begun to run and Bob was disgusted by the sight of him.

"What about your attorney?"

"Listen, man," he cried. "I said I'll talk. Now. Without the attorney."

"You sure about this?"

Spider nodded emphatically. "Yes. Sit down and I'll tell you everything."

At that instant, Ziegler burst through the door and glared at Spider.

"Forget it, Bob," he said, turning his attention toward the private investigator. "Cox is telling us everything."

Then he looked at Spider, who had straightened up in his seat and was looking absolutely terrified.

"It's too late, Spider," he sneered. "The deal's off."

CHAPTER 37

By the time Sheriff's homicide detective Murray Ziegler wound up in an interview room alone with John "Snake" Cox, the prisoner had already given at least one version of what happened to Jim and Daryl that hot August night. In a meeting with his attorney the night of his arrest, he had agreed to tell the truth and to allow his attorney to document the story.

For the most part, that story went like this:

On the evening of August 12, 1978, just after dark, Daryl Barber and Jim Boucher and someone known only as Mike came to the McDonald's restaurant in Daytona Beach, where they met up with Snake. At the time of the meeting, Snake was with another man named Robert MacDonald, but better known as Buford.

According to Snake, Buford was well known on the beach. Although Snake could not remember Mike's last name or any other identifying details regarding the man, he did remember that when Mike approached he told Snake that Jim and Daryl were very interested in buying some marijuana. He wondered if Snake might be able to help locate someone who could accommodate the boys.

Snake, always willing to help a couple of tourists in need, had agreed to work up a deal. So Jim and Daryl, Mike and Snake, had gotten into Daryl's car and driven around Daytona Beach looking for a marijuana dealer. Being as how such proprietors do not advertise openly, the foursome spent much of the night and into the early hours of August 13 without ever finding such a dealer. Finally, near daybreak, the group gave up and returned to Snake's trailer park at 681 North Beach Street in Daytona Beach.

Snake then exited the car and asked Jim and Daryl and Mike to come back later that afternoon. Certainly by then he could find someone to consummate the deal, and the boys could purchase the marijuana they apparently wanted so badly.

Then, according to this first version of Snake's recalling of the events that day, late in the afternoon Jim and Daryl and Mike returned to Snake's trailer. Snake got into the car and the trio immediately began looking for a place to buy the drugs.

Finally, at about five o'clock that evening, Jim and Daryl—with Snake's help— found a dealer named Kenny who agreed to sell Daryl one kilo of marijuana for five hundred and fifty dollars. Jim contributed about two hundred dollars cash to the deal but Kenny would not accept the traveler's checks. Again, ever willing to assist the beleaguered tourists, Snake offered to pay cash for Jim's two hundred dollars in traveler's checks.

Then, in an even more gracious gesture, Snake agreed to loan the boys one hundred and fifty dollars so that they would have a grand total of five hundred and fifty dollars in cash. Just enough for the drug deal. Of course no one could have expected Snake to merely trust the Michigan teenagers to repay him the one hundred and fifty. So he had worked out a deal with Daryl whereby he would take the Chevy Nova as collateral for his generosity.

According to Snake, everyone involved agreed on the deal and Kenny produced a brick-size, tightly packed kilo of marijuana in exchange for the boys' cash. After that, Snake took the boys back to the motel, the name of which Snake had long since forgotten. As the boys climbed out of the car, with Snake at the wheel, Jim and Daryl assured Snake they would return to his trailer within two weeks to repay the loan and repossess Daryl's car. At that time, Daryl wrote a note—which Snake had by some twist of fate misplaced—giving Snake permission to use the car until the loan was repaid.

Snake then used the car to drive to Biloxi, Mississippi, where he picked up his wife and brought her back to Daytona Beach. He used the traveler's checks, which he made a special note of saying he had paid cash for and which were legally his, to pay rent at the trailer park and to pay for the trip north to Biloxi.

After that he had waited for the boys to return with the money but he had never seen them again. And so, Snake decided, since the loan was never repaid, the car was legally his.

That was the story.

But when Snake's attorney asked him if he'd be willing to take a polygraph test and tell the entire story once again but this time hooked up to electrodes that could detect even the slightest amount of anxiety, Snake flat-out unequivocally refused. His reason was that in an unrelated incident some time earlier he'd had a bad experience while taking a polygraph test. Since then, even though he might want to take such a test, he had been physically unable to do so.

As Ziegler read the details of Snake's story he figured he knew what the bad experience was. It probably had something to do with the fact that Snake had lied while taking the test.

And so because of his refusal to take such a test and because of the shady details surrounding the story, after reading it in Snake's presence, Ziegler had tossed the document into the trash can.

"Buncha lies, Cox." Ziegler had spat the words in Snake's direction. Then he had lowered himself to Snake's level and glared at the man. "You know what's happening next door, Cox? Smith's about to spill his guts and when he does, when we get the truth about where the boys are, the other one of you scumbags will be headed for the electric chair."

Snake said nothing and kept his gaze focused on a neutral spot on the empty wall.

"You hear me, Cox?" Ziegler had yelled. "You talk to us or you take the chair. And this isn't any game we're playing here. This is real life, Cox. Talk or take the chair."

Being older and more experienced at a criminal's life, Snake had known instantly that Ziegler was not bluffing. He had thought his options over for what Ziegler estimated to be less than five seconds and then he had started to talk.

"All right, man, you win. I'll tell you what happened and where you can find 'em."

There had been no missing the fact that Snake was not happy about having to talk. But his words were coming fast and Ziegler had known instinctively that he was about to tell the truth.

"Just a minute," he'd said.

And then the detective had gone next door and ended the conversation between Bob and Spider. If Snake wanted to talk, then Spider could sit in jail and rot for the next ten years on death row until someone was finally willing to pull the switch.

After Ziegler made his announcement that Snake was willing to talk, Bob stared at Spider and shook his head sadly.

"Stupid move, Smith," he said. "You had every chance in the world."

Then he notified the bailiff that he was finished with the prisoner and he followed Ziegler into the next room.

"Get your pen and paper ready, Brown," Ziegler whispered as they made their way inside. "This ought to be good."

They sat down and stared at Cox, who looked like a caged lion with a bad case of rabies. Bob was thankful the man was wearing handcuffs.

"We're listening, Cox," Ziegler said. "Tell us what happened."

And so on December 12, at 12:50 P.M., exactly four months after Jim and Daryl had disappeared, Snake began to talk. This time, his story was significantly different from the first one he'd told.

The way Snake told it now, on the evening of August 12, he was sitting inside the McDonald's hamburger restaurant in the boardwalk area of Daytona Beach when he was approached by Spider Smith. Spider led him outside to the car he had arrived in—a red Chevy Nova with a black vinyl top. Inside the car were two teenage boys. Spider then pulled Snake away from the car so the boys could not hear what he was saying. At that time, he suggested that they take the boys to a party, do some smoking, and while they were at it, rip 'em off.

Spider then went back to the Nova and talked to the boys, and within a short time he reported back to Snake that the boys were willing and ready to find a party. At that time, Snake and Spider entered the boys' car and sat in the backseat. For a time, they sat in the McDonald's parking lot and smoked marijuana while talking about parties in the area. Then they had driven around Daytona Beach, all four of them still smoking marijuana in the car.

Ziegler raised an eyebrow toward Brown. Both detectives knew that the Michigan boys were not drug users and this detail sent up more than a red flag in Ziegler's opinion.

Snake continued. Somehow—and Snake couldn't remember exactly how—the group had wound up in the vicinity of the Strickland Rifle Range on Williamson

Boulevard in Volusia County. The area was dark and deserted, and all four occupants exited the car. At about this time, Spider pulled out a .25 caliber automatic handgun from his waistband and ordered Jim and Daryl to hand over their money and their traveler's checks.

At this point in the story Snake was unclear about whether it was him or Spider who was responsible for the specifics of what happened to the boys. Either way, after Jim and Daryl had been robbed, they were ordered at gunpoint to remove their belts.

Bob was scribbling notes furiously but when Snake mentioned the part about the boys having to remove their belts he suddenly stopped. All through the hours of staking out various locations and searching boating docks and cemetery plots and biker bars and making deals with shady characters named "Larry," Bob hadn't spent much time thinking about the ultimate truth, about what actually might have happened to the boys. And now he wasn't sure he wanted to hear the details.

He took a deep breath and bent over his notes. As long as Snake was telling the truth about what had happened to the boys, he would have to pay close attention. He had been paid to find the boys and as of yet they had still not been found.

Next, Snake was saying, the boys' belts were used to tie their hands behind their backs and then they were placed in the backseat of Daryl's car. Snake and Spider then climbed into the front seat and noticed the motel keys on the car's dashboard. "Thunderbird Motel, Room 109," the keys read. So with Snake driving the Nova, the group headed for the Thunderbird Motel.

But before they pulled out of the deserted area, Snake and Spider agreed that there was a problem they had to take care of before they could go anywhere. As long as the boys were sitting in the backseat they might try to alert someone that they needed help. Because of that, Snake pulled off the road once again. Jim's and Daryl's hands were untied and—for reasons Snake did not supply—their shoes were removed. Then they were placed in the trunk of the Nova.

Snake took a deep breath.

"Go on," Ziegler shouted. "This isn't story-telling hour, here. We don't have all day."

Snake glared at the detective and resumed his story.

Once the boys were in the trunk of the car, he and Spider had gotten back inside and continued the drive to the motel. When they arrived, he and Spider entered the boys' room and removed all their personal belongings including Jim's camera and both boys' suitcases and clothing.

With the boys still in the trunk of the car, Snake and Spider left the motel and drove around for quite a while deciding what to do with their victims. Finally, they came to an isolated area approximately half a mile off Highway 92 on Indian Lake Road. Snake stopped the car. Both men climbed out and one of them opened the trunk.

Seeing that the boys were no longer moving, Snake said, he and Spider came to the conclusion that Jim and Daryl had died while in the trunk. He and Spider then removed the boys' bodies and dumped them in a well-hidden wooded area.

"That's it," Snake said, leaning back in his chair as if he had just finished presenting an oral report on the benefits of good nutrition.

Ziegler stared at Snake for a full five minutes saying absolutely nothing.

There were many parts of the story, huge sections, in fact, that he did not for one minute believe. Those were details that Ziegler definitely intended to get hold of eventually. But overall, the story had a ring of truth to it.

There was one way to be sure.

"You ready to take us to the bodies?" Ziegler finally asked. Bob put down his pen and felt his breathing quicken.

"That's what you want? The bodies?"

"That's it, Cox. And if it doesn't check out you can just as soon fry for all I care."

"I know where they are, man. If you don't believe me then let me take you there. I'm ready when you are." Snake sounded defiant and hurt as if after admitting to a double homicide and after first lying about the facts the night before, he somehow still expected the detective to trust him.

As it turned out Ziegler was not ready for several hours. He contacted the judge and shortly before six o'clock that evening finally received permission together with deputy Joe Deemer and private investigator Bob Brown to take a handcuffed Snake to the spot he had described and search for the bodies of Jim Boucher and Daryl Barber.

Spider, meanwhile, had been returned to his cell, where by that evening he had received even more bad news.

His attorney, Dick Kane, had withdrawn himself from the case. So with no attorney and no idea that Snake was about to lead three investigators to the bodies of the boys, Spider spent the night huddled in the corner of his cell. He was utterly and completely alone.

Sometime before six o'clock, Bob Brown got the word to James Byrd, who in turn telephoned the Bouchers.

"I told you I'd get to the bottom of this," he said, shamelessly taking credit for Bob's work. "And I think we've finally gotten there."

"Did you find them?" Faye's voice was little more than a frightened whisper and she quickly moved out of earshot of her younger children.

"Not yet. But they've apprehended the second man, John Cox, and he's told investigators the whole story about what happened."

"Are they alive?" It was the last time Faye might be able to ask such a question, the last time there would be any uncertainty about whether her son was dead or not. Tears began trickling down Faye's cheeks and she closed her eyes in anticipation of the investigator's answer.

"No, Mrs. Boucher. I'm sorry." Byrd paused politely. "If Mr. Cox's story is correct, the boys died the same night they arrived in town. They were robbed and killed by a couple of the deadliest, dirtiest guys in the state of Florida."

Faye felt weak as if she might faint. Black spots were dancing before her eyes, and her legs were beginning to go numb. "But," she stammered, "they still haven't found them, right?"

"Right. They'll be going tonight. To the place Mr. Cox remembers leaving the boys' bodies."

Faye was sobbing now, wanting so badly for it all to be a nightmare. For four months she had convinced herself that the worst thing a mother could face was not knowing where her son was.

But she had been wrong.

This was worse. The ache in her gut would never go away, never be eased by the hope that someday he would come home. No, he would never come home again. Her oldest son was dead. And there was nothing in the world worse than that.

"Mrs. Boucher," Byrd said softly. "I'm sorry. Someone will be in touch after they find the boys' bodies."

Faye was crying so hard she was barely able to speak. "Will they find them today?" she managed to ask.

"Tonight, ma'am. They're going to look tonight."

Faye thanked him and hung up the phone. Then she collapsed to the ground, allowing her entire body to lie motionless while she screamed her son's name. Roy heard her first and came running from the back room.

"Oh, my God, Faye! What is it?" His face was white and Faye looked up helplessly, raising one hand and placing it inside her husband's larger one.

"They're dead, Roy." Her voice was weak. "They're both dead."

Roy closed his eyes and clenched his fists.

"No!" he screamed. "Not my Jimmy. Please, God, not my Jim."

At that instant the younger boys appeared and saw what was happening. Timothy and Stephen knew from the way their parents were acting that finally they had gotten word about Jim. Neither boy had to ask the question in both their minds because they already knew the answer. Their brother was dead.

"Is Jim dead, Daddy?" John asked, his childlike voice frightened, tears spilling onto his freckled face.

Roy looked at his youngest son and something inside him snapped. Throughout the past four months Roy had remained stoic, hiding his emotions so that he would not burden his hurting family. But now, with his family falling apart around him, Roy could do nothing but give in to his pain. He put his arm around his younger sons, sank to his knees alongside his wife, hung his head, and cried.

With Darkness encroaching, Ziegler and Deemer escorted the shackled Snake to a squad car. Bob Brown drove behind them, and following Snake's directions, they headed for Highway 92. Several miles out of the city limits and far beyond any buildings or signs of civilization, in an area covered with dense, deep Florida scrub brush, Ziegler turned the car onto Indian Lake Road.

Within half a mile, the road narrowed down and became little more than a glorified trail. At that point, Snake motioned for Ziegler to turn left on what appeared to be a fire trail that was even more narrow. As Ziegler drove, maneuvering slowly along the uneven dirt trail, branches from the overgrown brush scratched at the squad car. He turned to Deemer, seated beside him.

"No wonder we never found the bodies," he muttered.

"Yeah," Deemer said. "Only thing comes out this way is snakes and spiders."

"You got that right."

With Bob following closely behind they traveled the trail four-tenths of a mile. Suddenly Snake held up his hand.

"Right here," he said.

The cars stopped and the detectives climbed out, helping Snake to his feet. They watched as he walked a few yards ahead of the cars and then pointed toward a clearing in the brush.

Speaking in a tone of voice that suggested he was talking not about the bodies of two teenage boys but about, say, a spot where he'd last seen his missing sunglasses, he said, "We put 'em right there."

The detectives moved to the spot and peered into the clearing while Snake remained a few feet behind. It was 6:50 P.M. and there was very little light left so Ziegler flipped on his flashlight. There, scattered around what appeared to be a blue, woolen blanket, were dozens of bones.

"Look," Deemer said, pointing his flashlight to another area. The men looked and each of them could see what Deemer had found.

There were two skulls, lying side by side on the damp earth.

Bob turned away first. If everything checked out, his job was officially finished. It was the first time any of his investigations had resulted in the discovery of a dead body.

"Well, we won't be needing body bags on this one," Ziegler said. "Only thing left of those kids is a box full of bones." He turned toward Deemer. "Get on the radio. Tell 'em looks like Snake's story checks out. We'll rope off the area and then come back tomorrow when it's daylight. I'm betting we'll have to go over this whole area with a magnifying glass before we're through."

With Snake back in the squad car, Bob watched as Ziegler and Deemer roped off the area. Before they left, Ziegler turned to Bob.

"Only reason we're here right now is 'cause of you," he said. "I appreciate good work when I see it and this was one helluva good job, Brown."

Bob nodded his thanks.

Normally at this stage of an investigation he would feel elated, thrilled beyond words. But this time, with the image of Jim and Daryl's skeletal remains still in his mind, he felt only an emptiness. He worked private investigation so he could put an end to the pain people were feeling. And all along he had thought that would be true of this case, also. Once the parents knew where their sons were—dead or alive—at least they would no longer have to wonder. Because of that, Bob figured solving the case would end their pain. But now he knew without a doubt that he had been wrong.

If anything, their pain had just begun.

CHAPTER 38

The phone rang in the Barber home at nine thirty that evening. By then the Bouchers had made arrangements for their younger children, and the two couples had gathered at the Barbers' where they had done little more than wait by the telephone for most of the evening.

Ron Barber answered the call. It was James Byrd, putting in overtime, he said, and giving the impression that he had been losing sleep over the case while waiting for this moment.

"They found them, Mr. Barber," Byrd said.

Faye and Roy had composed themselves and shared the news with the Barbers hours earlier so Ron knew what to expect. But still, hearing the words from the investigator was like being punched in the stomach. Ron felt the air leave his body and he suddenly found it nearly impossible to breathe.

"Are they dead?" he asked. The others sat silent and still, their eyes glued to Ron's.

"Well, positive identification hasn't been made yet, but everything matches up. I'd say there's no mistaking the fact that it's them, Mr. Barber."

Ron closed his eyes and the others knew the answer. At long last their sons had been found. The searching and waiting and wondering was over. But there was no sense of victory, no elation over the fact. Their desperate need to know had been replaced with an even deeper pain, a raw anguish that was more awful than any of them had ever imagined.

"Have they made any arrests yet?" Ron knew that officially the private investigation was over. But now there would be bodies to identify, arrests to be made, and trials that would have to take place. The process had really only begun.

"They have two suspects in custody. One seems to be working with the authorities. He's the man who led the sheriff's deputies to the bodies. But both men will face murder charges. You can be sure of that, Mr. Barber."

Ron thanked the man for his work on the case.

"Well, it wasn't easy," Byrd said. "Took a lot of time and, as you know, a lot of money." Byrd cleared his throat. "Of course, we didn't want it to end like this. But at least you know the truth, now."

"Yes." Ron had the strange feeling that someone else was talking for him and that none of this was really happening to him.

"By the way, the story will be on the eleven o'clock news tonight," Byrd said. "Sheriff's going to read a press release."

And so by 10:50 that night, the Barbers and Bouchers and Faye's parents had gathered in front of the television set. As it turned out, the story was one of the first on the newscast that night. They watched, their eyes wide in horror, as Detective Ziegler explained to reporters that they had found the skeletal remains of two people, believed to be the Michigan teenagers who had been missing in Daytona Beach for the past four months.

At the mention of the word skeletal, Faye gasped and put a hand over her mouth. None of them had thought about what the elements might have done to their sons since their bodies had been disposed of that past summer.

Roy stared blankly at the television set and reached for Faye's hand. He listened to the story, took in the details, and paid careful attention to everything that was said. But when it was over he still had the unusual feeling he was listening to a story about someone else's sons.

Marian began crying and turned away from the screen, burying her head in Ron's shoulder. Even though there were no pictures of the scene or of the boys' remains, she could no longer watch.

At the end of the story, the newscaster said that although details of the boys' deaths had been given to authorities, they were not yet available to the public. Immediately, Ron stood up and dialed James Byrd's number. The investigator was still in his office.

"I understand the sheriff has the details about what happened to the boys," he said. "We want to know everything they do. As soon as possible. Can you have them call us or give us a number so we can call them."

"Well, uh," Byrd said. "I can tell you this much. The boys were robbed before they were killed. But that's about it. Anything more and you'll have to call the sheriff's department yourself."

Ron was beginning to feel annoyed. After all, they had paid this man more than sixty thousand dollars to find their sons. Now, even though he had gotten the job done, there was no reason why he couldn't cooperate and help them find the information they needed.

"What are you trying to say?" Ron asked.

"Well, officially speaking the investigation is over, Mr. Barber. You'll probably have a lot more questions as this thing goes through the legal system. And starting now those questions will have to go through the proper channels."

Ron was speechless. In a voice that after so much bad news finally had no emotion left, he thanked the investigator and hung up the phone.

That evening they discussed their next move, agreeing that Faye would be the one to initiate contact with the authorities. But for the most part, there was no sobbing or screaming or crying that evening.

Instead, there was a terrible emptiness—as if everything that had happened that day, the information from Byrd and the newscast on television, had never really happened. They were in shock, each trying to adjust to the idea that their sons had been found.

The problem was, until they could actually identify the boys none of what was happening seemed real. Each of them had spent their life savings so that they could get their sons back. Dead or alive, there had always been the hope that somehow they would see their boys again.

But now, all that was left were some skeletal remains. What all of them had really wanted was to see their sons' faces, feel the flesh of their arms, the warmth of their bodies—everything that had always been their sons.

But no investigation and no amount of money would ever bring them back now. They had bones and belts and blankets. But their boys were gone forever.

Early on the morning of December 13 a special crime scene unit from the Florida Department of Criminal Law Enforcement flew into Daytona Beach from Tallahassee. The team, led by Dr. Dan Morse, a forensic scientist from Florida State University, included Daytona Beach Police officer Mikelson, sheriff's deputies Joe Deemer and Murray Ziegler, and sheriff's captain Howard McBride. Present also were a representative from the Halifax Fire Department and two additional forensics scientists from the FDLE.

And of course, the group included Bob Brown, who had every right to continue on with the investigation until positive identification could be made on the remains. And after all the work he'd done on the case, the others were more than willing to have him along.

In all, there were eight people in three vehicles who converged on the scene first thing that Wednesday morning. The process was painstakingly slow. Bones from the two bodies were found over an area of forty square feet. At first this caused the investigators to wonder if they weren't perhaps dealing with more than two bodies.

But within the first few minutes of the search, Dr. Dan Morse quickly figured out what had happened. In his opinion, as the boys' bodies had lain on the blanket side by side slowly decomposing, animals had moved in and dragged away their various body parts.

Bob was sickened by the thought of animals eating the dead flesh of the missing teenagers. He tried to push the thoughts from his head. Working under the assumption that Dr. Morse's theory was correct, they began scanning the ground like surgeons searching for minuscule blood vessels.

They used screened devices and sifted surface soil, rinsing what remained so that they could reclaim even the smallest bones. Working with this process, they found finger and feet bones, wrist and ankle bones. The larger bones were easier to see, but in order to find them some of the brush had to be cut back.

While several men continued with the search, others were assigned the job of photographing the bones and the place where the bodies originally had lain. Apparently they had been placed under a blanket and although they were not buried, their bodies had made a slight depression in the ground. Pictures were

THE SNAKE AND THE SPIDER

taken of that area also to prove that although the bones were found scattered across an area that was forty square feet, they had at one time been placed side by side under a blanket.

As each bone was found, it was numbered and registered into a log that detailed every bit of evidence collected from the scene. The entries read something like this:

10:07 A.M. Left femur. Found seven feet, six inches north of the central location.

10:08 A.M. Right seventh rib. Found two feet, three inches west of central location.

And on it went, the central location being the spot where the depressions left by the bodies were found in the ground. In addition to the bones they collected two blankets and several items of clothing including two pairs of blue jeans and two T-shirts.

Finally, just before sunset that evening, the tired crew packed up the evidence they had collected and left the scene. The skulls, teeth, and other skeletal remains of the victims were sent to the crime lab headquarters in Tallahassee where they would be restructured and analyzed in attempt to determine numerous details including the cause of death.

By that time Michigan State Police had already sent both boys' dental charts to the crime lab in Tallahassee so that identification could be made immediately.

The Barbers and Bouchers knew that there was a possibility the remains were not those of their sons. But on Thursday afternoon when they took the call from a technician at the crime lab, they were not surprised at the news.

The dental records had been compared with the teeth found at the scene. Confirmation had been made. The bodies were those of Daryl Barber and Jim Boucher.

More than one week later, Spider Smith was sitting in his cell doing little more than existing. He still had not been assigned a new attorney and he had not been in contact with anyone regarding the missing boys. He had no idea if Snake had indeed told the truth about what had happened or even if he had talked at all. It was possible, he guessed, that Snake hadn't said anything to the detectives and that they were merely playing a waiting game with him, trying to force him to talk.

Well, Spider wasn't talking. As far as he was concerned there was no reason to tell anyone what happened. All that talk about the electric chair was, in Spider's opinion, little more than a scare tactic. After all he'd been sitting here eight days and no one had said anything about the death penalty.

Of course, by then Spider had been officially charged in the deaths of both boys. But that in itself did not worry Spider terribly. As long as Snake hadn't said much to the detectives there was no way they could prove he was guilty of murder.

Spider had spent long, lonely hours thinking about his good friend, Snake, and how likely it was that he would talk about this problem they shared. And after a great deal of time spent worrying about the issue, Spider decided Snake probably wouldn't say anything at all. But it bothered him that there had been no way to find out what really had been said in the interview room that afternoon.

And by Friday, December 22, Spider's need to know had grown so great that he finally asked a bailiff for a newspaper. Didn't matter how old it was, he just needed a paper. Perhaps if Snake had talked, he would find a story there with the details.

The bailiff grabbed an old copy of *The Tampa Tribune* dated December 15 and tossed it to Spider. Spider flipped through the paper, convinced he would find nothing. But then, at the top of page 2-B, he saw this headline: "Information from Suspect Led to Bodies of Boys."

Spider began reading the article in terror.

It spanned the width of the page and detailed how John Cox, Jr., alias "Snake," had led investigators to the remains of two Michigan teenagers. Then it told how Cox had informed the police of what had happened to the boys, all of which had led to the arrest of Earl "Spider" Smith, who was currently sitting in Volusia County Jail, where he was being held without bail.

When Spider finished reading the article, he read it again. With each word, Spider's fear diminished and his anger grew—until finally he wadded the paper up in a tight ball and threw it at the wall.

"That's a buncha bull!" he shouted. At which time the bailiff reentered the room and asked Spider if there was a problem.

"You bet, man!" he screamed. His eyes were wide and he looked more than a little wild. The bailiff stepped back a bit.

"What's the problem, Smith?" he asked calmly. He had been watching over Spider for weeks and had never seen him get this angry.

"I'll tell you what the problem is. I want to talk to one of the detectives," Spider shouted. "You know who I mean? The guys working on this murder thing I'm caught up in. It's time they know the real story about what happened."

The bailiff assured Spider that he would do his best, and then Spider began to pace. He paced his cell for nearly two hours until the bailiff returned, this time with news that Deputy Joe Deemer was waiting for him in the interview room.

"Good thing," Spider muttered as the bailiff led him away. "It's about time someone laid the facts out on the table. Time to tell the truth like it is, man."

CHAPTER 39

The idea that Spider suddenly wanted to talk came as something of a surprise to sheriff's deputy Joe Deemer. Even though he hadn't played the largest role in solving the case, he had been involved enough to know that Spider had been given numerous chances to talk and each time had backed down and told only bits and pieces. But this was the first time Spider had *asked* to be interviewed. Ziegler was out on another case and Bob Brown was back at his Orlando office. Since Deemer was very familiar with the case, he was more than happy to make the trip to county jail to hear what Spider wanted to say.

"Heard you wanna talk," Deemer said when Spider was ushered into the interview room. He was a laid-back detective in his late forties with a southern accent and a reputation for handling the nuts and bolts of a case. Nothing fancy. He was also perhaps the least intimidating officer at the sheriff's office, and in this case Deemer had a feeling his personality was going to work in his favor.

"You're darn right," Spider said angrily.

"Well, first I'm gonna have to read you your rights, Mr. Smith. Seein' as how you no longer have an attorney."

"Listen, you can read me whatever you want but when you're done I've got something to say, man. I mean it."

Deemer nodded casually and then read Spider his rights. "The part I want you to pay particular attention to is the fact that this conversation is gonna be recorded, Mr. Smith. You understand that?"

"Someone better record it. About time we got the truth out in this whole mess," Spider snarled.

"All right, just so you understand that anything you say can and will be used against you in a court of law. You can bet on it."

"I understand."

"And you don't want to wait until you get another public defender?"

"No!" Spider shouted. "I wanna talk now, man! Right now!"

"Okay. Have it your way. Mr. Smith, as of right now this conversation is being tape-recorded." "I understand."

"All right, then. Why don't you tell me what you know."

Spider leaned back in his chair and closed his eyes. "The whole thing, the whole night was like some kind of friggin' nightmare, man," Spider said.

And then, in vivid detail, Spider recounted that nightmare with a kind of clarity that shed an altogether different light on what happened that August night. And this time Deemer was fairly certain there was nothing at all that seemed shady or untrue about the story.

According to Smith, he had been prowling the Daytona Beach area near the boardwalk the evening of August 12, 1978, when he spotted the two Michigan teenagers. He approached them and smoked a few marijuana joints while talking to them about parties in the area. He tried to sell them about an ounce of pot, but both boys chose not to smoke any on the beach.

After a little while, according to Spider, he made up a story that there was a big party going on at the Days Inn down the street.

"It's open. Most of the guys are pretty cool about newcomers, you know?" Spider had said.

Then Jim and Daryl had asked Spider where exactly the party was and Spider had offered to take the boys there personally. After getting into the red-and-black Chevy Nova with the boys, Spider had made another suggestion.

"Hey," Spider had said, "I've got a buddy of mine not too far from here. What do you say we pick him up and take him to the party, too?"

Spider stopped the story here and paused a moment. He had committed himself now and he wanted to be sure to tell the entire truth. Exactly as it had happened. He assured Deemer that the buddy of his was none other than the hospitable Snake Cox himself. Spider continued the story from there.

At that point, Spider said, he led the boys to McDonald's where they met up with Snake Cox. Since Spider was determined to be completely honest, he told Deemer the truth about the meeting. He had gone up to Snake and told him about a couple of pigeons in the car outside.

The pigeons, Spider had told Snake, looked to be wealthy and extremely naive.

"Okay," Snake had said. "Let's go get 'em."

So Snake followed Spider and the two men climbed into the boys' car. After that they headed down the street and stopped for gas at a station near the corner of Atlantic and Broadway. During that time both Snake and Spider had noticed that Daryl had what appeared to be a wad of twenty-dollar bills in his wallet. Shortly after leaving the gas station, Snake suggested they stop by his trailer for some "party goods."

Jim had been worried about taking the side trip. "It's getting late," he had said. "How long will the party go?"

And Snake had assured him that the night was early and the party would last for hours yet. The boys agreed and drove to the trailer so Snake could get the goods. After a short while he returned with a paper bag, and once inside the car he pulled from the bag a .25-caliber automatic blue-steel pistol, which he handed to Spider. Snake kept a .38 caliber pistol for himself.

At this point in the story Spider racked his brains to remember which of them had pulled a gun on the boys first, but he simply couldn't recall.

"All I can say is one of us, maybe both of us, pulled our guns, on those boys, man," Spider told Deemer.

Jim and Daryl had been scared to death and they had followed Snake's directions, driving the car onto Highway 92.

"Now do what I tell you and no one'll get hurt," Snake had said. "Just keep driving."

The boys obeyed and when they reached a dark area they were told to pull off the road. They turned onto Indian Lake Road and drove for half a mile before Snake ordered them to stop the car. There, both boys were robbed of their wallets while Snake and Spider held guns to their heads. Snake moved away from the boys approximately one car length and motioned for Spider to follow him.

"Listen, man," Snake had said. "They know our names, they know where we live, they know where we hang out. We got no choice, man. We gotta kill 'em."

Spider, seeing no reason to object, took one boy by the arm and Snake took the other. It was pitch-dark but they forced the boys at gunpoint further down the road. The ground, as it is in much of central Florida, was muddy and in some places the mud was quite deep. As they walked, one of Jim's shoes got stuck in this mud and came off his foot.

"Hey, man, I lost my shoe," Jim had said. He was terrified but he was trying desperately to be brave.

Snake had laughed at this. "Where you're going you won't be needing shoes," he had said.

And then he ordered both boys to take their shoes off. Jim and Daryl, their eyes filled with fear, looked at each other and followed the command, taking off their shoes and tossing them in the bushes.

They walked along a little bit further and then they reached a clearing. The scrub brush was filled with cockroaches and crickets and other crawling insects but Snake didn't care. He ordered the boys to lie facedown in an area that was wet with several inches of mud and moss.

"You do one," Snake had said. "And I'll do one."

Spider took a deep breath at this point in the story and closed his eyes again. Never in his wildest dreams had he imagined recounting this story in all its truth before a sheriff's deputy with a tape recorder. But now he had no choice. He released an anguished sigh, opened his eyes, and continued.

Next, Spider said, he cocked the gun he was holding and held it to Daryl's head. But the image of the helpless teenager lying with his face in the mud and a gun to his head had been too much for Spider and he suddenly stood up.

"Can't do it like that, man," he had said.

So Snake laughed and picked up a tree limb which was lying nearby.

"Then do it like this," he had said.

He walked up to Daryl and began swinging the limb at Daryl's head until the boy was screaming in pain. Again and again Snake swung the tree limb at Daryl's head but the boy refused to die.

"Hang in there, Daryl," Jim had cried out to his friend. "Please hang in there."

Daryl could no longer talk by then but he moaned loudly and Jim knew he was still alive.

"I'm tired. You take a turn at him," Snake had said, handing the tree limb to Spider.

"You hit him, too?" Deemer interrupted the frightening tale.

"You bet I did. We had to kill 'em. That was the plan," Smith said. "And that stupid kid wouldn't die."

Spider said he took four hard swings at Daryl's head with the tree limb and then stood up and looked at Snake. "Look, Snake. This ain't working," he had said. "The kid's still alive."

"Maybe this'll do it, then," Snake had said. He walked up to Daryl and, holding his .38 in his hand, smashed it against the boy's skull. Daryl moaned again but was obviously still very much alive.

"Here, take this," Snake had said and he handed the gun to Spider. "Watch 'em till I go get the car."

Minutes later Snake returned with the car and he ordered the boys to take off their belts—a task especially painful for the beaten Daryl. Snake and Spider then used the belts to tie the boys' hands behind their backs. They put the boys in the backseat, ignoring the blood that was gushing from Daryl's head. But then before they pulled onto the main highway they changed their minds and ordered the boys out of the car.

Daryl was dizzy, his eyes dilated and his head swollen from the places where blood was pouring from his scalp. Jim used his body to hold his friend up and kept whispering words of encouragement to him. Snake saw what Jim was doing and suddenly smashed his gun over Jim's head. Then he removed the traveler's checks from Jim's wallet and shoved them at the trembling boy.

"Sign them," he had ordered, slapping the boy once across the face. "Fast!" As the boy scribbled frantically Snake continued to beat Jim, punching his face and using the gun to hit his head.

Deemer thought about this detail and decided it had a distinct ring of truth to it. The signature on the checks had been almost identical to Jim Boucher's actual signature. Perhaps the tiny inconsistencies were not caused by the checks having been forged by Snake but rather by the fact that Jim had been beaten continuously while he was signing them.

Spider continued with his story.

At that point, Snake collected the signed checks and opened the trunk of the car. Together Snake and Spider lifted Jim into the trunk and forced him to lie on his side, facing the rear of the car. Daryl, who had fallen to his knees, obviously suffering the side effects of a severe concussion, was then picked up and placed in the front part of the cavity facing the same direction as Jim.

Then Snake closed the trunk.

Unsure of what to do with the badly beaten victims in the trunk of the car, Snake drove back to his trailer where both men went inside and pondered what to do next. Finally, they agreed on a plan. There would be no trouble, no mess, no problems. They would take a piece of hose, some tape and drive the boys back to the deserted area off Indian Lake Road. Then they would gas them to death.

With Snake driving, they returned to the spot and drove half a mile down Indian Lake Road and another four-tenths of a mile down a fire trail. They stopped the car and opened the trunk. The boys were alive. Daryl was moaning loudly and trying to squirm free of the belt that bound his arms behind his back. Jim was crying softly, begging for Snake and Spider to let them go.

"Right, exactly what we're going to do boys. Let you go," Snake had said. Then he had laughed. "Tell you what. You boys count out loud to one thousand and when you're finished you can get out and you'll be free to go your own way. Got it?"

Both boys, as badly beaten as they were, nodded their understanding.

"You come out too soon and I'll kill you, you hear me, man?" Snake had asked.

Again the boys nodded and Snake slammed the trunk shut. Instantly, Snake took the hose and connected it to the tailpipe, sticking the other end into the trunk. Then he took the roll of tape and began sealing the seam of the trunk.

It was at that point that Daryl realized what was going on. Perhaps, as he had done most of his life, he was thinking of Jim, doing whatever was necessary to protect his friend even while he himself was in such bad shape. For whatever reason, obviously realizing that they were about to die, he began using his feet to kick the hose out of the trunk.

"That's it, man," Snake had muttered angrily.

He reached into the car's glove compartment and removed a hunting knife which Daryl kept there for safety reasons. He took the knife and began jamming it through the seam in the trunk until he must have felt it sinking into Daryl's chest.

He heard the boy cry out in pain and then suddenly the boy stopped trying to kick the hose out of the car. Satisfied, Snake dropped the knife and continued taping up the trunk. When he was finished he started the car, flooding the trunk with deadly carbon monoxide.

For the next two hours Snake and Spider sat on a nearby log, smoking pot and telling jokes.

At first they could hear the sounds of at least one of the boys kicking at the inside of the trunk with his feet. But after a short while there was only the sound of the car's engine in the background.

Finally, in the early hours of the morning while it was still dark, Snake walked back to the car and turned off the engine. Then he pulled off the tape and opened the trunk. When he saw that the boys were dead, he pulled their bodies from the car. With Spider's help they moved the boys into a clearing and lay them side by side. Since they didn't want anyone to see the bodies, they found a blanket in the back of Daryl's car and covered the boys. Then they left as quickly and quietly as they could.

"And that," Spider said, taking another deep breath, "is what really happened that night."

Joe Deemer hit a switch on the recorder, stopping the tape. As he removed it and placed it in an envelope, he said absolutely nothing to Spider. Finally Spider shouted in frustration at the lack of response.

"Well, man, ain't you gonna say nothin' 'bout that story?"

Deemer stared at Spider evenly.

"It's the coldest, most cruel story I've ever heard, Mr. Smith," he said. "But I'd bet everything I own—and I mean that—everything I own, that what you just told me is the truth, exactly like it happened that night."

Spider leaned back, a satisfied look on his face.

"You believe me, then?" he asked.

"Every word, Mr. Smith. Every word."

CHAPTER 40

When the others involved in the case found out about Spider's version of what happened to the boys, they agreed with Deemer on two very definite points.

First, they agreed that Spider was telling the truth. By late December members of a highly sophisticated autopsy team had reconstructed the skeletons of the boys and proven that there had been severe trauma to Daryl Barber's skull before his death. They had also located a rib from Daryl's left side which showed a knife mark that would support Spider's story that Snake had stabbed the boy. In addition, an expert in forgery had proven that Jim had indeed signed the traveler's checks. The shaky signature on the checks had no doubt been the result of the beating he had received while he signed them.

Secondly, and perhaps more importantly, they agreed that Spider's decision to confess to the murder would be used against both him and Snake when the time came for trial. Because by the end of the year Spider had made what members of the prosecution believed to be a fatal mistake. Literally. He had opted for a trial in lieu of a guilty plea.

Of course, a trial for either Snake or Spider had been something State Attorney Watson thought they might very well be able to avoid. Especially after Snake and his attorney, Howard Pearl, had agreed to their deal.

In light of the details provided by Spider, Snake had agreed to plead guilty to two counts of first-degree murder in exchange for his life. That is, he would receive a life sentence without the possibility of parole but because of his assistance in finding the boys' bodies and because he was willing to plead guilty, he could avoid the death penalty.

Watson was thrilled with this deal would put Snake in a high-security state prison for most of his life while sparing the boys' families and the taxpayers the pain and cost of a trial.

He had hoped that Spider would be equally willing to plead guilty and accept these conditions. Instead, after Spider had spilled his guts for Deemer and the tape recorder, he had spent the next few days sitting around his cell convincing himself that he truly was not responsible for the boys' murders.

In fact, as he pondered his poor childhood and the influence Snake had had over him, he had decided that any reasonable jury would probably find him innocent of murder charges. So what if he faced the death penalty? He could win a trial and avoid any punishment at all. But if he pleaded guilty he would spend the rest of his life in prison. And for what? For helping Snake take care of a little business. The way he saw it, it was Snake's idea to kill the boys and Snake's fault the deed had been done.

And so, despite the risk of the electric chair, on February 9,1979, Judge James Foxman of the Seventh Judicial Circuit Court of Volusia County appointed Attorney Thomas Bevis to represent Spider in the case of the State of Florida versus Earl Lee Smith.

Bevis was a young attorney with a surprisingly successful record despite the types of criminals he often defended. He wore dark-rimmed glasses and nondescript suits to trial, all of which led people to sometimes overlook him in a courtroom. But Bevis's voice was laden with emotion, and once he began speaking a jury couldn't help but give him its complete attention.

Because of his youth and relative inexperience, Bevis took a number of court-appointed cases and usually tried to make the best of them. Many times he even won cases for defendants who hadn't seemed to have a chance at acquittal. But after analyzing the details of the case against Spider Smith, Bevis could probably sense the prosecution's victory ahead.

Here was a case in which his defendant had been fingered as an accomplice by a man who had willingly pleaded guilty to first-degree murder. If that wasn't damaging enough, Spider himself had given a two-hour oration in the company of a sheriff's deputy and a live tape recorder in which he admitted to participating in the murders. Bevis had heard the tape and he must have figured Spider did a better job proving himself guilty than any prosecutor he'd ever worked against.

Still, he was obligated to work the case and he was going to give Spider the best defense he could muster. He would try to focus on the angle of Snake being a manipulative ringleader type who had coerced Smith into assisting with the murders. But it wouldn't be easy and the attorney couldn't have expected in his wildest dreams to win.

Spider, meanwhile, did not care one way or another about his attorney or the opinions he held regarding the case. He figured the facts would speak for themselves. The murders hadn't been his idea so naturally he would be found innocent of the charges and released. Then he could get back to the beach life he so badly missed while sitting in his windowless cell at the Volusia County jail.

Bob Brown had stayed in contact with Ziegler and Deemer, the chief investigators for the prosecution, and he knew that the case against Spider was better than airtight. It would take a truly terrible set of legal fumblings to manage anything less than a first-degree murder conviction against Spider.

Now that Bob was back working private investigations and no longer chasing down murder suspects, he'd had quite a bit of time to reflect on the case involving Snake and Spider and the missing teenagers. Most private investigators, especially those who typically handle only domestic cases, would probably have resigned from the case as soon as they realized there was criminal activity involved. In the private investigation field it was not thought to be sound practice to continue in an area that for safety reasons was best left in the hands of the police.

But Bob knew that if he had abandoned the investigation after learning about Snake and Spider's involvement, the boys might never have been found. He thought about the times he had placed himself in danger, the times he boldly approached biker gangs and allowed himself to be pushed around in the dark shadows of the Boot Hill Saloon. And he thought about Larry, the way God had answered his prayers by providing such a man who could turn up the where-abouts of Snake Cox. But also the way Larry could have gotten both of them in deep trouble when he kidnapped Fat Man.

It had been an exciting case, no doubt. Bob knew he would never regret the fact that he had stayed with the case through the end. Despite the danger, he had never been afraid. Cautious, yes. But not afraid. And because of his efforts and the answers to his prayers two very deadly criminals would be put behind bars for a long time. Except, of course, for Spider.

According to Ziegler and Deemer, after the trial Spider wouldn't spend too much behind bars. The reason being that he was, they believed, headed straight for the electric chair.

And by the spring of 1979 no one involved in the case was losing much sleep about the fact. Especially one particular guard who happened to be working the night shift at the county jail when Spider and one of his newly made criminal buddies decided to have a little fun.

Apparently, in Spider's twisted opinion, a fun night in the cell meant assisting another man in capturing this certain guard, disarming him, beating him, and subjecting him to a gang rape.

When the guard was asked to testify about this hideous incident in a trial completely separate from that of the double murder involving the Michigan teenagers, he was barely able to talk. He said that Spider had done unspeakable things to one of his specific body cavities and that he had finally stopped fighting the rape because Spider had threatened to "bite my jugular vein if I cried out for help."

When Bob Brown and Deemer and Ziegler got word of that incident, they were thrilled that Spider had opted for a first-degree murder trial. Because when he lost, and they believed it was merely a matter of when and not if, he would surely get the death penalty. And by that time each of the three, not to mention the jail guard and many other people who had followed the case, would have personally fought for the chance to pull the switch on Spider Smith.

The person who intended to see the deed done, regardless of who did the pulling, was Assistant State Attorney Gene White, one of the most brilliant prosecutors in Watson's office. After reading the case file and listening to the tape recordings of the confessions from both Snake and Spider, White had to agree with Spider's attorney. The whole idea of going to trial was ludicrous, given the evidence against Spider Smith, which had been graciously provided almost in its entirety by Spider himself.

Still, he was aware that the governors of both Florida and Michigan had been involved in this case and that they were watching carefully to see that justice was served. He prepared for the case as if it had gaping holes that needed to be shut. The fact that the holes in this case were invisible and a few pieces of mending thread were all that was needed to sew them up did not matter in the least. Gene White was taking no chances.

Almost from the beginning White decided to sidestep the investigation conducted by Bob Brown. Although Bob's work was detailed in the court file, there were parts that would certainly be subject to scrutiny by the defense. Especially the parts about paying witnesses and kidnapping people who were then forced into giving information. Gene White appreciated Bob's work immensely and was thankful for his unorthodox techniques. But he would just as soon not have to justify them before a curious jury.

Also, early in his preparation for the case he spoke with the parents of the boys. He wanted to know the victims, know their families. That way when he spoke of the cruelty of the murders, the devastation their deaths had caused, he would be speaking from the heart.

White liked to speak from his heart and he was brilliant at doing so. Typically jury members would listen as he wove the tale of the crime and when he reached the climax they would have tears in their eyes. In a case like this one there was no need for dramatics. The facts provided all the drama anyone would ever need to convince the jury of Spider's guilt.

As the months went on and the Barbers and Bouchers waited for the trial, they spent considerably less time together than before. It was time to get on with their lives, however empty and painful they had become.

For the Bouchers there were the younger children, who seemed to need constant attention. Especially John, whose nightmares had gotten worse despite the fact that the bad guys were now in jail. The other boys were struggling with their schoolwork, and with everything else falling apart, Roy's health had continued to fail. He was in the hospital numerous times in 1979 while the defense filed one continuance after another.

Kristi, it seemed, was the only bright spot for the family. Now a cheerful toddler, Kristi would make her way throughout the house humming and gurgling and babbling words that couldn't quite be understood. Because she never knew her older brother, she was too young and too innocent of the facts to grieve like the others.

Still she could tell when her mother was upset, and sometimes she would tilt her head and stare at the tears in Faye's eyes as if to offer some childlike comfort. Faye was grateful for Kristi and knew that in part the reason she was surviving the nightmare was because of the little girl.

The Barbers found themselves dealing with Daryl's death somewhat differently. Because their other children were grown and had moved out of the house, they tried to resume life as it had been before Daryl was killed. There were times when Marian simply could not and did not want to talk about Daryl. It was the only way she could go on. But there were other times, especially at night, when she would pull out pictures of Daryl and cry for hours at a time for her youngest son.

Throughout 1979, regardless of how they dealt with their grief, both couples had determined one thing for certain. No matter how many delays the defense was given, they would attend the trial and see Spider Smith convicted for his part in killing their sons. If necessary, they would testify as to the character of their sons, although the prosecutor had told them that they would probably not have to do so.

But they would be in the courtroom when Spider Smith received his punishment. The way they saw it there were two reasons to punish Spider: first, for killing their sons; and second, for insisting on a trial and thereby forcing them to relive their sons' final, terror-filled moments. They knew Gene White was going for the death penalty and they wished him luck.

Finally, the number of delays the defense could file ran out and on Monday, January 14, the trial of the State of Florida versus Earl Lee Smith got underway in Judge James Foxman's courtroom. A jury of nine women and three men had been selected and promised by both attorneys that the trial would not take up much of their time.

The Barbers and Bouchers had arrived over the weekend and were some of the first people to show up in the courtroom that morning. In addition, the press filled the courtroom. Since the boys' skeletons had been found and since it had been learned that the governors of two states had been pushing for this case to be solved, the trial had received national attention. If the prosecutor did not intend to tell the story of a mild-mannered private investigator who stumbled onto the deadly path of Snake and Spider, the newspapers had already done so. Bob Brown had become something of a local hero for his efforts, and the reporters intended to cover the trial daily to see the story through.

Much to the delight of the press, Bob Brown was also in the courtroom. He had taken personal time away from his other investigations to see the fruition of his labor come to pass at the capable hands of prosecutor Gene White.

When Spider walked into the courtroom he looked toward the boys' parents, seated in the front row of spectators, and glared at them.

"My God," Faye whispered to her husband. "Look at his eyes." But Roy had already noticed them. He had seen the way those brown eyes were flat and lifeless as if the person behind them did not possess even one bit of remorse or guilt or any other kind of emotion.

The jury was seated and by 10:15 that morning Gene White rose like a man intent on stopping a serious injustice and began to deliver his opening statement. He told the jury that the state would first prove that the Michigan teenagers had been murdered. Then they would prove how the investigation—and here he did not even mention Bob Brown's name—had been conducted and how police in Tampa had impounded Daryl Barber's car after finding it at Snake Cox's trailer. Finally he told them how this investigation led to Cox himself taking detectives to the site where the boys' bones were recovered and how Snake's confession had in turn led to that of Spider Smith.

"You will see the photographs," White said, pacing in front of the jury and sounding as if he was talking about something that had happened to his own two sons. "You will see the bones and the condition of the bones."

He stopped a moment and shook his head sadly. "This will be the evidence the state will present to you. A double murder was committed for money and to cover up the act of robbery.

"Spider and Snake," White waved toward the spot where Spider was sitting, "these cold-blooded men, were responsible for the deaths of those boys. I will appreciate your time and your perfect attention while we go about proving this to you."

It was time for Bevis to take the floor and he did so with as much enthusiasm as he could muster. As Gene had been talking he had seemed to be nodding along in agreement. There was no denying any of the assertions the prosecutor had made, and for the hundredth time Bevis must have wondered why his client hadn't simply agreed to a plea bargain. Even if it meant serving a life term in prison.

Bevis introduced himself to the jury and told them that everything was not always as it seemed. Yes, there had been a double homicide and, yes, someone was responsible. But the unanswered question, the question the jury was mandated to answer, was who that responsible party was. More importantly, Bevis reminded them, it was up to them to determine who that responsible party was not.

He spent nearly thirty minutes alluding to the fact that sometimes, on occasion, a person might do something that is completely out of character, completely against their nature because of coercion by another person. This was the case, he said, in the incident that August night involving his client, Earl Smith.

Gene White was not surprised that during his opening statement Bevis never referred to his client as Spider, the name that even the defendant preferred to use. The rationale was obvious. Perhaps if the jury could get a picture of Earl Lee Smith, the poor little young man who had been forced to commit a crime against his will, then they would have a shot at an acquittal.

Because it said a great deal about the twenty-one-year-old defendant's character, calling him by his nickname could do nothing but damage his case.

Of course, it didn't really matter what Bevis called his client since Gene White had long since decided that Spider was the only name he would use to represent the defendant.

The trial lasted just four days.

During that time Prosecutor White presented only seven of the fifty witnesses he had subpoenaed. The reason for this was simple. The case against Spider was so perfectly sound there was no reason to waste further time boring the jury with needless testimony.

Among the seven witnesses were forensic specialists who had examined the skeletal remains of the boys in December 1978. Their testimony proved that Daryl had been severely beaten before his death and that he had been stabbed on the left side. Then Deemer had taken the stand and given vivid details of Spider's confession which matched up with the physical evidence in a way that left no holes whatsoever. When he was finished testifying, the tape of Spider himself talking about the murders was played for the silent courtroom.

So sound was the state's case that when it came time for the opposition to present its case, Bevis stood up and announced that the defense would not be calling any witnesses.

This came as a surprise to the Barbers and Bouchers, seated in the courtroom and taking in every detail of the trial. But Gene White knew what Bevis was doing. Since there truly were no witnesses who could undo the damage done to the defendant, the only way to win was to convince the jury to convict Spider of a lesser charge than first-degree murder. He would do this during his closing argument by replaying the same lines he had fed the jury during his opening remarks. Still, Gene White was not the least bit concerned.

White went into his closing arguments like a man driven to win a race in which he was the only participant. He rehashed the evidence that had been presented over the past four days and then stopped for a moment, turning his attention fully on the boys' parents.

The jurors, all of whom had been hanging on his every word and intonation, followed his gaze and saw that the boys' mothers were crying. Since the jury was made up primarily of women, most of whom were mothers themselves, there was no estimating the effect the boys' grieving mothers left on the jurors.

White next turned his attention toward Spider and began to recount the story of what happened to the boys as it was told by Spider during his confession. The prosecutor knew the story by heart and he told it now with feeling.

When he was finished, he looked at the jury.

"Is there any chance that Spider fabricated this?" he asked. "No! I'd rather a hundred times have a confession like this given to officers than have to rely on an identifying eyewitness who may have only seen a suspect for a couple of seconds. This is a hundred times more reliable than any eyewitness."

Finally the prosecutor talked about whether a person could be guilty of first-degree murder even if he hadn't been the ringleader.

"If you participate in a robbery and the victim dies," White's voice rang through the courtroom passionately, "if you do that and the victim dies and if you're present at the scene participating, you are guilty of first-degree murder. Whether you intended to kill them or not."

He concluded his argument as zealously as he had begun it.

"Your duty is clear," he said, his voice lower now and his gaze intent on the eyes of each of the jurors. "Not pleasant by any means but clear. First-degree murder. Any other verdict, any other verdict at all, would be a mockery."

At 11:02 A.M. Bevis took the floor and straightened his glasses. His argument was lengthy since there were no defense witnesses and what Bevis was about to say would have to provide his defendant's entire case. At first Bevis focused on the incredible responsibility of a jury to return a fair verdict.

"Right now you have more power and you possess more power than you will ever possess for the rest of your life. You virtually hold the life of a fellow person, a human being, in your hands.... That is why it's so critical. That is why there are two sides. And now you will hear the defendant's side of the story."

Then Bevis launched into an attack on the facts in the case, drilling in the idea that Snake, or John Cox as Bevis called him, had been the guilty party. In this way he recreated the entire set of events, focusing entirely on Snake's role in the murders and completely ignoring Spider's.

"The state proved that John Cox made the decision to rob the boys after he saw the money that was exposed at the service station. The state proved that John Cox decided how this was to be done," he said, his voice rising.

"The state proved that John Cox gathered the tape, gathered the hose.

"The state proved that John Cox inserted the hose into the exhaust pipe, inserted it into the trunk, and taped the trunk.

"The state proved that John Cox did these murders!" Bevis turned and pointed dramatically at Smith. "Ladies and gentlemen, no other evidence links that man to this crime except for his own statements."

With that, Bevis delved into an area that Gene White had not expected him to discuss. He said that not only had Smith gotten caught up in the atrocious acts of John Cox, but that Smith had never intended to make the confession to the sheriff's deputy.

"The defendant was psychologically coerced into making a confession to investigators and for that reason it should be wholly disregarded.

"Don't penalize Earl Smith for not testifying in this case, for not giving evidence in this case," Bevis said before sitting down. "He has nothing that he needs to prove to you. The proof must come from the state. And the proof that the state has given has proved only that John Cox is guilty of first-degree murder. They did not prove a single thing against Earl Smith. Consider that when you deliberate on their verdict."

The jury received its instructions at two o'clock that afternoon, and whatever its members did consider it did not take much time. They reached a unanimous decision in less than an hour.

When the boys' parents, who had been waiting out in the hallway, heard that the verdict was in after so little time, they were thrilled. Gene White had told them that the more quickly the jury returned the better the chances that they had earned a conviction.

When everyone had filed back into the hushed courtroom, Judge Foxman asked the jury foreman to read the verdict.

The woman held the slip of paper steadily in her hands and began to read.

"This court finds the defendant, Earl Lee Smith, guilty of two counts of first-degree murder...."

Instantly, both sets of parents embraced and began crying. The judge tapped his gavel on the bench several times and called for order so that the other counts could be read. Spider was also found guilty of two counts of robbery and two counts of kidnapping. Sentencing was set for the following day, Friday, January 18.

Gene White stood up to leave and as he did he caught Spider's glance. For the first time since the trial had begun, Spider looked something other than sure of himself. Now, in light of his conviction, Spider actually looked afraid.

White turned away and headed toward the Barbers and the Bouchers and congratulated them.

"Of course, it's not over yet," he added. "There's still the sentencing."

"What do you think, Mr. White?" Roy asked. He looked thin and pale and Gene could see the damage the ordeal had done to him. He felt for the man and for the others who missed their sons so badly. But justice had been served and he would do his best to see that it was done again in the morning.

"About the death penalty?" White asked with a grin. "Honestly, I think it looks pretty good."

CHAPTER 41

On the morning of January 18 the courtroom was more full than it had been at any time during the trial. The news had hit the papers and television stations that Earl "Spider" Smith had been found guilty of first-degree murder. Now everyone wanted to know if the prosecutor would successfully argue in favor of the death penalty.

The arguments began only moments after Judge Foxman took the bench. Prosecutor Gene White spoke first and immediately began discussing the obligation of the jury to send Smith to the electric chair "because that is how our law in this state works."

He quoted Jesus as saying, "Render unto Caesar what is Caesar's," and he spoke of civic responsibility.

"This is a duty," he said, his face contorted in emotion. "Like people who go off to war. A sacred duty and one which we must fulfill. You as a jury do not sit there as individuals. You sit as a representative of the community. You cannot sit there and think, well, what do I personally feel? You are a representative faced with a duty."

He took a breath and looked sympathetically toward the boys' parents. "If you will recall, during the whole course of this trial we had to carefully avoid any mention of the parents and their feelings, the boys and their feelings, so that we could give you the cold, hard facts.

"And this is the only time you will ever hear a consideration of the victim."

He spoke in a gentle voice now, one that would be appropriate in, say, a funeral parlor during viewing hours. He was compassionate and caring and completely aware of the parents' grief. And where the jurors were concerned his emotion was contagious.

"These people," he said softly, "are not a technicality. They are not a name by which we prove simply that they did live and they did die at the hands of another. Take Jim Boucher, for instance. He lived. He had a family. He had feelings.

"And Daryl Barber, he was a human being. He had feelings and a family. Consider these things. The facts now face the defendant squarely and on an equal basis with the emotions of the case. And when we consider what the boys suffered, it is clear that Spider Smith should receive the ultimate penalty."

White talked about Snake and how, yes, he should deserve to die, too.

"But he's remorseful at least. He has shown some signs of rehabilitation by leading authorities to the site where the boys' bodies were left to rot."

He stared at Spider angrily. "Spider, on the other hand, has shown us no remorse whatsoever. When he gets out in twenty-five years or maybe in fifty years, couldn't it happen again? I ask you to consider this. Couldn't it happen again, to someone like your family or mine?"

White shook his head and looked gravely serious.

"I wouldn't want to take the chance," he said. "Is it worth putting another family through what these poor people have had to go through this past year? I think not. You weigh the facts and I suggest that there is not one reason, not one single reason why the defendant should not receive the penalty of death."

Bevis looked crushed by the prosecutor's argument. He stood up slowly and faced the jury. There was only one way to argue on behalf of Spider Smith now. He would have to beg for mercy.

"This is not a pleasant task for me," Bevis began honestly. "And I am sure it is not pleasant for you, either. But you must know something now. Your hand is on the switch. And it's a big, electrical switch."

The jury looked disinterested in whatever Bevis was about to say, their expressions hard and firm. Unmoving, White would say later, as if their minds had already been made up.

Bevis could read this as surely as if they had said as much themselves, and he decided not to waste any time. He went right for the heart of his message, insinuating that everlasting guilt would fall on any juror who would vote for the death penalty.

"When you vote to send this man to his death, you pull that switch just as surely as that executioner will pull it four or five or six years from now when that man walks down that last corridor to the electric chair."

He moved closer to the jury and raised his voice. "This is the most important decision you will ever make in your lifetime. For God's sake, consider it."

Then he spoke of the technicalities again, the reasons why his client should not have been convicted of first-degree murder and the reasons why he should not have to suffer the penalty for such a crime.

But the jury looked bored and Bevis quickly turned his comments back to those that were more emotional.

"If you condemn Earl Smith to die he will go on death row." Bevis nearly shouted the words. "And for what? For what? Retribution? Is that what's in your heart? Do you think that's going to bring those boys back? Do you want three people to die instead of two? Would that make society feel better? Would it help those grieving parents?"

He paused a moment and took a deep breath.

"Believe me," he said, his voice once again at a normal level, "I feel sorry for those people. I can't imagine what they've been through. But do you think having the blood of a third person on their hands will make them feel any better?"

Bevis shook his head sadly and began to pace in front of the jury, discussing the history of the death penalty and what were by his standards the cruel ways in which it was often carried out.

"There is no such thing as a merciful execution," he said, stopping suddenly and facing the jury. "I've seen that chair, I've been in there. Let me describe it to you a little better."

There was silence in the courtroom as Bevis continued. For the first time, the jury appeared to be listening intently, riveted at the thought of hearing details about the electric chair.

"First," Bevis began, "a metal cap will be brought down on his head. Then a mask, a cloth bag, will be placed around his head. He will be strapped in an open chair and an electrode will be placed on his left ankle with a jellylike solution to conduct the electricity."

Spider squirmed uncomfortably in his chair as his attorney continued.

"He will be facing twelve witnesses in another room through a glass panel. Then, the executioner will come in, a person known to no one but the governor and the prison warden. And he will pull the switch."

Bevis paused again. "At that moment, several thousand volts of electricity will course through this man's body, causing him to violently jerk at the restraining devices."

The jurors seemed to flinch at the thought.

"And the smoke will sizzle up from his burning flesh and then, only then, will the state have its pound of flesh."

Bevis was quiet a moment and when he spoke again his voice was barely more than a whisper.

"Is that what you want? Will that bring those boys back? I ask you to commit one final act of mercy, for to do otherwise would serve no purpose, moral, legal, or otherwise.

"Don't pull that switch," Bevis said and he might as well have been on his knees.

The jury, which included at least one Christian minister, then spent seventy-five minutes deliberating on the idea of pulling the switch.

When they returned to the courtroom, Judge Foxman ordered everyone to their seats. The Barbers and Bouchers held hands while the jury foreman read the decision. All of them knew that regardless of what the jury recommended the decision was ultimately up to the judge.

"We, the jury in the case of the State of Florida versus Earl Lee Smith, do hereby recommend that the defendant be electrocuted until death as penalty for two convictions of first-degree murder."

Gene White turned toward the boys' parents and nodded his approval and from across the courtroom Bob Brown felt his breathing quicken. He had brought about the arrest of a man who was about to be sentenced to die for his crime and there was no describing the array of emotions he was feeling. In the front row of the spectator section, the boys' parents squeezed the hands they were holding a bit tighter.

"Very well." Judge Foxman nodded and cleared his throat. He directed his attention toward Spider.

"In that case you, Earl Lee Smith, being now before the court and attended by your attorney, Thomas Bevis, and having had a fair trial by the jury of your countrymen and having been found guilty of the crime of murder in the first degree with a recommendation of death by the jury, will face your penalty. What have you to say?"

Smith stared at the floor and ignored the judge's question.

"Saying nothing, it is the sentence of this court that you be incarcerated until such time as you will be electrocuted until you are dead. May God have mercy on your soul."

The boys' parents closed around each other, blocking out the circus of media cameras hungry for an emotional moment. Then the Barbers and Bouchers did an amazing thing. They bowed their heads and prayed.

"Lord, we thank you that justice has been done in this courtroom," Roy said softly. "But we ask you to work in the life of Earl Smith and John Cox so that at some point they may become remorseful for what they have done."

He paused a moment, tears filling his eyes. "Thank you that finally this ordeal is over. And please God, wherever Daryl and Jim are right now, let them know that we love them. And how very much we miss them."

The pain for the Bouchers and Barbers did not end however, that January morning in the Florida courtroom. The media continued to run stories about the murders and at one point Timothy Boucher, who was fifteen at the time, came home from school in tears.

"They told me Jimmy was cut up in tiny pieces after he was killed!" Tim cried angrily. "How come you didn't tell me, Mom?"

Faye was shocked at this and asked Timothy to explain himself.

"Everyone at school's been reading the papers and they said Jim's bones were found all over the place. He was cut up in tiny pieces."

Faye sighed, finally understanding where her son's confusion lay. Throughout the course of the investigation and the trial she had sheltered her other children from the details of what happened to Jim and Daryl. Now she knew she would have to be honest.

"Tim, the boys were not cut up, believe me." She put her hands on her son's shoulders and looked directly into his eyes.

"Then what's this about police finding their bones scattered throughout the brush."

"Your brother and Daryl lay there for a long time before anyone found them. Eventually their bodies started to decompose and the animals got to them. That's why their bones were scattered about."

Of all the horrible things she might have said, she had never imagined saying such a thing to one of her children. She pulled Tim into a hug and held him for a long time while he sobbed in her arms.

The grief did not stop there.

Despite the fact that Spider had been sentenced to die, his attorneys continued to fight for an appeal on whatever grounds they could conjure up. Because of that, the bones of Jim and Daryl were not released to their families for proper burial.

"They're state's evidence, ma'am," an officer explained to Faye when she called once to demand that their bones be returned. "It could be years."

And it was.

Over the years several attempts were made to earn an appeal for Spider's death sentence. Finally, in 1988, attorneys argued that Spider's terrible childhood was responsible for his role in killing the two teenagers. Attorneys cited the fact that Spider's mother had been raped prior to his conception and that he had been forced to witness his stepfather's suicide.

After listening to the argument, Judge Foxman finally agreed to overturn the death sentence.

"Although this man definitely deserves to die for the crime he has committed, the time has come to put an end to the legal circus surrounding this case. There needs to be an end at some point and I have decided the end will be here. I hereby overturn the death sentence as it was assigned to Mr. Smith and sentence him to life in state prison."

The decision came as a shock to the Barbers and Bouchers, who attended the appeal hearing as they had many others in the past.

There was more bad news after that.

By 1991, shortly after the boys' bones had finally been returned to their families, it became evident that although Snake and Spider were now both relegated to life sentences, the courts would likely set both men free as early as 1996 because of time off for good behavior and the fact that prisons in Florida are overcrowded.

When the dust had settled all that was left was an even greater emptiness for the couples.

Not only had their sons been murdered and left to rot in Florida scrub brush, but now the criminal justice system had let them down.

In the wake of these events, Roy Boucher grew even sicker than he'd been before, the diabetes ravaging his already weak body. Finally, in 1992, he died with Faye by his side holding his hand.

The Barbers, no longer wishing to be reminded of the painful memories, moved away from Metamora in the mid-1980s and when Daryl's bones were finally released they were buried near his parents' new home in northern Michigan.

As for Faye, by 1993 her remaining children were nearly grown but she was constantly haunted by one aspect of Judge Foxman's decision to overturn Spider's death penalty.

"He told us that it was time to put it behind us, time to move on so that finally the nightmare would be over," she said once. "But those were our sons who were killed, a part of ourselves. My husband is dead now, my children scarred for life. The judge thought the nightmare would be over just because he overturned the death penalty. But he was wrong. The nightmare will never, ever be over."

READER LETTER

Dear Friends,

Back when my writing career started, I was a reporter for the *Los Angeles Times*. I began in the sports department, writing game stories and profiles of prominent athletes. I was quickly promoted to a general assignment reporter, writing features and covering prominent crime cases for the front page of the Sunday paper. The position was the most coveted on staff, but there was nothing glamorous about following the grim details of abduction, tragedy, and murder. Many nights I lay awake, praying for peace, staring at the ceiling, unable to sleep. I could usually find a redeeming character in each true story I covered – the detective who held tight to her faith, the private investigator with the Bible verse on his desk. I was intrigued enough to adapt a number of these stories into books. But the darkness in these stories was more than I could bear. After writing four true-crime books, I knew I needed a change.

Not only did I want to escape the darkness of crime stories in Los Angeles. I wanted to be part of the light. I wanted to tell stories with real struggles and trials, real tragedies and triumphs – but I wanted to tell them in light of redemption. I wanted to write stories that gave people a reason to believe.

I wanted to be a bearer of light.

And so that is what I became. I began writing redemptive hope-filled fiction and I trademarked it Life-Changing Fiction ™. I have 25 million copies of those novels in print now, and miles of letters from readers who have found hope and light reading my stories. But many of them – many of you – wanted to know where my writing journey began. I often get asked that question when I speak and at every book-signing.

For that reason I acquired copies of these early works that had been out of print for years, though they remained available via second-hand retailers and the internet for significant sums of money. In rereading them, I wasn't pleased by the offensive language that was added without my consent when they were first published. After a fresh edit, I decided to make them available again to those who wanted to read them. Also, sometimes there is benefit in reading a cautionary tale, a story about innocent people caught in the crossfire and people who chose darkness and bore the consequences. That said, these stories are not for everyone. Though there is always a redemptive character, they are not stories of redemption. While these are different from the books I now write, they still remind us that life often turns on the smallest of hinges and that seemingly innocent choices can provoke dramatic consequences—including the loss of life itself.

They are true stories of choices and consequences, true stories of tragedy and darkness in a world that desperately needs light. There is no knowledge of light without darkness, no sense of good without evil, and no understanding of our desperate need for God without understanding how far gone we truly are.

I know that's true in my own life, and I am grateful for the journey God has led me on and the grace I've been shown along the way. For those wondering how I got my start as an author, it all began here and with the three other true crime books (*Deadly Pretender, Final Vows, and Missy's Murder*) I wrote as a young mom. Every road has it's beginning, and I'm thankful for mine. But I'm immensely and eternally grateful for the love of God that called me to a brighter place and ultimately allowed me the opportunity to write Life-Changing Fiction ™. Bad things still happen in the lives of my characters because that's the reality of our fallen world. There's death and extraordinary hurt and pain. But that is not the end of the road or of the story. Amidst the darkness, there is a great light. There is hope. There is redemption.

Thank you for allowing me the chance to share a bit more of my journey as an author and participating with me as we bring light into a dark world. And no matter where you are in your personal journey, please never ever forget that your life is precious to me and to the One who created you.

You can connect with me on Twitter @KarenKingsbury.com or on Facebook. I'd love to hear from you.

Karen Kingsbury

ABOUT THE AUTHOR

Karen Kingsbury is America's favorite inspirational novelist. There are more than 25 million copies of her award-winning books in print, including several million copies sold in the past year. Karen's recent dozen titles have all debuted at or near the top of the New York Times Bestseller's list. She is also a public speaker, reaching more than 100,000 women annually through various national events. Karen lives and works outside Nashville, Tenn., with her husband, Don, and their five sons, three of whom were adopted from Haiti. Also living nearby is their only daughter, Kelsey, an actress in inspirational films and married to Christian recording artist Kyle Kupecky. For more information visit www.karenkingsbury. com. Karen is also on Facebook (facebook.com/AuthorKarenKingsbury) and Twitter (@KarenKingsbury), where she regularly interacts with nearly half a million reader friends.